W9-CLQ-875

THE BATTLE OF THE BULGE

THE PHOTOGRAPHIC HISTORY OF AN AMERICAN TRIUMPH

John R. Bruning

Zenith Press

First published in 2009 by Zenith Press, an imprint of MBI Publishing Company,
400 First Avenue North, Suite 300, Minneapolis, MN 55401 USA

Hardcover edition published 2009. Softcover edition 2011.

Zenith Press titles are also available at discounts in bulk quantity for industrial or sales-promotional use. For details write to Special Sales Manager at MBI Publishing Company,
400 First Avenue North, Suite 300, Minneapolis, MN 55401 USA.

To find out more about our books, visit us online at www.zenithpress.com.

ISBN-13: 978-0-7603-4126-1

The Library of Congress has cataloged the hardcover edition as follows:

Bruning, John R.
The Battle of the Bulge : the photographic history of an American triumph / John R. Bruning.
p. cm.
Includes bibliographical references and index.
ISBN 978-0-7603-3568-0 (hb w/ jkt)
1. Ardennes, Battle of the, 1944–1945—Pictorial works. 2. United States. Army—History—World War, 1939–1945—Pictorial works. I. Bruning, John R. II. Title.
D756.5.A7B78 2009
940.54'219348--dc22
2009015305

All images official U.S. archives photos and author's collection.
Maps by Philip Schwartzberg, Meridian Mapping, dedicated to his uncle, Pfc. Harry Hochstadt, Company A, 347th Infantry Regiment, 87th Infantry Division, ETO. Private First Class Hochstadt was awarded a Combat Infantryman Badge and a Bronze Star.

Printed in China

For Richard, Eric, Jenn, and Julie.

This book exists because of your patience

and belief in me.

CONTENTS

MAPS

PREFACE

WHAT CAN I SAY ABOUT THE BATTLE OF THE BULGE that hasn't already been said a million times? On my bookshelf alone, I have sixty-five books on the subject. Fine historians have spent a lifetime studying these bloody thirty days in the dead of World War II's final winter. They have expounded on the subject in far more depth than I ever could.

So for this book, I want to tell you the story through the photographs taken by brave and dedicated combat cameramen. They risked their lives countless times to get these photos and endured all manner of privation and suffering alongside their GI subjects. Many of these priceless images have languished in dusty archives, forgotten and slowly fading away, a fate similar to the very veterans captured within their frames. There are still a few aging survivors to be found here and there, but, sadly, one walk through a local cemetery will probably uncover many more. Let them be your connection, and cling to it in the years ahead, lest this country shed their memory like it so often seems willing to do with its history. Let your eyes linger on these photographs until the details come into sharp relief. They will tell so much of this story.

I will not lie to you and tell you I am an unbiased historian. I am an American, and I have spent the past three years with a unique association with an infantry battalion in my neck of the woods. I lived with these guys in the hell that was New Orleans in the aftermath of Hurricane Katrina. I've slept beside them in freezing deserts. I've been slammed into walls and dumped into icy puddles by them as the leader of their opposing force (OPFOR) while they have prepared to return to battle once again. I see their commitment. I see their love of country and the devotion they have for their brother-in-arms. I've also seen the petty infighting, the jostling

Private First Class Margerum, a native of Philadelphia, walks back toward Bastogne two days after Christmas, 1944. Though the fighting took place on another continent, the roots of the U.S. Army are here in America and can be found in every community across the nation.

Technician 3rd Class Donal B. Calamar, one of the select group of Signal Corps cameramen who captured the war in Europe on film, appears here with the 167th Signal Company, recording the Ninth Army's crossing of the Roer River in February 1945. The photographer was Technician 5th Class M. A. Nicholson.

for rank, the slackers, the braggarts, and the shirkers. I've seen the effect combat has on the human mind; it has led to suicide attempts, addiction, broken families, and shattered lives. Choosing the warrior life comes with a price that most of us will never fathom.

And as I've gone back to study and write about the infantry in the Ardennes, I am struck by the similarities between the men I know and call my brothers and the men within these pages who staved off the worst evil the world ever faced.

The legacy of these anonymous GIs from every corner of the country and every conceivable walk of life serves as a guide through the shoals of our own era. The lesson? Americans don't quit. They don't cave in. They don't get intimidated. They master fear. They master panic. And the best of them see opportunities in the chaos. Not all of them, of course, exhibit these qualities, but enough do, and they make the stand that saves the day and brings to close another crisis.

Therein lies the story I want to tell. It is easy to revere success and study its many trappings. But to truly understand the character of an army, watch it when it is faced with adversity and despair. See how it

An infantry platoon assaults forward under heavy fire near the Roer River, 1945.

Over the past seventy years, the heart of the infantryman has not changed. Only their uniforms are different.

reacts then. Does the desperate human being run for safety? Does the regiment fold in the wake of a crisis? Does the army unravel as tanks shatter its front and press into the rear? In those moments, the true character of an army emerges, and it stands or falls on that character and nothing else.

How these veterans reacted in the snow-covered forests and hills of the Ardennes stands as the ultimate symbol of who Americans are as a nation and a people. An army reflects the society that created it, and over time only their uniforms have changed. The commitment, courage, and endurance in the face of extreme adversity remains the same. Thanks to the Bulge, those are the attributes that today still run deep in the U.S. Army's gristle and bones.

The name of this Signal Corps cameraman, one of the first into northwestern Europe, was not recorded, but the caption notes he landed on D-Day.

Firepower and mobility, two of the U.S. Army's primary concepts—neither of which have changed since World War II—were embodied in this wartime creation, the Sherman Calliope. This was a standard M4 with a multiple rocket launcher system attached to the turret.

INTRODUCTION

☆ ☆ ☆ ☆ ☆

THE BATTLE OF THE BULGE ranks as the single largest battle ever fought by the United States Army. More men, vehicles, supplies, equipment, aircraft, and effort went into this thirty-day battle than into any other in American history. It was larger than Gettysburg, larger than the Gulf War, larger than the landings in Normandy that ignited the fuse that carried the army halfway across Europe to the blood-stained snow of the Ardennes.

Thirty-one American divisions—fully a third of the U.S. Army raised during World War II—saw action in this battle. As a result, it was a quintessentially American moment. It was also a test: could this conscript army from a pacifistic democracy defeat the best remaining men and machines a totalitarian government could produce?

The story of the Bulge is the story of panic, fear, and physical misery. It is the story of how a generation of draftees, National Guardsmen, and a small core of regular officers and NCOs faced those three elements as snow piled around their foxholes and the incessant drumming of artillery splintered the woods that gave them shelter. It is the story of men, frozen and hurting, far from home with little hope of seeing it again until the killing finally ended.

The Nazi offensive into Belgium that December was the desperate gamble of a dictatorship on its last legs. Had our fathers and grandfathers failed, the world we knew after Hitler ended his life would have been vastly different. The outcome of the war would not have changed, but failure in the Bulge would have redrawn the postwar map and made the Cold War even worse. This makes what happened in the Ardennes all that more important.

An aerial view shows an American armored column soon after it had been shelled by the Germans during the Battle of the Bulge.

The Bulge made heroes of ordinary Americans. Private First Class Patrick E. Shea of Pendleton, Oregon, served with the 1st Battalion, 329th Infantry Regiment, 3rd Infantry Division, at Rochefort, Belgium. During a counterattack, a German unit surrounded his company, which fought on for two days. Shea personally drove off two columns of German troops with his Browning Automatic Rifle. Such personal acts of bravery, most now lost to history, helped stem the tide in the Ardennes that winter. The photographer was Myers of the 165th Signal Company.

When the United States Army first clashed with the Germans in North Africa in 1942 and 1943, its failures were magnified and its successes ignored. The British, ever prickly about the U.S. role in the alliance they shared, referred to the U.S. Army as "Our Italians." The press eviscerated the army, and the British (read: Montgomery) took credit for its victories. The taint of this injustice lingers in the postwar historiography of the campaigns our fathers and grandfathers fought. The GI was derided as a mediocre soldier who prevailed only because of material advantages the Germans never had. The Germans, in turn, were venerated as tactically the best army on the planet.

Nonsense. The American way of war as applied in the 1944 campaign represented nothing less than a paradigm shift in land combat. The Germans never understood

Men of the 70th Infantry Division were photographed in action in eastern France in late 1944.

Removing a fallen comrade.

that, and those few that did never could invent an effective means to stop the U.S. Army. Hitler's plan for the counteroffensive in the Ardennes reveals all those misunderstandings, and they cost the Germans dearly.

In truth, the story of the Bulge reveals what the GIs knew and were too humble or traumatized to talk about to later generations: These young Americans made fine soldiers. They were inventive and adaptive. They took initiative in the chaos, and even when forced to react to the Germans, they threw plenty of surprises at their enemy. A platoon here, some engineers there, and perhaps a couple of marooned staff officers were all it took to lay an ambush, delay the German spearheads, and knock out a tank or two. And this wasn't an isolated event. All over the front, tiny groups of Americans coalesced around small-unit leaders to delay, harass, and poke the Germans in the eye. Their efforts played a vital role in defeating the Third Reich's last offensive and turned it into a death spasm instead of a victory march.

At the start of World War II, the German Army was the world's juggernaut. The U.S. Army ranked nineteenth, but only got that slot after the Dutch surrendered in 1940.

Part I

THE REICH'S LAST HOPE

★ ★ ★ ★ ★

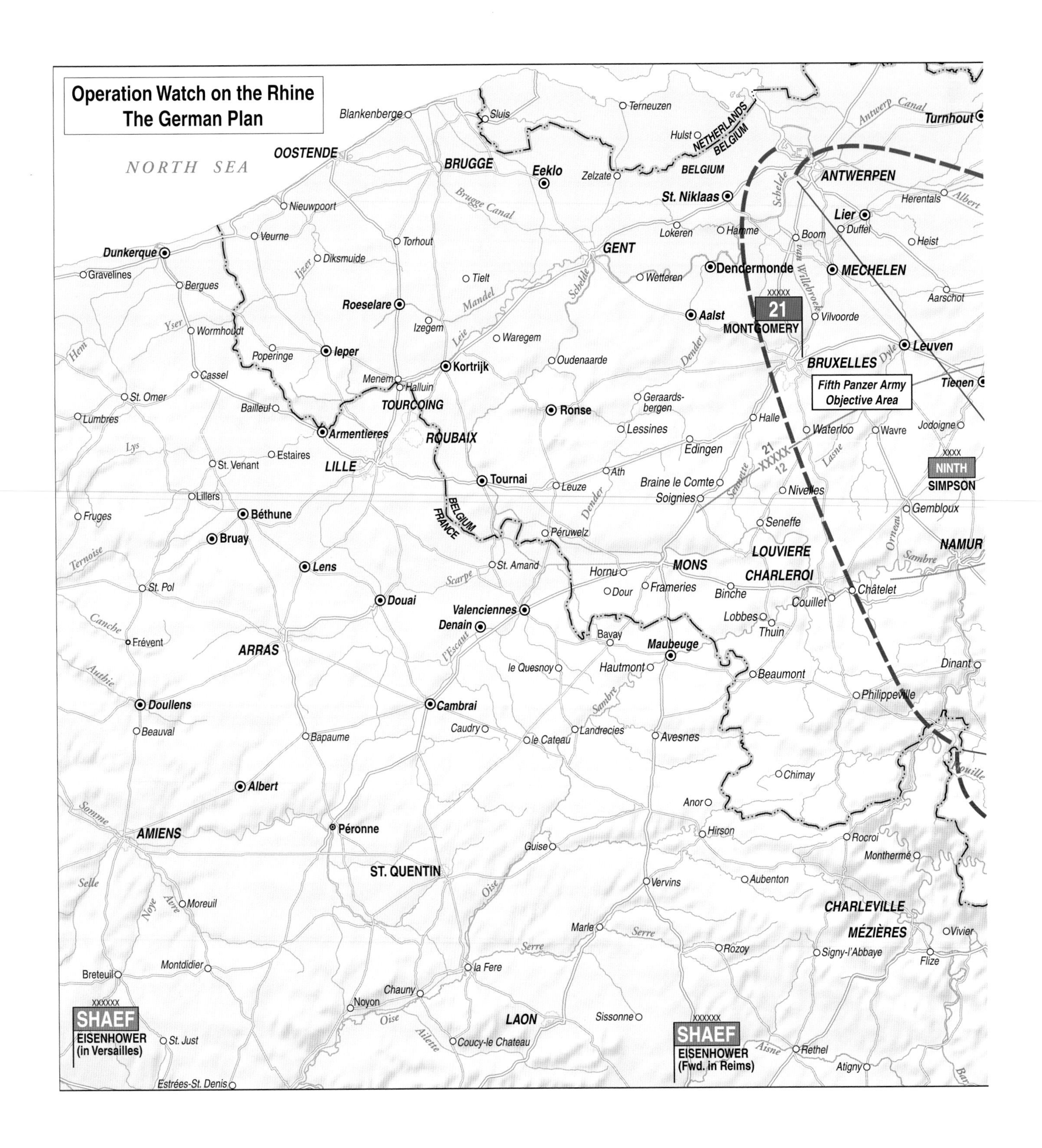
Operation Watch on the Rhine
The German Plan
NORTH SEA
OOSTENDE
Blankenberge
Sluis
Terneuzen
Hulst
NETHERLANDS
BELGIUM
BRUGGE
Eeklo
Zelzate
ANTWERPEN
Turnhout
Antwerp Canal
St. Niklaas
Herentals
Albert
Nieuwpoort
Brugge Canal
Lier
Duffel
Veurne
Torhout
Lokeren
Hamme
Boom
Heist
Dunkerque
GENT
Diksmuide
Dendermonde
MECHELEN
Gravelines
Tielt
Wetteren
Bergues
Roeselare
Mandel
Aalst
21
MONTGOMERY
Vilvoorde
Aarschot
Wormhoudt
Izegem
Waregem
Leuven
Poperinge
Ieper
Kortrijk
Oudenaarde
BRUXELLES
Cassel
Menem
Halluin
Fifth Panzer Army
Objective Area
Tienen
St. Omer
TOURCOING
Geraardsbergen
Ronse
Halle
Lumbres
Bailleul
Armentieres
ROUBAIX
Lessines
Waterloo
Wavre
Jodoigne
Estaires
Edingen
St. Venant
LILLE
Ath
NINTH
SIMPSON
Tournai
Braine le Comte
Soignies
Leuze
Nivelles
Lillers
Béthune
Fruges
Bruay
Péruwelz
Seneffe
Gembloux
LOUVIERE
NAMUR
Lens
St. Amand
Hornu
MONS
CHARLEROI
Dour
Frameries
Binche
Châtelet
St. Pol
Douai
Couillet
Valenciennes
Denain
Lobbes
Thuin
Frévent
Bavay
Maubeuge
ARRAS
le Quesnoy
Hautmont
Dinant
Beaumont
Philippeville
Doullens
Cambrai
Caudry
Landrecies
le Cateau
Avesnes
Beauval
Bapaume
Chimay
Albert
Anor
AMIENS
Péronne
Hirson
Rocroi
Guise
Monthermé
ST. QUENTIN
Vervins
Aubenton
Moreuil
CHARLEVILLE
MÉZIÈRES
Marle
Vivier
Rozoy
Signy-l'Abbaye
Flize
Montdidier
Breteuil
la Fere
Chauny
Noyon
LAON
Sissonne
SHAEF
EISENHOWER
(in Versailles)
St. Just
Coucy-le Chateau
SHAEF
EISENHOWER
(Fwd. in Reims)
Rethel
Atigny
Estrées-St. Denis

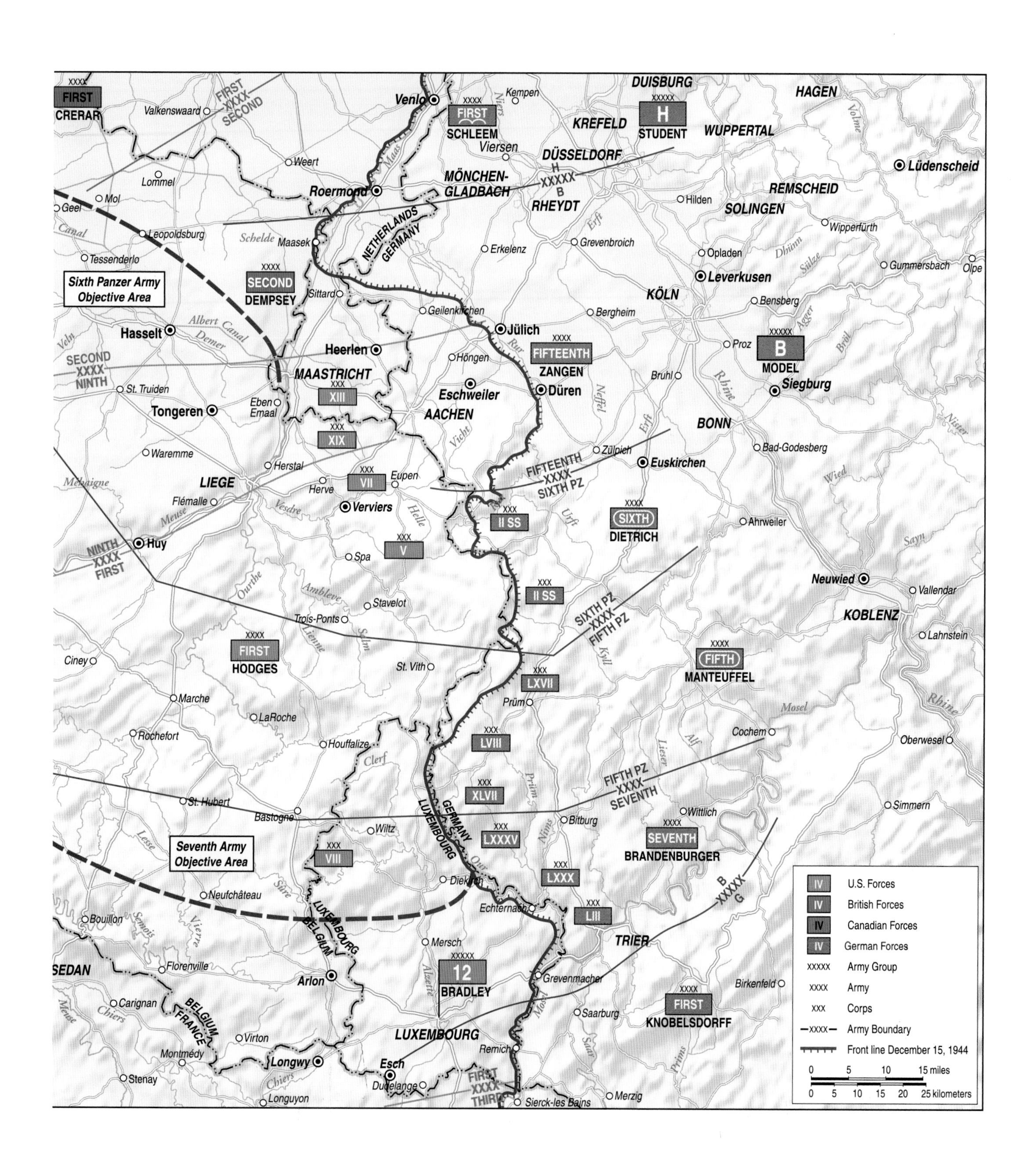
Sixth Panzer Army Objective Area
Seventh Army Objective Area
FIRST CRERAR
SECOND DEMPSEY
FIRST SCHLEEM
H STUDENT
B MODEL
FIFTEENTH ZANGEN
SIXTH DIETRICH
FIFTH MANTEUFFEL
SEVENTH BRANDENBURGER
FIRST KNOBELSDORFF
FIRST HODGES
12 BRADLEY
XIII
XIX
VII
V
VIII
II SS
LXVII
LVIII
XLVII
LXXXV
LXXX
LIII
DUISBURG
KREFELD
DÜSSELDORF
WUPPERTAL
HAGEN
MÖNCHEN-GLADBACH
RHEYDT
REMSCHEID
SOLINGEN
KÖLN
BONN
KOBLENZ
AACHEN
MAASTRICHT
LIEGE
TRIER
LUXEMBOURG
SEDAN
NETHERLANDS GERMANY
GERMANY LUXEMBOURG
LUXEMBOURG BELGIUM
BELGIUM FRANCE
Venlo
Roermond
Heerlen
Hasselt
Tongeren
Huy
Verviers
Jülich
Düren
Eschweiler
Euskirchen
Leverkusen
Siegburg
Lüdenscheid
Neuwied
Arlon
Longwy
Esch
Bastogne
St. Vith
Spa
Stavelot
Malmedy
Eupen
Houffalize
Wiltz
Diekirch
Echternach
Bitburg
Prüm
Cochem
Wittlich
Grevenmacher
Remich
U.S. Forces
British Forces
Canadian Forces
German Forces
XXXXX Army Group
XXXX Army
XXX Corps
—XXXX— Army Boundary
Front line December 15, 1944
0 5 10 15 miles
0 5 10 15 20 25 kilometers

By 1944, Hitler's mental state had significantly deteriorated. So had his relationship with many of his closest associates, including Hermann Göring (at right) and Sepp Dietrich.

1

HITLER'S DEADLY GAMBLE

BY THE FALL OF 1944, Hitler harbored no illusions as to the future of the Third Reich. His empire lay in ruins; enemies drove at him from every direction. It would all be over by December. They had two options as Hitler saw it: retreat or pray for a miracle.

Hitler knew there would be no escape for him and his loyal officers. The Allies would hang them all. So, even as his armies retreated on all fronts, he conceived what he hoped would be history's military comeback: a strategy that would wipe out three years of defeats with a single, decisive victory. Germany would crush the Western Allies first, then turn and fall on the Russians with the full might of its army. No more split-front fighting. They would stop the Soviets at the German border and battle for a negotiated peace.

That was Hitler's grand strategic vision that formed the cornerstone of the Ardennes offensive. It was also pure fantasy.

In June, the Americans, British, Canadians, French, and Poles assaulted Hitler's Atlantic Wall and breached it in a single day, moving inland off the Normandy beaches on D-Day to establish an unshakeable foothold on the Continent once again. It had been four years since the last Allied soldier had wielded a rifle in northwest Europe.

Through the summer, the Allies battered away at the German defenders in Normandy. Finally, at

Hitler realized Germany could not defeat the resurgent Red Army. He saw his only hope in crushing the Western Allies, then negotiating a peace with Stalin.

Loading up prior to D-Day in Southampton Harbor.

A well-concealed emplacement on Hitler's Atlantic Wall. For all the concrete poured, men deployed, weapons accumulated, and ammunition stored, the Atlantic Wall failed to hold for even a day. Ultimately, it proved to be a tremendous waste in manpower and resources.

Omaha Beach, June 6, 1944.

Saint-Lô, the Americans achieved a breakthrough at the end of July. The German front crumbled, and in desperation Hitler ordered a counterattack even as his armies in Normandy faced total annihilation.

The counterattack, aimed at capturing Mortain and sealing off the American breakthrough, ran headlong into the 30th and 4th Infantry Divisions. It was here that the U.S. Army proved decisively that it had come of age at last. The Americans stood fast and slaughtered the panzer grenadiers. Artillery and tank destroyers wiped out many of the remaining German tanks in Normandy. Of seventy German tanks that managed to break

An American infantry patrol creeps forward among the dead outside of Saint-Lô, July 1944.

A street fight is in progress in Mortain in August 1944. It was here the Germans tried to counterattack and pinch off the American breakthrough.

The German counteroffensive at Mortain failed. Its disastrous results paved the way for the Falaise Pocket debacle. Here, GIs walk past a knocked-out Panzer IV in Mortain. The Mark IV, as the Allies knew it, served as the backbone of the Wehrmacht's panzer force.

The ruins of Saint-Lô. After taking the wrecked city, the U.S. Army finally broke out of the bocage country and started the race across France.

The Republic P-47D Thunderbolt became the quintessential fighter-bomber of World War II. While serving with the Eighth and Ninth Air Forces, the P-47 wrought havoc on both the Luftwaffe and the Wehrmacht. The German infantrymen referred to them as "Jabos."

through the American first line of defenses, two-thirds became burning coffins for their crews. The attack failed and helped break the back of the German armies in Western France.

The counterattack thwarted, Allied armored columns spread across the French countryside like mailed fingers clutching at the German jugular in the West. By mid-August, the Americans seemed poised to deliver that greatest of military victories—a total encirclement. The U.S. Army provided the hammer, and the British, Canadians, and Poles formed the anvil. In between the Allies stood the German army, which fought with a desperate fury fueled by the knowledge that its very survival lay at stake.

Called the Falaise Pocket, this final battle of the Normandy campaign claimed the lives of ten thousand German soldiers. Another fifty thousand surrendered to the Allies. Just escaping the Allied noose was all the Fifth Panzer Army and Seventh Army could do during those bloody days. In the end, they left behind almost all their artillery, flak, and antitank guns—some ten thousand pieces in all, plus most of the motor transport for the two armies. Fewer than a hundred panzers made it out of Normandy.

At Falaise the Allies destroyed the German armies on the Western Front. Though thousands of soldiers survived the battle and made it out of the pocket by crossing the Seine, they left behind the vast majority of their heavy weapons, trucks, and armored vehicles. None of these could be adequately replaced by the Third Reich's war machine in 1944. As a result, when the Ardennes offensive began a few months later, most of the panzer divisions were still not anywhere close to full strength.

Combat Command B, 7th Armored Division, encounters an ambush during the drive across France. The 7th Armored would later play a key role in the Ardennes Offensive.

Another wonder weapon was the Messerschmitt Me-163 Komet short-range rocket fighter. On hard landings, the Komet's fuel tanks sometimes ruptured, spilling its caustic fuel into the cockpit and virtually melting the pilot trapped inside.

Hitler's propaganda machine pinned the nation's hopes for victory on the new generation of wonder weapons then in development. This included the famous Messerschmitt Me-262, whose jet engines made it a revolutionary new aircraft. Production totaled just over a thousand by war's end, but the aircraft's radical technology was never reliable, and in the field they had major serviceability issues.

The German retreat from France in the late summer of 1944 was frantic and brutal, harried by Allied artillery and air attacks. Unnecessary—and, at times, necessary—equipment was cast aside as desperate German soldiers fled across the Seine to regroup. Abandoned and destroyed equipment and dead soldiers and horses littered the roadsides.

It took the Allies most of the summer, but they shattered the German defenses on the Western Front. Now they just needed to follow it up and catch the fleeing Nazi army before it could reach the haven of the Siegfried Line. This was the German version of the Maginot Line, a series of concrete bunkers, pill boxes, antitank ditches, and minefields that defended the Third Reich's western frontier. If the remains of the Fifth Panzer Army and the Seventh Army could get behind these defenses, it could earn Germany a reprieve from total defeat. The infantry and panzer divisions could regroup, replace their losses, and rebuild behind the safety of this defensive belt. The Allies would be unable to end the war quickly, and maybe a stand on the Siegfried Line would hold up the American and British armored columns long enough for Hitler's wonder weapons—rockets, buzz bombs, and jet fighters—to tilt the balance of power in Germany's favor.

Tens of thousands of lives lay at stake. The race was on.

The remains of a German vehicle convoy hit by Jabos—the Ninth Air Force's venerable P-47 Thunderbolt fighter-bombers.

2

SHOESTRINGS AND BOOTSTRAPS

★ ★ ★ ★ ★

A HUNDRED THOUSAND GERMANS staggered out of the Falaise Pocket with barely more than their uniforms and boots. Behind them, they left a bacchanal of horrors in their wake. Amid the burnt trucks, cast-off equipment, and abandoned guns, thousands of their dead comrades lay bloated and rotting in the summer heat. The German Army of 1944 still relied on horses for its mobility, and through the disaster of Falaise, these animals suffered terribly from artillery and strafing Allied fighter-bombers. Their corpses littered the path through the Allied noose. No veteran of this battle would ever forget the wretched stench of the dead or the sight of the swarms of flies and rats that feasted on them.

Somehow, the Germans managed to get those hundred thousand men across the Seine River, despite intensive air attacks on the bridges and ferries that carried these bone-weary, beaten soldiers to the temporary safety the far side of the river offered them. Only a few units crossed intact. Most were broken fragments mixed with stragglers from other units. After they crossed, these bits and pieces formed ad hoc battle groups—kampfgruppen—and those that still had the will and the means to fight did their best to slow down the Allied advance. Meanwhile, here and there the Germans pulled divisions out of the line and sent them to refit behind the Siegfried Line. The Wehrmacht would try one last time to pull itself up by its fraying bootstraps.

Men of the 101st Airborne secure an area of bocage country after a sharp firefight. The 101st would play the leading role in the defense of Bastogne during the climactic moments of the Ardennes offensive.

For the American soldiers and tankers, the end of the summer represented both a trial and a release. With

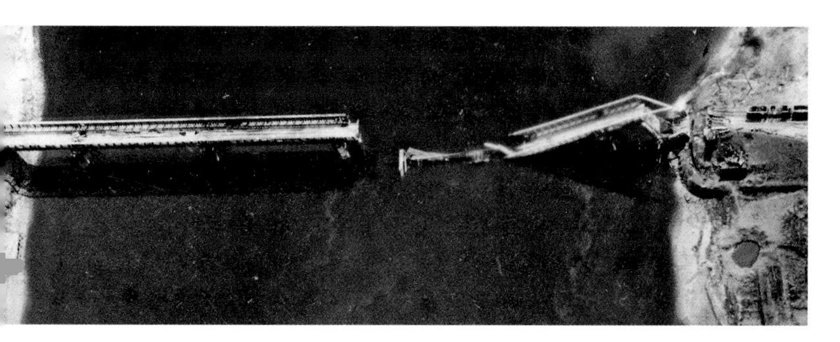

Two of the Seine River bridges, as seen by the Ninth Air Force. The Ninth did its best to isolate the battlefield and destroy every bridge over the Seine, but the Germans were still able to get most of their men across to safety.

the breakout accomplished, they had liberated themselves from the hellish close-quarters fighting in Normandy's hedgerows, where the Germans had inflicted grim casualties and imparted many lessons to those who survived. Units like the 30th Infantry Division, a National Guard unit from Tennessee and the Carolinas, emerged tempered and skilled, its NCOs now combat veterans who understood how the Germans fought.

Most recently, six hundred men from the 30th Infantry Division held off repeated German attacks on Hill 317 at Mortain earlier in August. Though half of the men fell, they held this key piece of terrain. When their relief finally reached them, they found the American foxholes surrounded by heaps of dead and dying

The fighting in the Normandy bocage country ranks as some of the most brutal close-action fighting the U.S. Army experienced during World War II.

Exhausted GIs take a short break from the fighting. The Normandy campaign and the breakout tested the limits of human endurance.

Germans. The 30th later earned the title "Eisenhower's Praetorian Guard." It would play a pivotal role in the Bulge a few months later.

The Americans, led by Gen. George S. Patton's Third Army and Gen. Courtney Hodges' First Army, drove east, frequently going around stiff German resistance in order to continue the pursuit. At the same time, the push forward taxed human endurance. The heat, a very dicey supply situation, and frequent German ambushes took their toll. The men who fought through the breakout and the drive across France remember it as one grim town after another, each providing its own sad story of loss and horror.

The big picture back at Supreme Headquarters Allied Expeditionary Force (SHAEF) looked good except for one thing: the supply situation. It was impossible to bring enough fuel, food, oil, ammunition, and equipment into France over the Normandy beaches. The few ports in Allied hands—most notably Cherbourg—had been totally destroyed by the Germans and had yet to be returned to fully operational status. When the Allies landed in southern France in August, the situation got a little better with the capture of Marseilles. Nevertheless, the farther the Allies pushed into France, the more serious the supply problem became.

The French infrastructure made the situation worse. For months prior to D-Day, the Royal Air Force and U.S. Army Air

Cherbourg was supposed to become a major supply center for the U.S. Army. When the Americans finally captured the port city, the Germans had done so much damage to the harbor that it was months before it could be fully utilized again. Here, American engineers work to get the docks operational again.

One of the many forts defending Cherbourg. The Germans fought furiously, despite knowing they had little hope of rescue.

With Cherbourg not fully operational, the Allies were forced to send their supplies over the beaches. But as the drive across France continued, the beachhead could no longer adequately support the armies in the field, leading to the supply crisis in September.

Forces (USAAF) had teamed up to isolate the Normandy battlefield from the German fatherland. The medium bombers took out bridges and laid waste to railyards and vital road junctions. The fighter-bombers blew up secondary bridges and destroyed rolling stock and locomotives. The campaign had gone so well that when the Allies broke out of Normandy, their progress east was hampered by the air forces' own successes. Transporting the supplies that did come off the beach grew harder and harder since the rail system was a mess and not enough rolling stock had survived the onslaught. Consequently, the Allies had to supply their forward units by truck over an ever-increasing distance. The British simply didn't have the wheels to do it. To keep their offensive moving up into Belgium and Holland, Gen. Dwight D. Eisenhower gave the order to strip several freshly arrived American divisions of their motor transport, including the Timberwolves of the 104th Division, recently of Camp Adair, Oregon. Their trucks, half-tracks, and jeeps kept the British moving.

In some ways, the Ninth Air Force did its job too well. Its Martin B-26 Marauder medium bombers knocked out hundreds of bridges and destroyed France's rail infrastructure. Once in Allied hands, the bridges and railroads had to be repaired if the armies in the field were to be supplied properly.

The Allied tactical air forces almost completely destroyed the rail infrastructure of Western Europe. Rolling stock and locomotives served as prime targets for roaming fighter-bombers.

Locomotives were especially favored targets by American P-47 and P-38 pilots. Later in the war, the Germans studded their trains with antiaircraft guns, making them much more difficult targets.

To keep the British Army mobile, the United States had to send Montgomery hundreds of trucks and other vehicles brought into France by newly arrived infantry divisions, including the 104th, which had trained at Camp Adair, Oregon.

The French road system became an issue in bad weather, further bogging down the supply convoys bound for the Allied spearheads driving for the Siegfried Line.

At the same time, the U.S. Army organized a massive resupply effort, largely with African-American service troops. Dubbed the Red Ball Express, these dedicated men delivered almost 12,500 tons of supplies a day via dedicated roads that were closed to all other traffic. The Express ran from Cherbourg to a gigantic forward supply base at Chartres. From there, other transportation units carried the supplies to the twenty-eight combat divisions then fighting the Germans in northwest Europe. The Red Ball Express operated from August 25, 1944, until mid-November, when the British captured the Belgian port of Antwerp.

The Allies took other desperate measures to keep the supplies moving. The pre-D-Day planning had counted on a pause along the Seine River in order to build up the resources

General Benjamin O. Davis Sr. addresses men of the Red Ball Express. The Red Ball Express delivered 12,500 tons of supplies a day along a dedicated road that was closed to all other traffic.

Anonymous heroes studded the supply echelon's ranks. Here, Pfc. Thomas Glasby, a native of Greenville, South Carolina, is congratulated by Col. Fred Van Duzee, the executive officer of the First Army's quartermaster section. Glasby had been driving with a truck convoy delivering gasoline to forward units in the Ardennes Forest four days after the start of the offensive. The column ran into Germans, who set his vehicle on fire. Rather than bailing out and running for it, Glasby realized that his rig could cause the entire convoy to go up in flames. He stepped on the gas and drove his burning vehicle another hundred yards to get it clear of the other trucks. Then he dismounted and pulled cans of gas out of the back of his truck to keep it from blowing up.

General Dwight D. Eisenhower, commander of all Allied forces in Europe.

necessary for a push to the German frontier. That plan died in the flames of the Falaise Pocket. Instead of waiting, General Eisenhower saw opportunity in haste. The supply situation would have to be winged. And it was. Beyond the Red Ball Express, artillery units and engineer battalions were used to haul supplies. Others stripped off whatever vehicles they could afford to lose so that others could drive them forward. Despite every ad hoc effort, gasoline and ammunition shortages plagued the frontline units by early September. Patton's lead armored elements survived on a logistical shoestring.

The shortage would soon reach crisis levels. Eisenhower, Field Marshal Bernard Law Montgomery, commander of the British forces in northwest Europe, and his American counterpart, Gen. Omar Bradley, all saw the writing on the wall. The Allies simply did not have the resources to continue a full-front offensive. Either the British got the available supplies and continued their drive toward Northern Germany, or the Americans did and continued their offensive into eastern France and Belgium, crossed the Rhine, and drove into the heart of the Third Reich. Which path offered the best chance to end the war before the end of the year?

Though they lost thousands of vehicles and artillery pieces, the Germans still managed to get much of their manpower out of the Falaise Pocket. These men would form the core of the Third Reich's efforts to rebuild the armies on the Western Front during the fall of 1944.

3

MUD AND PILLBOXES

IN EARLY SEPTEMBER, the Allies estimated that the summer's fighting in France had cost the Germans 200,000 men and almost all their 2,300 tanks and AFVs. Another 230,000 Germans remained behind, guarding various French ports despite being sealed off from the Reich by the American breakthrough. On the Eastern Front, the Russian summer offensive ripped apart the Wehrmacht's Army Group Center and inflicted another 900,000 losses. The Third Reich was bleeding to death trying to hold onto the last shreds of its empire.

Germany could not avoid defeat. The Allied strength ensured that. But when and how would the Third Reich yield? That was the question on everyone's mind as Patton, Hodges, and Monty drove their men forward to the German border that September.

Montgomery believed that a reverse Schlieffen Plan—a full-scale, forty-division drive into northern Germany through Belgium and Holland—would be the quickest way to end the war.

The Americans wanted a dual drive, with Monty in the north and Bradley pushing into the Reich south of the Ruhr River Valley. Then the supplies dried up, and Ike had to make a choice: send what was available to Monty, or give it to Patton and let him keep racing the Germans back to the Siegfried Line.

Patton had been making remarkable progress. His armored and infantry divisions reached out into the heart of France, reaching the old World War I battlefields by the end of August. Reims fell on the 30th. On September 1, the 4th Armored Division crossed the Meuse River. Other divisions pressed on across the Moselle and stretched out to the fortress city of Metz on the dregs of their fuel stocks.

continued on page 31

The advance continues as American troops liberate the fortress city of Liège, Belgium.

In one of those little-known ironies of World War II, Field Marshal Bernard Law Montgomery rarely squandered an opportunity to denigrate his American allies, yet he used a Douglas C-47 Skytrain, made in the United States, as his personal transport.

Despite all its losses, the German Army remained a formidable fighting force, thanks to its small-unit cohesion and the firepower available to its infantry. Here, a German soldier hefts a panzerfaust, a one-shot antitank weapon. The Third Reich's shoulder-launched antitank weapons proved far superior to the U.S. Army's, and in some cases American units hoarded captured panzerfausts and panzershrecks for use against their former owners.

After bailing out from their stricken track, a tank crew takes cover while a medic works on one of the men during an ambush in France, fall of 1944.

Field Marshal Montgomery advocated a primary role for himself in the conquest of the Third Reich through the fall of 1944. His ego and his poor relationship with his American counterparts almost got him fired in January 1945.

On September 1, 1944, Patton's most trusted division, the 4th Armored, crossed the Meuse River at Saint-Mihiel, near the old World War I battlefield where many of the American senior-level officers had first seen combat.

An engineer guides a 4th Armored Division M4 onto a pontoon bridge over the Meuse River. Building things quickly, including bridges, was one of the U.S. Army's biggest assets during World War II. By the fall of 1944, U.S. engineers could construct a bridge strong enough to handle armor in a matter of hours. The Germans had no such ability, and it cost them dearly during the Ardennes Offensive.

Men of the Third Army approach the fortress city of Metz while supported by an M4 Sherman tank. By the fall of 1944, experienced units understood the importance of tank-infantry cooperation, and they became quite adept at combined operations, utilizing armor, artillery, and close-air support in close concert to shatter any resistance they encountered.

continued from page 27

In fact, as Patton's tanks rolled, the gasoline shortage grew so severe that elsewhere along the lines, the advance to the German frontier started to falter. Patton's Third Army managed to stay in the game only through some serious good luck. At Sens in late August, Patton's men captured one hundred thousand gallons of gas in thirty-seven train loads. This was enough to keep going to Chalons-sur-Marne, where another hundred thousand gallons of gas fell into his hands. Strangely, these windfalls were not reported to SHAEF! Patton kept dogging the Germans with their own fuel.

U.S. Army engineers bridge the Moselle. Not only were American engineers the best in the world; they had access to the best equipment. Allied bridging gear was second to none during the war.

British troops scale a demolished bridge in Vernon, France. While the Americans pushed east for the Siegfried Line, the British advanced northward along the coast into Belgium and Holland.

This couldn't last. Ike knew it, and when Montgomery proposed an airborne assault designed to capture a bridgehead over the Rhine River into Germany, he decided to roll the dice. Meanwhile, all along the front lines in Belgium and northeastern France, the last spasm of the pursuit finally came to an end. In the Ardennes Forest, the First Army penetrated part of the Siegfried Line on a long ridge called the Schnee Eifel. There, its soldiers and tanks stumbled and came to a stop, fuel-deprived and exhausted from the past month's fighting.

The Germans won the race. Safe behind their pillboxes and antitank ditches, they furiously rebuilt and regrouped. Ike saw no chance of ending the war through the southern drive. He ordered Monty to execute his plan.

The Germans won the race. Eisenhower turned to Montgomery's plan for salvation. In mid-September, the Allies launched Operation Market-Garden, which remains one of the most famous actions of World War II, thanks to the movie *A Bridge Too Far.*

Eisenhower wanted to beat the Germans to the Siegfried Line defenses (known as the "West Wall" by the Germans) during the race across France. He feared that if the German armies could get behind this network of pillboxes, fixed artillery emplacements, antitank obstacles, and barbed wire, its units could gain time to replace the losses suffered during the summer's fighting in Normandy.

British troops watch over the Nijmegen Bridge, one of the key objectives of Operation Market-Garden. Montgomery hoped to seize a bridgehead over the Rhine, from which his army group could strike into the Third Reich's industrial heartland and end the war by Christmas.

In an example of Allied cooperation at its finest, U.S. Army paratroops from the 101st Airborne ride aboard American-made M2 half-tracks driven by British soldiers of Monty's XXX Corps during the fighting in Holland, September 1944.

On September 17, 1944, Montgomery launched history's largest airborne operation, code named Market-Garden. Using three parachute divisions, he intended to secure a series of bridges stretching up to Arnhem and the Rhine River. The British XXX Corps would then charge into Holland, secure each of the bridges captured by the airborne troops, cross the Rhine at Arnhem, and pour into the Third Reich's industrialized Ruhr Valley.

It failed miserably, and when the smoke cleared, any chance that the Allies could end the war by Christmas had evaporated. With the heady pursuit over, the front coalesced into a continuous line from the North Sea down to the Swiss border.

By early October, as the supply situation began to stabilize, the advances on the Western Front came only with a sanguine toll. To the far north, the British 21st Army Group struggled in Holland as they tried to hold onto the gains made during Market-Garden so that operation wouldn't go down in history as a complete fiasco (it did anyway). On the right flank of the British, the U.S. Ninth and First Armies fought horrifically bloody battles at Aachen and the Hürtgen Forest. The Germans, now defending their own soil, found fresh resolve and took a heavy toll on the Americans as they battered their way forward.

South of the Ninth and First Armies, Patton's Third Army, the Seventh Army, and the First French Army struggled to clear all of France to the German border. At times,

Once Market-Garden failed, Montgomery faced a new challenge: defending the narrow corridor XXX Corps had opened from Eindhoven to just south of Arnhem, across the Nijmegen Bridge. Surrounded on three sides by Germans, the British found themselves in a tight situation and were unable to advance much farther for the remainder of the year.

Following Market-Garden, the supply situation improved, and the drive into Germany from eastern France continued. Unimaginative leadership led the First Army into a head-to-head fight with entrenched Germans in the Hürtgen Forest. The American divisions committed to the battle suffered appalling losses and gained little ground for their efforts. It was the low point of American operations in Western Europe.

The Battle of Aachen found the U.S. Army locked in a bitter urban fight with an entrenched and determined foe. Here, a medium machine gun team from the 26th Infantry Division rakes a fortified building during the battle. Aachen became the first major German city to fall to the Western Allies.

The cost in lives and treasure for Aachen and other such victories remained depressingly high.

Light tanks formed the backbone of the 1940 panzer corps. In spring weather, they were able to negotiate the narrow roads that twisted through the Ardennes with relative ease. That would not be the case four years later when the Germans tried again.

The Germans captured Sedan in 1940 through a lightning-quick strike through the Ardennes Forest. In 1944, Hitler sought to repeat history.

the shoestring supply situation thoroughly hampered the American and French advance. Simultaneously, the Germans tried to hold things together long enough to get reorganized and rearmed behind the Siegfried Line.

And it was here that Hitler saw his chance. While his generals struggled with just how to even save the situation on the Western Front, the Führer's great Hail Mary took shape. Like most plans, this new one contained echoes of the past.

In 1940, the Germans had surprised the French, Belgian, and British armies by sending their panzers through the rugged, hilly terrain of the Ardennes Forest. The area had been lightly defended by Belgian and French cavalry units that did not have the firepower to stand against the German panzers. They retreated in disarray, and the Germans crossed the Meuse River and split the Allied armies in two. This breakthrough carried the panzer units all the way to the coast, forcing the British and many French divisions to withdraw from the Continent at Dunkirk. It was the decisive blow that led to the fall of France, and the surprise attack in the Ardennes served as the key moment in the campaign.

Hitler decided to try again. This time, though, he mixed in a little of the strategic reasoning behind the 1918 Ludendorff offensives. In 1918, the Germans launched a series of last-gasp offensives on the Western Front that they hoped would end the war in their favor. The Germans aimed their first blow against the British, hoping to drive a wedge between them and their French allies. For a time, it looked like that might work. The British retreated

One of the key components to the German victory in 1940 was the Luftwaffe's overwhelming superiority in the air. By 1944, the Luftwaffe could not stand against the mighty USAAF and RAF. The German soldiers and Waffen-SS troops gathered for the Ardennes Offensive that fall could count on minimal air support at best.

In 1940 the Luftwaffe revolutionized airpower-infantry cooperation. The ultimate close-support platform that year, the Junkers Ju-87 Stuka, still soldiered on in the Luftwaffe's ground-attack units at the time of the Ardennes Offensive. However, they'd become so obsolete that to send them into battle on the Western Front would have been a death sentence for the crews. Instead, the remaining Stukas fought against the Russians on the Eastern Front. What air support was available for the Sixth SS and Fifth Panzer Armies would come in the form of single-engined fighter-bombers.

When Montgomery captured the port of Antwerp, it looked like the Allies could resolve all of their supply issues at last. However, he neglected to clear the Schelde Estuary. It wasn't until early 1945 that the last Germans were captured or killed around the approaches to Antwerp, making the port finally useable for the Allies. Nevertheless, Hitler hoped to retake the city in the Ardennes offensive, splitting the American and British armies, then turning to defeat each in detail. The plan was sheer fantasy.

Hitler's bizarre racial views colored his entire perception of the United States, its army, and its ability to wage a modern total war. Those misconceptions played an important role in how Hitler crafted his Western Front counteroffensive.

in disarray and made plans to defend the coast ports that could get them out of the country in a worst-case scenario. The French fell back toward Paris. A gap opened between the two Allies, but the Germans could not capitalize on it.

Hitler hoped to do the same thing in 1944. He wanted to hit the U.S. Army in the Ardennes, push across the Meuse River, then drive northwest and capture Antwerp. In the process, he would cut off the British from their lines of supplies and from their American allies to the south. If the Wehrmacht could pull this off, Hitler believed the destruction of the trapped and marooned 21st Army Group would cause the demise of the Anglo-American alliance.

There were all sorts of problems with this plan, not the least of which was a repeat of the same mistake the Germans made in 1918. They attacked the wrong army. In 1918, the French Army barely could man its trenches. The previous year it had mutinied, and the British had to take over an increasingly large stretch of the front, as the French could not defend their own country anymore. The staggering losses at Verdun and the Chemin des Dames ensured that.

Instead of finishing off the French in March 1918 with the Ludendorff offensives, the Germans wasted their efforts on the much stronger and more resilient British. That error remains one of the classic lost opportunities in modern military history. Had that first hammer blow hit the French, the war might have ended in a very different way.

In 1944, Hitler assessed the Americans as the weaker ally in Western Europe. He based this on his own racial views, a total misunderstanding of the American way of warfare and its command arrangements, and an outdated view of the army's quality and capabilities. At the same time, he magnified the capabilities of the British Army in his head and missed whatever real opportunity lay in the West that fall. Hitler had always believed the Americans to be weak, viewing them as racially mixed degenerates, obsessed with jazz music and vice, a corrupt democracy with no martial spirit. He also thought that like his own army, the U.S. Army would have to get permission from President Roosevelt himself to make any serious withdrawals in Europe in the face of a major counteroffensive. That would take time, and the delay would give the Germans the chance to exploit their breakthrough and get across the Meuse. Hitler did not understand that FDR and the Pentagon basically left the conduct of the war to the theater commander, Dwight D. Eisenhower. That meant the U.S. forces could react much more rapidly to any sudden threat than Hitler thought.

By 1944, Hitler's low opinion of the U.S. Army had been overcome by events. After two years of hard fighting, the Americans had learned priceless lessons, its veteran units hardened by months in battle. As the U.S. Army continued to gain strength, the British Army began to shrink. Without the United States' manpower reserves, Great Britain essentially ran out of replacements for 21st Army Group by the fall of 1944. To keep the divisions in the field going, other units had to be cannibalized. Five years of global warfare had exhausted America's primary ally.

Roosevelt, the president of Turkey, and Churchill meet in Cairo in 1943. Unlike Hitler, President Roosevelt never micromanaged his field commanders. Hitler assumed Roosevelt controlled the U.S. Army in the same manner he controlled the Wehrmacht and that such a command situation would delay the American response to the Ardennes offensive. It was yet another misconception that laid the groundwork for failure.

As to the quality of the U.S. divisions in the West, Hitler and the Germans in general held a low opinion of them. This was not unusual, and it stemmed from the Battle of Kasserine Pass in 1943. Here, the U.S. Army faced a significant German armored counterattack for the first time and suffered several serious routs before containing the attack and throwing it back. The British, who conveniently forgot that they'd had their hat handed to them for three straight years by the Germans and had only won their first decisive victory against them a few months before at El Alamein, crowed and cackled over the American setback. They derided the Americans as "our Italians" and leaked stories to the press about how poor a showing the Yanks put up in the northwest African countryside. Those stigmas lingered for decades, so it is not surprising that Hitler held the views he did in 1944.

It was through the outstanding leadership of men like Gen. Omar Bradley (shown with General Anderson) in North Africa that the U.S. Army absorbed and put to good use the lessons learned in this first campaign against the Wehrmacht. The army the Third Reich faced in 1944 was vastly different from the one it first engaged in 1942.

The U.S. Army cut its teeth in North Africa. Branded by the mini-disaster at Kasserine Pass, its reputation never really recovered, and the British continued to hold a low opinion of their American allies through the rest of the war. More importantly, so did Hitler and many senior Wehrmacht leaders.

General von Arnim surrendered almost 250,000 Axis troops in Tunisia in the spring of 1943. Hitler's distorted view of the U.S. Army's capabilities required him to have a selective memory and forgot such disasters.

He was dead wrong of course. The weak link in the autumn of 1944 was not the U.S. Army, which was growing in strength, experience, and capabilities on almost a daily basis by the fall of 1944. As the Americans grew ascendant, the British peaked and struggled. Five years of costly battles all over the globe had drained the Empire of its manpower, resources, and finances. The manpower situation grew to crisis proportions, and by the fall of 1944 the British Army had to cannibalize other divisions to keep replacements flowing to the 21st Army Group in Holland. While tactically and strategically capable, the British in 1944 wielded an army that lacked depth. The Germans could have exploited its brittleness, but instead Hitler looked first to the Americans.

The counteroffensive would be made through the Ardennes, just like the now-legendary days of 1940. To negate the threat of Allied airpower, Hitler decided that the attack would begin only when cloaked by bad weather. The best remaining troops, tanks, and Waffen-SS

From the first battle for France in 1940 through the torturous mountain campaigns in Italy, the British Army had fought a long, debilitating war with the Wehrmacht. By 1944, Montgomery's 21st Army Group embodied all the lessons learned, but suffered from an acute manpower shortage, as well as low morale in some of his divisions that had seen combat with him in North Africa, Sicily, and Italy.

When Montgomery brought some of his veteran divisions to England after the hard fighting in the Mediterranean theater, many of his men felt they were shouldering an unfair load of the war effort. He appealed to them before D-Day and told them the Empire needed their skill and dedication. Nevertheless, they were right. Some British and Commonwealth units had remained either in England or India and had yet to close with any enemy. Units such as the 51st Highlanders had seen more than their share of the fighting. The resentment this stirred lowered morale.

Bad weather and deep woods were the only things that could keep Allied air recon from discovering the German troop and armor buildup on the Western Front. The winter weather cooperated, and the Ardennes Forest provided ample cover for the Sixth SS and Fifth Panzer Armies.

units would be gathered and concealed around the Ardennes under strict radio silence. To prevent the Americans from catching on that they faced new units in the area, the arriving German divisions received orders that forbade them from patrolling. This minimized the risk of prisoners falling into U.S. hands and telling their captors their unit assignments.

To make the decisive thrust for Antwerp, the German plan envisioned a series of front-shattering attacks by infantry that would then be exploited by panzer and Waffen-SS divisions. Those armored thrusts would be beefed up by the latest and deadliest tanks in the German arsenal, including the Tiger II (or King Tiger), the Jagdpanther, and the Jagdpanzer IV. These nearly impregnable steel monsters would sow havoc across the American front as they ground their way forward.

All this would require an enormous logistical effort, something that the German Army always seemed to mishandle. By 1944, stocks of fuel and artillery ammunition dwindled to almost nothing. The Reich had to scrape the bottom of the barrel just to come up with a few

Waffen-SS troops during the counterattack at Kharkov in early 1943. The Waffen-SS units were among the most feared soldiers in the world. Fanatically loyal to the Hitler regime, they proved to be ruthless and utterly determined in combat.

A British Bren Gun Carrier rolls through Prague at the end of World War II. By 1945, the Brits depended heavily on American lend-lease equipment for keeping its army rolling forward, but this was one of their few homegrown designs to soldier on through the war.

The Jagdpanther was one of the deadliest tank destroyers of World War II. Its effectiveness was limited by its lack of maneuverability, its weight, and its reliability. In the Ardennes, such heavy armored vehicles became a liability at times when the available roads could not support their weight.

hours' worth of fuel for the training of each panzer crew assigned to the new offensive. Even worse, the fuel shortage threatened to put Antwerp out of reach. To solve this problem, the Germans counted on capturing American fuel depots as they advanced. This was Hitler's great gadget play: break through the American lines in the Ardennes, cross the Meuse River into more open countryside, and capture the most important port in northwest Europe, Antwerp. With the Allied armies split, just like in 1940, the Germans would turn north and finish off the Brits. Then Hitler could turn his attention east, wait for his wonder weapons to reach the front in numbers, and aim for a negotiated peace.

There were so many miscalculations, bad judgment calls, poor-planning-related errors, and compromises in the basic plan that it is hard to fathom how any sentient human being could ever think this would work. The fact is, Hitler's mental capacity in the fall of 1944 had suffered serious blows. His health was failing; his doctors injected him with a daily drug cocktail that in retrospect must have impacted his mind. There is speculation that he suffered from the final stages of syphilis and perhaps Parkinson's disease as well. He had also barely survived the July 20 assassination attempt when a bomb went off only a few feet away from him. The blast possibly left him with a traumatic brain injury, which contributed to his sudden outbursts of rage and other side effects. The explosion also injured his arms, shoulder, and legs. He was not a man capable of functioning as an effective commander in chief.

It is not surprising that a mind in this condition produced a plan so riddled with bad assumptions. In the weeks to come, those bad assumptions played out with disastrous effect on the German armies in the west.

A two-seat night-fighter variant of the Me-262 was just entering production when the war ended. Designed to be the wonder weapon that would drive the Royal Air Force's Bomber Command from the skies over the Third Reich, it never reached operational service in enough numbers (and reliability) to make any difference at all in the outcome of the war.

A B-17 Flying Fortress returns from a mission over Germany. The Germans were able to assemble two panzer armies right under the nose of Allied aircraft. It was a remarkable feat, especially given the fact that the USAAF controlled the skies over Germany during daylight hours and the RAF's Bomber Command dominated at night.

4

WATCH ON THE RHINE

★ ★ ★ ★ ★

THROUGH NOVEMBER AND EARLY DECEMBER, the Germans carefully amassed their remaining panzer and Waffen-SS divisions around the Ardennes Forest. Hidden in the woods from the prying eyes of Allied spy planes, the panzer crews tended to their tanks, gathered fuel and ammunition, and bided their time.

To conceal what was happening, the Germans curtailed their patrolling so as not to reveal the presence of new units in the Ardennes. They also observed strict radio silence, which proved very effective. The Allies never tumbled onto the fact that so much power had been gathered in the Ardennes. In fact, it ranks as one of the greatest deception campaigns of the twentieth century. When the panzers started rolling, they caught the Americans completely by surprise.

By early December, the Germans could count on twenty-four divisions to be ready for the counteroffensive. Ten of those twenty-four were armored. Divided into three armies, the Sixth Panzer, the Fifth Panzer, and the Seventh, a motley group of volksgrenadier and infantry divisions would launch the first assaults on the American lines. Once they tore open the front, the panzers would pour through.

The Sixth Panzer Army (which would officially become the Sixth SS Panzer Army after the Battle of the Bulge), commanded by an old friend of Hitler's named Gen. Sepp Dietrich, received the toughest assignment. Dietrich's command included four hard-bitten Waffen-SS panzer divisions, including the 1st, 12th, 9th, and 2nd. These dedicated and politically reliable units formed the core of Hitler's plan. Supported by heavy armored units, a parachute division, and numerous volksgrenadier divisions, the SS panzer units would form the northern strike force for the Ardennes offensive. The Fifth Panzer Army, commanded by another politically reliable general, Hasso von Manteuffel, would support and protect Dietrich's left flank, exploiting any breakthroughs south of the road center at Saint-Vith. On the far left, the Seventh Army would use its infantry divisions to secure the southern shoulder

Sepp Dietrich, close to Hitler since the late 1920s, was beloved by his men and reviled and disdained by Wehrmacht officers. He never distinguished himself as a strategist or tactician.

General Dietrich (in profile) examines a map as refugees file past. When Dietrich died after the war, over twenty thousand people, mostly veterans of the SS who served under him, attended his funeral and memorial service.

The lull before the storm.

A veteran infantryman writes home to his family wearing not a shred of winter camouflage. This would be a serious problem during the Ardennes counteroffensive—one that the GIs themselves were forced to solve with ad hoc solutions, such as wearing bed sheets over their uniforms.

Though the Germans wanted to replace the venerable Panzer IV with the Panther, production of the newer medium tank never achieved high enough levels to make that happen. As a result, the prewar-designed Panzer IV soldiered on and remained a key component of every panzer unit until the end of the war. Here, a Panzer IV is seen on the Eastern Front getting buzzed by a Fieseler Storch liaison aircraft.

An M4 company trains in the Southern California desert prior to its deployment to the ETO. The M4 Sherman, equipped with a modified version of the World War I French 75mm gun, served as the U.S. Army's standard medium tank. In the Ardennes, the M4 was seriously outclassed by newer German designs, including the Panther and the Tiger I and II. Nevertheless, the M4 crews gave a good account of themselves even when the odds were against them.

The M10 (known as the "Wolverine" to the British) served as the standard tank destroyer through 1944. Equipped with a 76mm cannon, it was much more effective against German panzers than the short-barreled M4 Shermans. U.S. Army doctrine distinguished between tanks and tank destroyers. Tanks provided mobile firepower support for the infantry while tank destroyers knocked out enemy armor.

of the advance. Manteuffel possessed a powerful fAorce that included the elite Panzer Lehr Division, rebuilt after its almost total destruction in Normandy. He also had the 2nd, 9th, and 116th Panzer Divisions at his disposal.

A checkerboard of exhausted, depleted units and fresh-faced ones just arrived from the States faced these two German armies. Since the fighting in September, the Ardennes had become a quiet sector, and the U.S. Army used it as almost a frontline rest area for divisions that had been chewed up elsewhere. Hodges and his First Army had become responsible for the Ardennes following the Battles of Aachen and the Hürtgen Forest earlier in the fall, and the truth was that the First Army had suffered a lot of casualties during those weeks. Mixed in with the veteran and exhausted 4th, 28th, 1st, and 2nd Infantry Divisions were the new arrivals. The 99th Division, nicknamed the Checkerboard Division, reached the front only a few weeks before the start of the battle. On the Schnee Eifel, amid the pillboxes of the

Every American tank battalion included a company of light tanks. By 1944, these light tanks were hopelessly deficient when facing any sort of German armored threat or antitank weapon. In the Ardennes, the light tank companies took heavy losses.

An M5 Stuart, the standard American light tank in the Ardennes, of the 27th Cavalry. The M5 was an upgraded version of the earlier M3 Stuart, which first saw action with the British Army in the North African desert in 1941. The M5 served as the primary armored vehicle for the U.S. Army's cavalry squadrons during the final year of the war. It was subsequently replaced by the M24, which arrived in numbers during the final weeks of the Battle of the Bulge.

Siegfried Line, the brand new 106th Division conducted a relief in place and took over an extended section of the front only days before the German onslaught.

Altogether, the Americans had eighty-three thousand men with 242 tanks and 182 tank destroyers covering a ninety-mile front in the Ardennes. To support the GIs in the trenches, the divisions in the area could count on 394 artillery pieces.

Across the front, the German first wave waited for their attack orders some 250,000 men strong. They possessed 382 tanks and 335 assault guns. Behind them, the exploitation units contained another 55,000 men and 561 tanks. They would pour forward into the American lines only after the 2,623 artillery and rocket pieces behind them unleashed the largest German barrage seen on the Western Front.

After several postponements, the Germans readied their gear, stood by their tanks and loaded their nebelwerfers—the multiple rocket launchers that made such dreadful howling noises that the men called them "Screamin' Meamies"—and howitzers. Operation Watch on the Rhine, history's greatest gadget play, would begin on December 16, 1944. The Americans, huddled in their foxholes carved out of the forest floor, had no clue of the blow about to fall on them.

M10s in action during the drive across France. With their open turrets and thin armor, the M10 could not stand toe-to-toe against the much more heavily armored German tanks. Instead, the crews used the M10s maneuverability and speed to minimize their own weaknesses.

The German nebelwerfer multiple-launch rocket system, dubbed "Screaming Meemies" for the sound its incoming rockets made, was a feared and deadly indirect-fire weapon.

Part II

THE NORTH SHOULDER

★ ★ ★ ★ ★

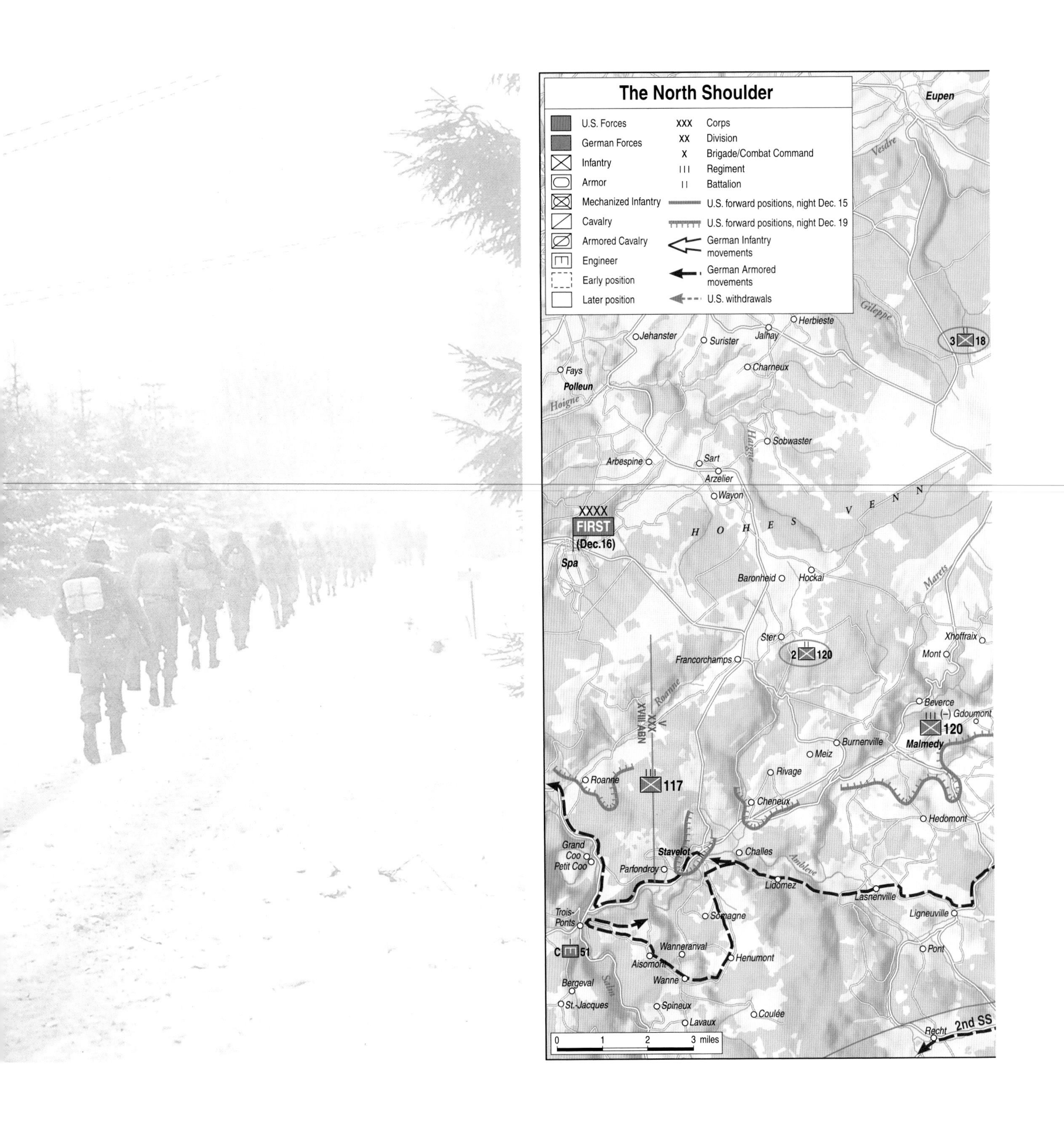
The North Shoulder
U.S. Forces
German Forces
Infantry
Armor
Mechanized Infantry
Cavalry
Armored Cavalry
Engineer
Early position
Later position
XXX Corps
XX Division
X Brigade/Combat Command
III Regiment
II Battalion
U.S. forward positions, night Dec. 15
U.S. forward positions, night Dec. 19
German Infantry movements
German Armored movements
U.S. withdrawals
Eupen
Vesdre
Gileppe
Herbieste
Jalhay
Jehanster
Surister
Charneux
Fays
Polleun
Hoigne
Sobwaster
Arbespine
Sart
Arzelier
Wayon
HOHES VENN
XXXX
FIRST
(Dec.16)
Spa
Baronheid
Hockai
Marets
Ster
Xhoffraix
Mont
Francorchamps
Roanne
XVIII ABN
Beverce
(–) Gdoumont
120
Malmedy
Burnenville
Meiz
Rivage
Roanne
117
Cheneux
Hedomont
Grand Coo
Petit Coo
Stavelot
Challes
Parfondroy
Amblève
Lodomez
Lasnenville
Ligneuville
Trois-Ponts
Somagne
Pont
51
Wanneranval
Aisomont
Henumont
Wanne
Bergeval
Salm
St.-Jacques
Spineux
Coulée
Lavaux
Recht
2nd SS
0 1 2 3 miles

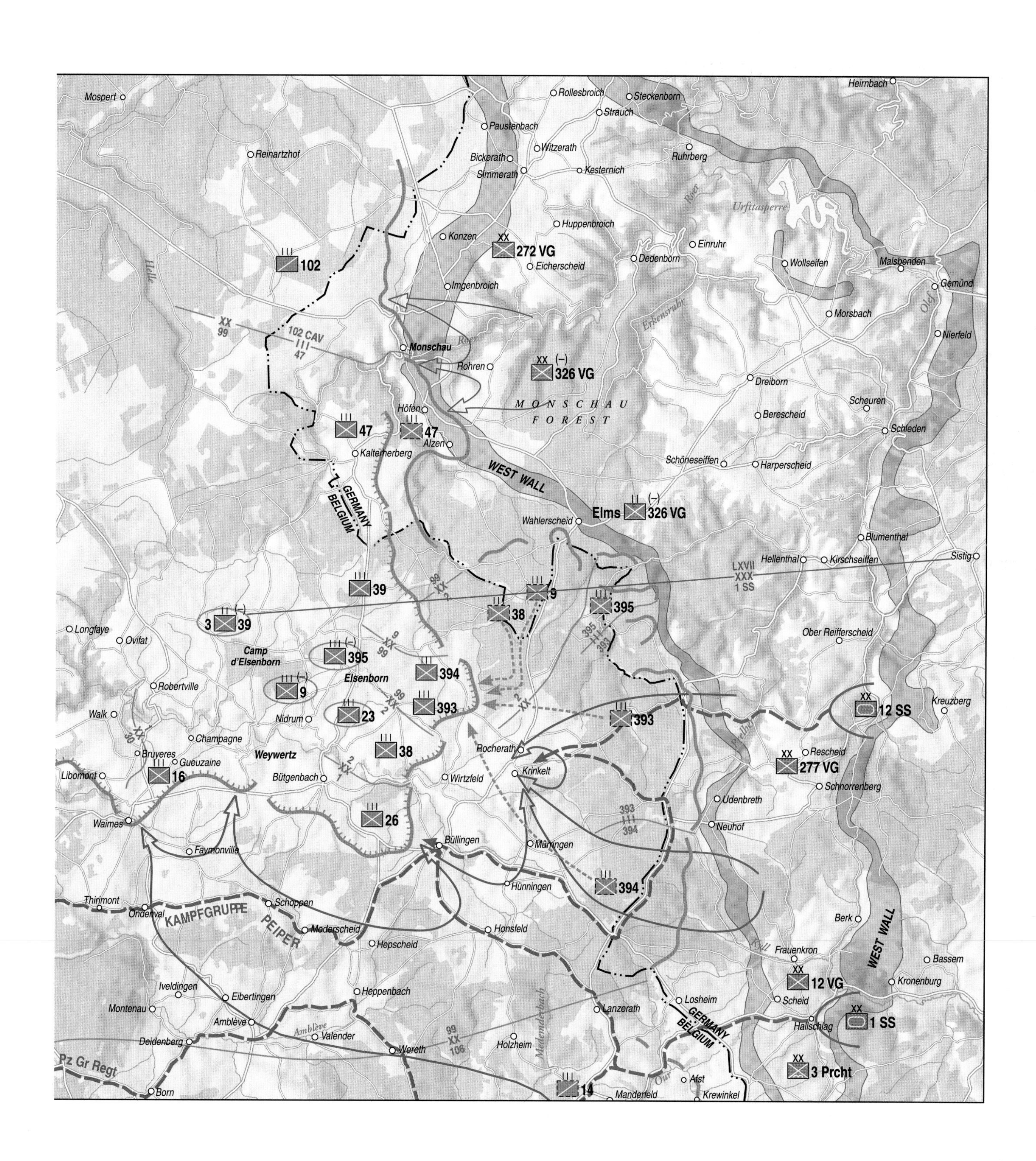
Mospert
Rollesbroich
Steckenborn
Heirnbach
Strauch
Paustenbach
Reinartzhof
Bickerath
Witzerath
Simmerath
Kesternich
Ruhrberg
Roer
Urftasperre
Huppenbroich
Konzen
272 VG
Einruhr
102
Eicherscheid
Dedenborn
Wollseifen
Malsbenden
Helle
Imgenbroich
Gemünd
Erkensruhr
Olef
Morsbach
99
102 CAV
47
Nierfeld
Monschau
Rohren
326 VG
Dreiborn
MONSCHAU
FOREST
Höfen
Scheuren
Berescheid
47
47
Alzen
Schleden
Kalterherberg
WEST WALL
Schöneseiffen
Harperscheid
GERMANY
BELGIUM
Elms
326 VG
Wahlerscheid
Blumenthal
Hellenthal
Kirschseiffen
Sistig
LXVII
XXX
1 SS
39
9
38
395
3
39
Longfaye
Ovifat
Ober Reifferscheid
Camp d'Elsenborn
395
394
Elsenborn
Robertville
9
393
12 SS
Kreuzberg
Walk
Nidrum
23
393
Champagne
Rocherath
Resscheid
Bruyeres
Gueuzaine
Weywertz
38
277 VG
Libomont
16
Bütgenbach
Wirtzfeld
Krinkelt
Schnorrenberg
Udenbreth
393
394
Waimes
26
Neuhof
Faymonville
Büllingen
Mürringen
Hünningen
394
Thirimont
Schoppen
Ondenval
KAMPFGRUPPE
PEIPER
Berk
Moderscheid
Honsfeld
Hepscheid
Kyll
Frauenkron
Bassem
WEST WALL
12 VG
Kronenburg
Iveldingen
Eibertingen
Heppenbach
Losheim
Scheid
Montenau
Lanzerath
GERMANY
BELGIUM
1 SS
Amblève
Hallschlag
Amblève
Valender
Medendorbach
99
106
Deidenberg
Wereth
Holzheim
Pz Gr Regt
3 Prcht
Our
Afst
Born
14
Manderfeld
Krewinkel

With the front quiet, U.S. cavalry troopers take a few minutes to attend mass with German locals in the late fall, 1944.

5

JOHN BUFORD'S GHOST

IN MID-DECEMBER, LT. COL. ROBERT E. O'BRIAN JR. had a hunch. As commander of the 38th Cavalry Reconnaissance Squadron, he'd been tasked with defending the ancient city of Monschau, which served as an important part of the local road network. One north-south road passed through town, intersecting with an eastward running route that could take the traveler to Rohren (still held by the Germans) or southeast to Hofen and the 3rd Battalion, 395th Infantry.

O'Brian held an important part of the line, and his hunch led him to believe that the Germans might counterattack him. As a result, in the final days before Watch on the Rhine began, he kept his troopers busy digging trenches, clearing fields of fire, and laying mines and trip flares. He brought in eighty truckloads of barbed wire and made sure that all of his platoons and troops were wired in tight. For additional support, he placed a platoon of tank destroyers to overwatch the main roads leading into town. His M5 Stuart light tank company covered the town itself and the route leading east, while his troopers hunkered down on the hills and slopes east of town, scraping their fighting positions out of hip-deep snow and frozen ground in places. The work was hard and rugged, but O'Brian's men would be prepared. On the night of December 15, 1944, his troopers hunkered down in their holes, waiting to see if the squadron commander's hunch would play out.

An American barbed wire party. Lieutenant Colonel Robert O'Brian foresaw the threat to his command and made sure his men were wired in tight in the days before the German offensive.

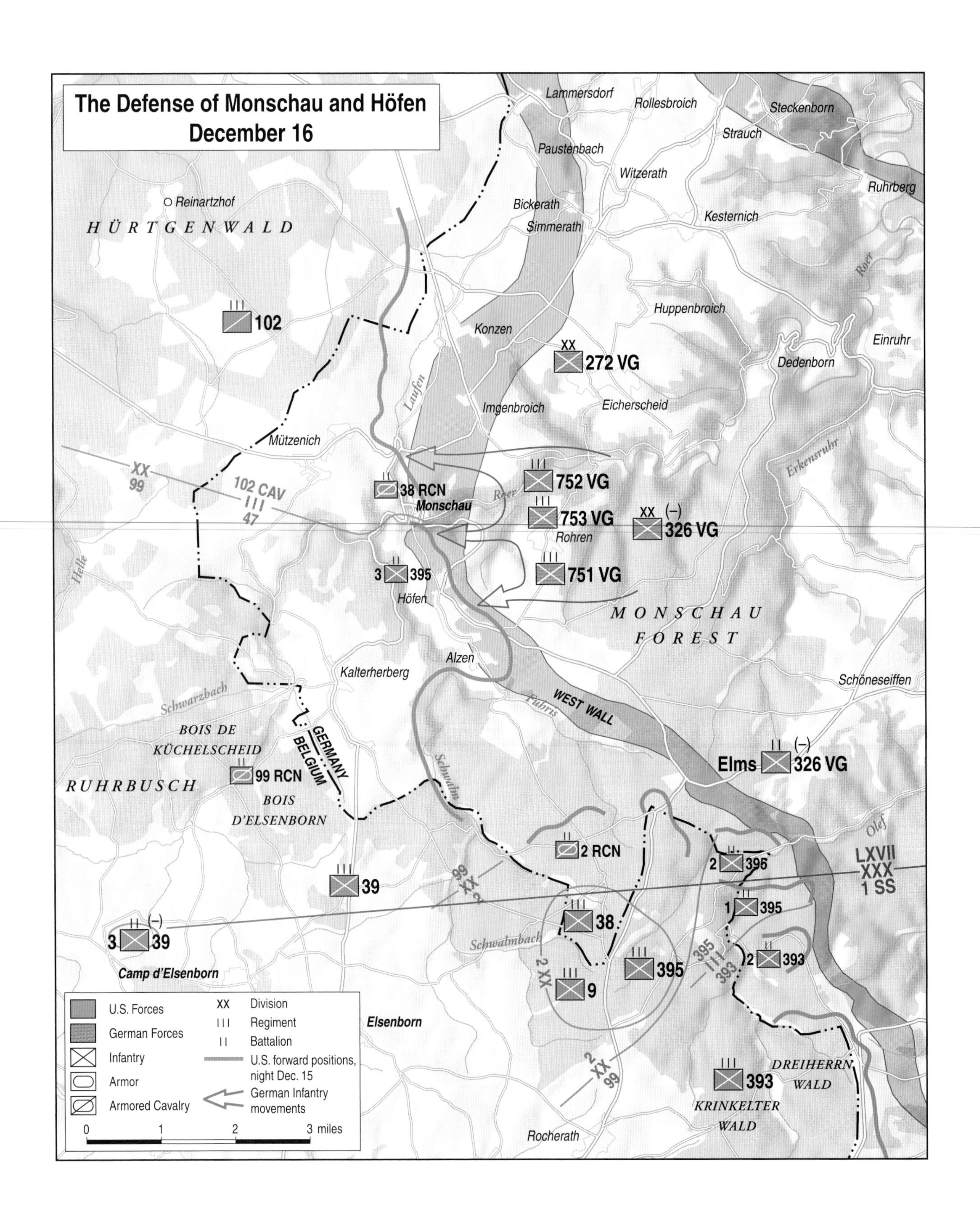

The Defense of Monschau and Höfen
December 16
Lammersdorf
Rollesbroich
Steckenborn
Strauch
Paustenbach
Witzerath
Ruhrberg
Reinartzhof
Bickerath
Simmerath
Kesternich
HÜRTGENWALD
Roer
Huppenbroich
102
Konzen
Einruhr
XX
272 VG
Dedenborn
Laufen
Imgenbroich
Eicherscheid
Mützenich
Erkensruhr
XX
99
102 CAV
III
47
III
752 VG
38 RCN
Monschau
Roer
III
753 VG
XX (–)
326 VG
Rohren
Helle
3
395
III
751 VG
Höfen
MONSCHAU
FOREST
Alzen
Kalterherberg
Schöneseiffen
Schwarzbach
WEST WALL
Fuhrts
BOIS DE
KÜCHELSCHEID
GERMANY
BELGIUM
II (–)
Elms
326 VG
99 RCN
RUHRBUSCH
Schwalm
BOIS
D'ELSENBORN
Olef
2 RCN
2
396
LXVII
XXX
1 SS
III
39
99
XX
2
1
395
III
38
3
39
Schwalmbach
395
III
393
2
393
395
2
XX
9
Camp d'Elsenborn
U.S. Forces
German Forces
Infantry
Armor
Armored Cavalry
XX Division
III Regiment
II Battalion
U.S. forward positions, night Dec. 15
German Infantry movements
0
1
2
3 miles
Elsenborn
2
XX
99
III
393
DREIHERRN
WALD
KRINKELTER
WALD
Rocherath

Across no man's land, the men of Sepp Dietrich's Sixth Panzer Army made their final preparations for Operation Watch on the Rhine. Sepp Dietrich was a street fighter. An NCO during World War I, he returned home and embraced the chaos of postwar Germany. He became one of the earliest Nazi adherents and one of Hitler's oldest confederates. As a combat leader, he was despised and derided by the blue-blooded Prussian elite that formed the nexus of the Werhmacht's officer corps. They thought he owed his position entirely to his relationship with Hitler, and that anyone with his Luddite level of intelligence was best left in the NCO corps, not commanding entire SS armies. Perhaps so, but the fact was Dietrich commanded almost reverence among his men. Time and again, he inspired them with his frontline example as well as his refusal to live better than they did. He shared their hardships and privations, and the Waffen-SS soldiers loved him for it.

But by 1944, Dietrich's heart wasn't in it anymore. After Normandy, he knew the war was lost, and Hitler's insistence to continue it only got more of his men killed. After learning of Operation Watch on the Rhine that fall, he approached the Ardennes counteroffensive with a very pessimistic view of how things would go. He was not disappointed.

The Sixth Panzer Army was supposed to attack after a heavy initial bombardment along a front that ranged from about ten miles north of Monschau south to the Losheim Gap. The terrain here was low and swampy—impossible tank country. Behind and to the south of Monschau stretched the high ground of the Elsenborn Ridge. That ridge was the key to the Sixth's initial attack. Take it, and the roads to the south the panzers needed to get to the Meuse would be opened up. The Sixth Panzer had been assigned five main roads that would

Sepp Dietrich, Hitler's friend from the early days of the Nazi Party, had become disillusioned by December 1944. After the Normandy campaign, he no longer believed Germany could win the war.

Dietrich (far left) with his staff in Normandy. He led from the front throughout the war. His men loved him for it, even if his fellow German generals disparaged his tactical and strategic savvy.

The German rail net was under constant air attack by the fall of 1944. To move anything forward, especially during the day, invited destruction at the hands of roving Allied fighter-bombers. To counter that, the Germans heavily camouflaged their trains and tried to move at night as much as possible.

hopefully carry the panzers west to the Meuse River. Taking Elsenborn Ridge would open up three of those five routes to the river.

Dietrich assigned his LXVII Corps to launch the initial attack around Monschau. This would be the hinge of the entire Sixth Panzer Army's assault, and was designed to protect the right flank of Dietrich's main effort.

Originally, it was supposed to be carried out by the 272nd and 326th Volksgrenadier Divisions, supported by a battalion of behemoth Jagdtiger tank destroyers. Fate threw the first curveball of the game, though, when the Jagdtigers failed to arrive before December 16. They had been loaded aboard trains and sent forward. On the way, Allied fighter-bombers shot up the tracks. The Jagdtigers could not get forward in time to support the initial blows. The volksgrenadiers would make their attack unsupported.

The German LXVII Corps faced another problem on the morning of the 16th. The Americans had been driving forward with the 2nd, 9th, 78th, and part of the 99th Infantry Divisions right on the north side of the Ardennes, intending to grab the Roer River dams

An engineer prepares to demolish trees outside of Monschau. This was a quick and easy way to toss roadblocks in the way of advancing German armor.

One of the main weapons used by the U.S. cavalry squadrons was the M5 Stuart light tank. The M2 .50-caliber heavy machine gun could be used as an air-defense weapon as well as against German infantry or soft-skinned vehicles.

A 60mm mortar crew in action at Monschau. These light support weapons played a key role in the 38th Cavalry Reconnaissance Squadron's defense of the city.

before Christmas. Three days before the offensive's scheduled start, the 272nd Volksgrenadier Division had been sucked into a furious house-to-house urban battle in Kesternich. Part of the 326th Volksgrenadier Division had to actually go and reinforce it, which bled away much of the corps' initial strength in its own assault.

None of this mattered to the men in the frozen foxholes east of Monschau when the first German shells began to fall at 5:30 a.m. All up and down the ninety miles of Ardennes frontline, over a thousand German guns roared to life. Everything from mortars to 14-inch naval guns rained high-explosive death down on the American positions. Within minutes, the shells severed most of the communication lines that ran between the frontline units and their headquarters, or the artillery units.

Twenty minutes later, at Monschau, Sepp Dietrich's volksgrenadiers padded across the snow-covered forested hills and slammed into O'Brian's defenses. The American cavalry troopers were waiting, virtually unscathed by the opening bombardment thanks to their defensive preparations. In fact, O'Brian had ordered wire parties out to restore communications with their assigned field artillery battalions in the rear before the barrage had even ended.

They had not yet finished repairing the lines when the first volksgrenadiers from the 751st Regiment slipped into view. If the 38th Cavalry folded, V Corps headquarters would be vulnerable to an attack from the rear and flank. It was a seminal moment for the American cavalry, and like Gen. John Buford's troopers on Gettyburg's Seminary Ridge two generations before, they more than rose to the challenge.

The U.S. Army had learned to dig in deep every night after the day's advance. With the lines stable in the Ardennes, the Americans were well entrenched, and the initial German barrage, despite its strength and duration, caused surprisingly few casualties.

The German shelling destroyed the phone lines running to the American frontline units. As soon as the barrage lifted, signal teams went to work restoring communication.

An American infantryman reloads his M1 Garand rifle shortly after his platoon killed a number of their German counterparts. On the north shoulder, close-quarters combat in the snow, woods, and villages became commonplace.

A dead German soldier lies frozen in the snow. It appears that with the last of his strength, he withdrew a photo of his wife and held it in his hand as his life ebbed away.

A section of the 99th Infantry Division's line, seen on December 15, 1944. The 99th had joined the fight only a few weeks before the German offensive and was still considered a very green unit.

The first wave of Germans reached the outskirts of Monschau and ran right into the waiting M5 Stuarts from F Company. The tankers loaded their guns with 37mm canister shells, and when they opened fire, the massed effect of these gigantic shotgun-like blasts tore apart an entire volksgrenadier company. The survivors recoiled as their comrades, so vibrant a moment before, lay in gruesome horror around them. They left behind at least fifty, probably more like seventy-five, dead and dying men.

The 38th Cavalry suffered seven casualties. Sepp Dietrich's far-north assault had failed completely.

The initial German assault waves maneuvered through ground fog and sleet. The weather concealed them from long-range machine-gun and direct-artillery fire.

A few miles to the south, the 99th Infantry Division's 3-395 had weathered a dreadful barrage that saw at least 250 shells land in the battalion's area of operations around Hofen. At 5:50 a.m., the 2nd Battalion, 751st Volksgrenadiers, 326th Volksgrenadier Division charged through the morning fog across broken terrain and hit the 3rd Battalion, 395th Infantry, at five points almost simultaneously. The German main effort slammed into the junction between I and K Companies, which happened to be just east of Hofen. Without communications re-established with the artillery units in the rear, the battle that unfolded here pitted a green U.S. infantry battalion against a green German volksgrenadier division.

The volksgrenadiers surged for the American lines and ran straight into point-blank small-arms fire. Some of the U.S. BAR men held their fire until the Germans were not even ten feet away from their camouflaged foxholes. The dead heaped around these positions, and some of the stricken grenadiers actually tumbled into the BAR men's foxholes. Mortar shells fell, machine guns unleashed their fearsome destructiveness, and the grenadiers died in the snow. The attack continued, but American gunfire stopped each successive rush.

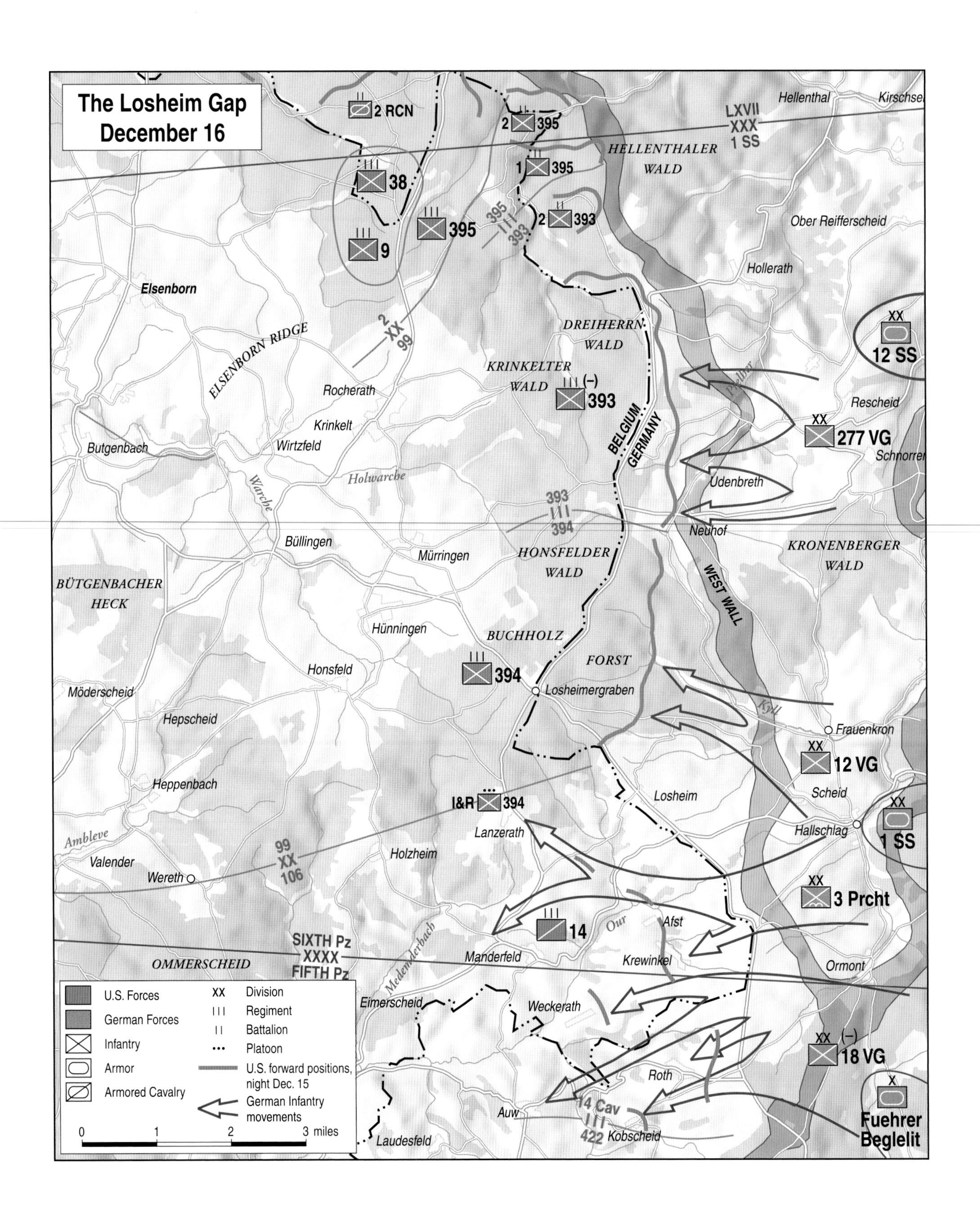
The Losheim Gap
December 16
2 RCN
2 395
1 395
38
9
395
2 393
LXVII
XXX
1 SS
HELLENTHALER
WALD
Hellenthal
Kirschseiffen
Ober Reifferscheid
Hollerath
Elsenborn
ELSENBORN RIDGE
2
XX
99
DREIHERRN
WALD
KRINKELTER
WALD
393
(–)
12 SS
Rocherath
Krinkelt
Wirtzfeld
Butgenbach
BELGIUM
GERMANY
Rescheid
277 VG
Schnorrenberg
Holwarche
Warche
Udenbreth
393
394
Neuhof
Büllingen
Mürringen
HONSFELDER
WALD
KRONENBERGER
WALD
WEST WALL
BÜTGENBACHER
HECK
Hünningen
BUCHHOLZ
FORST
Honsfeld
394
Losheimergraben
Möderscheid
Hepscheid
Frauenkron
12 VG
Kyll
Heppenbach
Losheim
Scheid
I&R 394
Hallschlag
1 SS
Lanzerath
Ambleve
99
XX
106
Valender
Holzheim
Wereth
3 Prcht
14
Our
Afst
Medendorbach
SIXTH Pz
XXXX
FIFTH Pz
OMMERSCHEID
Manderfeld
Krewinkel
Ormont
Eimerscheid
Weckerath
18 VG
Roth
14 Cav
422
Auw
Kobscheid
Laudesfeld
Fuehrer
Beglelit
U.S. Forces
German Forces
Infantry
Armor
Armored Cavalry
XX Division
III Regiment
II Battalion
••• Platoon
U.S. forward positions, night Dec. 15
German Infantry movements
0 1 2 3 miles

By the fall of 1944, the United States Army had the best artillery branch in the world. Flexible, responsive, and utilizing such devastating tactics as "time on target" barrages, the American artillerists could crush an attack with sheer weight of firepower.

At 6:50 a.m., an hour after the attack began, the battalion restored communication with the artillery units in the rear. Within minutes, the forward observers in the trenches called down hell itself on the Germans. Multiple battalions of 105mm howitzers and the massive 155mm Long Tom cannons joined the battle.

The grenadiers attacked with desperate bravery, and in some places they made it through the curtain of artillery to battle the Americans with bayonets and butt stocks. The men of the 3-395 held firm, refusing to be driven from their foxholes even as heaps of German dead piled around them. By 7:45 a.m., the attack had failed. Almost half the 2nd Battalion, 751st Volksgrenadiers, lay dead or dying in the snow.

As the grenadiers withdrew and regrouped, they left behind over a hundred and fifty wounded men. Some lay as close as two hundred feet from the 3rd Battalion's foxholes. Throughout the day, they groaned, and cried out in agony, unable to move. In places, the lesser wounded men scrabbled through the snow to give what succor they could to their dying comrades. Here and there, a German medic would brave American fire to rush forward and administer some morphine and first aid. But there weren't enough brave medics that day, and by nightfall the moans and pleas grew steadily weaker. By morning, the battlefield was silent; the wounded had frozen to death.

Young German airborne recruits examine a scoped sniper rifle. By the fall of 1944, the quality of most of the German airborne units had declined dramatically. After the appalling losses the fallschirmjäger regiments suffered in Normandy and in Italy, many of the replacement officers and men flowed in with little infantry experience. Antiaircraft officers found themselves suddenly commanding companies or battalions. In the Bulge, these inexperienced leaders made basic errors that cost their units dearly.

6

THE CHECKERBOARDS' STAND

☆ ☆ ☆ ☆ ☆

FARTHER TO THE SOUTH, the 99th Infantry Division's other two regiments weathered a series of desperate attacks. At first, the division's commander, Brooklyn-born Maj. Gen. Walter Lauer, did not consider the situation to be very serious. A visitor to his headquarters that morning found him playing a piano while his staff milled aimlessly around the command post (CP).

In the field, the miserable, half-frozen men in the foxholes in the 99th Division's front clung to their fighting positions as Sepp Dietrich's men battered away at them. The division's other two regiments, the 393rd and 394th, were spread terribly thin south of Hofen down to the Losheim Gap, where the Checkerboards were supposed to be tied in with the 14th Cavalry Group at the seam between their own V Corps and Troy Middleton's VIII Corps.

The German assault succeeded in places and threw the 99th Division into a state of confusion. Major General Lauer pulled his divisional headquarters out and withdrew to the rear. Some platoons found themselves cut off, fighting desperate, small actions around their snow-covered foxholes. On the 393rd's front east and northeast of Rocherath, the Germans managed to break through the American lines. The success of this attack posed a major threat both to the 99th and the 2nd Infantry Division to its north. If the attack here could be reinforced and exploited, the Germans could potentially open up the entire north shoulder of the offensive.

While with the 99th Infantry Division, Private First Class Sellers, a Signal Corps cameraman, snapped this iconic image of Pvt. Albert Hart as he slid a K-ration box over the muzzle of his M1 rifle to protect it from the snow. Hart belonged to K Company, 393rd Infantry, 99th Infantry Division, and hailed from Methuen, Massachusetts. Conditions along Elsenborn Ridge only worsened as winter set in.

The Germans hit the 393rd Infantry with two full volksgrenadier regiments. The battle raged all day as both sides fed reinforcements into it. By nightfall, the 3rd Battalion, 393rd Infantry was almost entirely surrounded, fighting for its very survival.

To the south, the 394th faced a major challenge when its men were hit by the 27th Fusiliers, which was part of the 12th Volksgrenadier Division. Part of the American right flank gave away, and the 27th Fusiliers pushed over a thousand yards into the regiment's position.

On a hill nestled between the 394th Infantry's extreme right and the 14th Cavalry Group's extreme left, sat the Intelligence and Reconnaissance (I&R) Platoon from the 3rd

Fort Eben-Emael on the Albert Canal, one of the key Belgian mega-forts defending the Liège area, became the German fallschirmjäger's first major success story during World War II. Instead of trying to take the fort with tanks, artillery, and infantry, the Germans landed paratroops and gliders on the roof of the fort in 1940. The fallschirmjägers fought their way inside and forced the Belgian garrison to surrender. Such actions contributed to the élan of the German airborne units.

Battalion, 394th Infantry. Led by Lt. Lyle Bouck, the platoon's eighteen men had dug in overlooking the main road through the Losheim Gap, and one that was of key importance to the Sixth Panzer Army. Here the terrain was better, more open, and not as a snowy as it was around Huren. The road was paved and in good condition, which made it a prime object for Dietrich's SS panzer units.

Dietrich assigned the 3rd Fallschirmjäger Division—German airborne troops—to open up the Losheim Gap so that his panzers could exploit the road and race to the Meuse on it. The 3rd Fallschirmjäger Division, led by Lt. Gen. Richard Schimpf, had suffered grievous losses in Normandy and the retreat from France. By the time it limped behind the Siegfried Line, only a quarter of its strength and men remained. To prepare for the winter offensive, the division reached out to some unusual places to find bodies. Replacement officers came from the rear echelon ranks of the Luftwaffe. The men also came from Luftwaffe support units and possessed only six weeks of training when they joined the unit. Minimal infantry experience combined with a sense of devotion to comrades and country made for a near-suicidal cocktail in the Ardennes Forest that December. It was an airborne unit in name only.

On the morning of December 16, after the initial shelling knocked out the I&R Platoon's only radio and jeep, a battalion from the 3rd Fallschirmjäger appeared on the road to Lanzerath right in front of Lieutenant Bouck's hill. Lanzerath served as the vital road junction for the

Members of the 1st Fallschirmjäger Division. In defensive situations, the fallschirmjägers could be tenacious foes. At Monte Cassino, Italy, in 1944, these German elite troops held out against incredible odds and delayed the Allied advance up the Italian boot.

A truck load of very happy fallschirmjägers after the Eben-Emael coup de main. After the Battle of Crete in 1941, however, the Germans abandoned large-scale airborne operations. The fallschirmjäger divisions became elite Luftwaffe ground troops under the overall command of Hermann Göring.

Losheim Gap, and the entire area represented the best tank country in the Ardennes Forest. Obviously, its capture would be pivotal to the success of Operation Watch on the Rhine.

The Germans moved to take the hill. Marching shoulder to shoulder, as if to channel the British Army of the Somme a generation before, the fallschirmjägers charged the hill. Bouck's men stopped them cold with a single M2 "Ma Deuce" .50-caliber machine gun, a few BARs, and M1 rifles. The Germans retreated, leaving heaps of their dead littering the hillside.

The Germans tried again. Bouck's men scythed them down. Scores died or fell wounded. The I&R Platoon held. All day long the pressure mounted, but the Germans could not dislodge Bouck.

Finally, a veteran German NCO rebelled against these bloody and blunt frontal assaults. He collected about fifty men and maneuvered on the flanks of the American position. After dark, they stormed the hill and captured Bouck's men. As they surrendered, the Germans finally had forced open a key entry point to the Ardennes and the Meuse River.

Bouck's stand had delayed the Germans for an entire day. Behind the 3rd Fallschirmjäger Division, Jochen Peiper and his 1st SS Panzer Division spearhead fumed and waited. The plan only gave them two days to go the sixty miles to the Meuse River, and now one of them was already lost.

By nightfall, even as the 3rd Battalion, 394th Infantry's I&R Platoon fought its epic

A sketch of a German fallschirmjäger. German airborne troops wore different helmets from Wehrmacht units and carried gear unique to their divisions.

The M2 .50-caliber machine gun proved devastatingly effective whenever it was employed against infantry. Weighing eighty-four pounds, it was a difficult weapon for infantrymen to carry and lacked the maneuverability of the lighter M1919 Browning air-cooled machine gun. Still, its stopping power and rate of fire made it one of the best machine guns of World War II.

Despondent men of the 99th Infantry Division, some wounded, march through the mud into captivity. These photos were snapped by a German combat cameraman in Hallschlag, Germany, just after the start of the offensive.

stand outside of Lanzerath, men of the Checkerboard Division suffered terribly. In places, squads and platoons found themselves overrun. Some escaped and evaded, slipping through the snowy woods to find ways around the German spearheads. Others went to ground and waited. Some died in place, fighting to the last bullet and the last measures of courage. But in nearly every position, the German gains were shallow and usually contained with local counterattacks.

On the 1st Battalion, 393rd Infantry's front, where the Germans outnumbered the Americans six to one, a sharp, surprise assault carried the fusiliers through B Company's lines. The company executive officer (XO), Lt. Eugene Kingsley, suffered two wounds, one in either arm, as he frantically tried to fight back in overwhelming chaos. It proved a losing battle, and his men fell or ran all around him. Finally, weak from his wounds, he surrendered with several of his wounded soldiers.

Along with a GI whose jaw had been shot away, Kingsley was marched to the rear as darkness fell over the torn and shattered forest. The Germans took him and the other wounded Americans to a makeshift aid station set up in a nearby church. As the medics worked on German and Yankee alike, somebody sat down at the church's organ and began to play. Over the blood-soaked scene of wounded and dying men, the soft, lilting tune of "Silent Night" erased distinctions of creed and nationality. Enemies moments before, the wounded men now found common ground in this haunting memory of home. In two languages, they began to sing along.

Gerow's V Corps came ashore on D-Day at Omaha Beach. Anxious to see the situation for himself, he became the first American corps commander to touch French soil that day. He later earned a Silver Star for his leadership throughout the Normandy campaign, which he capped by being the first American major general to enter Paris. Gerow died in 1972.

7

NORTH SHOULDER BLUES

FOR SEPP DIETRICH, the first day of Watch on the Rhine devolved into a series of frustrations and failures. The Sixth Panzer Army had used its volksgrenadiers to try to break the thinly held American lines and tear the holes needed to send the panzers thundering for the Meuse River. None of that had happened, and while the 99th Division had suffered heavy losses and had lost ground in places, it had not been shattered. The road through Lanzerath was finally cleared around midnight, which meant that Jochen Peiper and his 1st SS Panzer Division's spearhead kampfgruppe could start its deep penetration mission to the river. That offered some hope.

The problem was, aside from the one at Lanzerath, none of the assigned roads had been cleared yet. Dietrich needed to dislodge the 99th Infantry Division and push onto the Elsenborn Ridge. With the ridge in German hands, the full potential of the Sixth Panzer Army could be unleashed. Without it, the Waffen-SS troopers would have a tough time trying to develop their attack.

Gen. Leonard Gerow was the commander of V Corps. A Virginian, he joined the army before World War I and saw service during the Veracruz Campaign in Mexico. He later took part in the relief effort in Galveston, Texas, in 1915 after a hurricane devastated the town. During the Great War, he served as a staff officer in a Signal Corps unit.

This area of the Ardennes fell under the control of Maj. Gen. Leonard Gerow's V Corps from the First Army. Gerow, a Virginian who grew up in the cradle of Civil War Virginia, having been born in Petersburg, graduated from the Virginia Military Institute twelfth in his class of fifty-two in the summer of 1907. It was his corps that landed at Omaha Beach, and his handling of the D-Day invasion and the subsequent days as the toehold was expanded ranks as one of his finest military achievements. Respected by Eisenhower, Gerow led his corps across France and into Belgium. During October, it was his corps that made the thrust into the Hürtgen Forest, suffering calamitous casualties in the process.

As the situation worsened on December 16, Gerow realized that he needed to get help to the Checkerboard division as soon as possible in the morning. The problem was, General Hodges at First Army didn't see the German onslaught as anything more than a spoiling attack, designed to draw men and material from the Roer River dam campaign. He did not

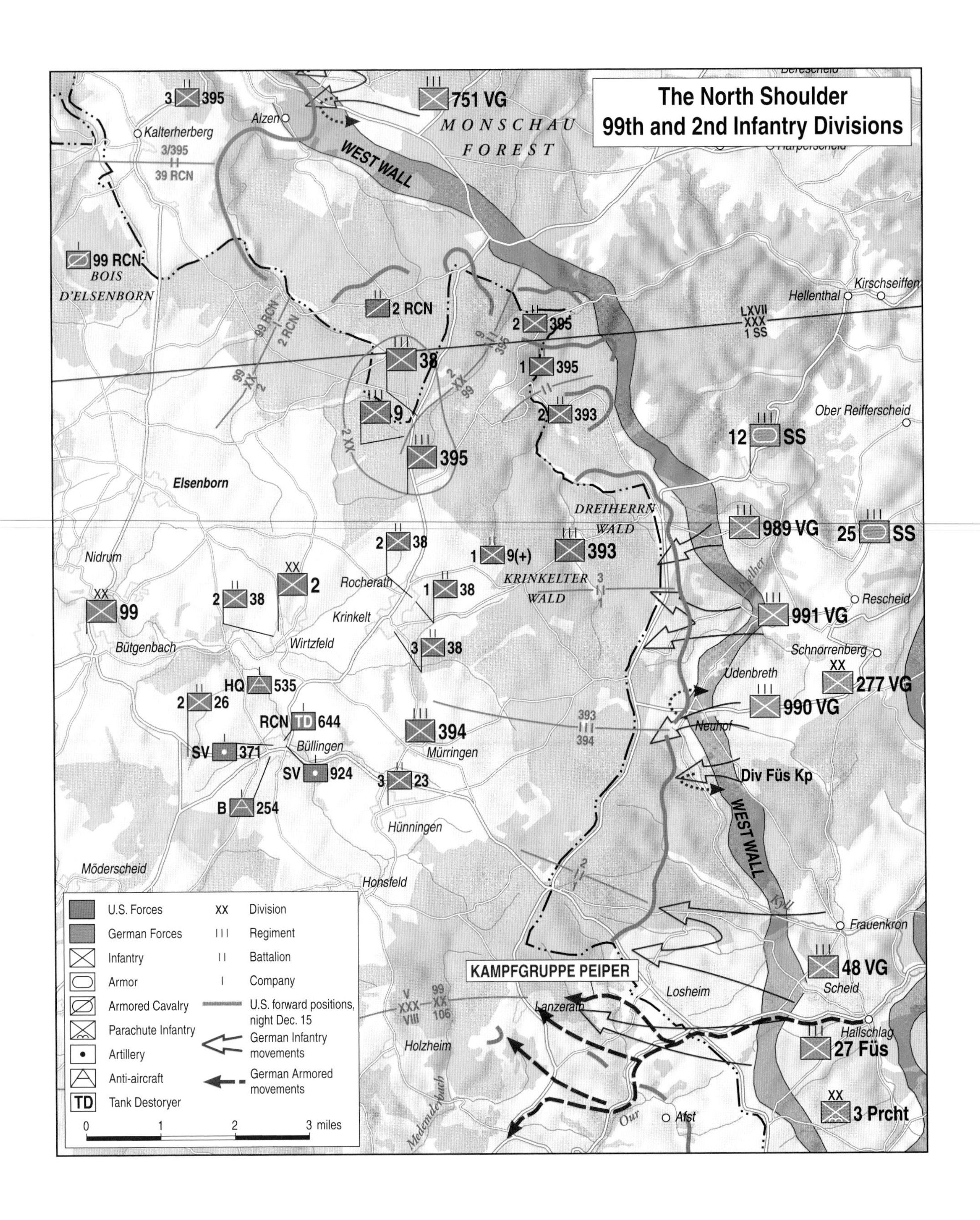
The North Shoulder
99th and 2nd Infantry Divisions
WEST WALL
MONSCHAU FOREST
751 VG
Alzen
Kalterherberg
99 RCN
BOIS D'ELSENBORN
2 RCN
Hellenthal
Kirschseiffen
LXVII
XXX
1 SS
Ober Reifferscheid
12 SS
Elsenborn
DREIHERRN WALD
989 VG
25 SS
KRINKELTER WALD
Rocherath
Krinkelt
Nidrum
Bütgenbach
Wirtzfeld
991 VG
Resscheid
Schnorrenberg
Udenbreth
277 VG
990 VG
Neuhof
Div Füs Kp
Büllingen
Mürringen
Hünningen
Möderscheid
Honsfeld
Frauenkron
48 VG
Scheid
KAMPFGRUPPE PEIPER
Losheim
Lanzerath
Hallschlag
27 Füs
Holzheim
Afst
3 Prcht
U.S. Forces
German Forces
Infantry
Armor
Armored Cavalry
Parachute Infantry
Artillery
Anti-aircraft
Tank Destoryer
Division
Regiment
Battalion
Company
U.S. forward positions, night Dec. 15
German Infantry movements
German Armored movements
0 1 2 3 miles

The fighting in the Hürtgen Forest was some of the bloodiest in American military history. The entrenched Germans used the woods to their best advantage, concealing machine gun nests, pillboxes, and antitank guns with brilliant camouflage. The battle virtually crippled several American divisions and seriously weakened the First Army and Gerow's V Corps.

want to call the advance off. That left Gerow's 2nd Infantry Division, which was advancing north of the 99th Division, in a very awkward position. Gerow wanted to pull the division back, but General Hodges refused to allow it on the 16th. First Army also took away Gerow's mobile reserve, a combat command from the 9th Armored Division. It was sent south to reinforce Troy Middleton's VIII Corps later on December 16. Without his armor, Gerow's options narrowed considerably.

That evening, Gerow sent his deputy corps commander, Clarence Huebner, to visit Maj. Gen. Walter Robertson, the leather-tough commander of the 2nd Infantry Division. They talked the situation over, and tacitly Robertson decided to back off on any further offensive

An M4 Sherman from the 741st Tank Battalion supports men of the 2nd Infantry Division. The 741st landed at Omaha Beach with amphibious duplex-drive (DD) tanks, taking brutal losses to both heavy seas and German fire. It served with the 2nd Infantry Division during the drive across France, where it played a pivotal role in capturing Hill 192 on the Vire River. For its service in the Bulge, the 741st received the Distinguished Unit Badge and Oak Leaf Cluster.

General Hodges decorates Gen. J. Lawton "Lightning Joe" Collins. Hodges' conduct with the First Army during the Bulge has been heavily criticized by postwar historians. The sudden German offensive placed an enormous burden on General Hodges, and some observers at his headquarters suggested the blow had overwhelmed him psychologically.

thrusts despite the First Army's orders. It proved to be a wise decision, especially since the 2nd Infantry Division was attacking right into the seam between the I SS Panzer Corps and the LXVIII Corps in what was known as the Wahlerscheid Salient. Any further advance would have stuck the division's head in a noose. Instead, Robertson planned to stay put and swing south if necessary to get his men out of the trap he had already sensed was closing around them.

In the morning of December 17, the 2nd Infantry Division would play a pivotal role on the north shoulder. In the meantime, Elsenborn Ridge would be defended at all costs. Gerow understood its importance, and he worked through the night of the 16th to send as much strength to defend it as possible. Artillery battalions began massing on the reverse slopes. Combat engineer units began to arrive. The 99th would not have to hold out alone much longer.

And so, as the first day of Hitler's last offensive came to an end, the north shoulder had held. The Germans suffered multiple defeats and had not been able to exploit any of their gains—yet. But December 17 would bring two opportunities to the Germans: the chance to grab Elsenborn Ridge, and a breakthrough with Jochen Peiper's four thousand ruthless and committed Waffen-SS panzer troopers.

Hodges remained in command of the First Army after the Bulge. His units were the first to cross the Rhine River in March 1945. At the end of the war, his men reached the Elbe River and linked up with the Red Army. Hodges had enlisted as a private prior to World War I. He received the Distinguished Service Cross in 1918 and became one of the few men in American military history to rise from the ranks and become a full general.

A BAR gunner lies in a shallow, snowy pit. American GIs lacked winter clothing and camouflage, which made them much easier targets than the generally better concealed and clothed Germans they faced.

8

WHERE MEDALS OF HONOR GREW

★ ★ ★ ★ ★

DAWN BROKE OVER THE FOG-SHROUDED FORESTS south on Monschau to reveal an American corps in crisis. The 99th Division's center and right had held the day before, but the 393rd and 394th Infantry Regiments clung precariously to their positions, and the Germans set right to work on them again. Except this time, instead of the volksgrenadiers, Dietrich sent in the 12th SS Panzer Division.

Northeast of Rocherath, Lt. Col. Paul V. Tuttle's 3rd Battalion, 23rd Infantry, swung in behind the crumbling 393rd Infantry late on December 16, supported by a platoon of tanks from the 741st Tank Battalion—the same unit that brought the Sherman duplex-drive (DD) tanks ashore on Omaha Beach during the D-Day landings. They set up a blocking position along one of two roads assigned to the 12th SS for its drive to the Meuse River. This was the northernmost route, Rollbahn A, which ran over the Elsenborn Ridge. The 23rd Infantry found itself in a critical position that morning as Gerow scrambled to throw together a cohesive defense behind them.

Along a small creek near Ruppenvenn, the regiment established its defensive line while under heavy artillery and rocket fire. The men dug in as best they could, but the snow and frozen ground made anything more than a shallow rifle pit almost impossible.

The next morning, the 12th SS and the volksgrenadiers attacked and shattered most of the 393rd Infantry.

Photographer Pfc. James Clancy, 165th Signal Corps Company, snapped this photo of Maj. Gen. Walter Robertson decorating Pfc. Walter Gach with the Silver Star near Saint-Vith just before the Battle of the Bulge began. Pfc. Glenn Campbell stands at right. Robertson ranks as one of the best American division commanders to emerge from the war in Europe. Courageous, talented, and adept at thinking on his feet, he organized an ad hoc defense of Elsenborn Ridge that derailed Sepp Dietrich's Sixth Panzer Army and helped unravel the entire German counteroffensive.

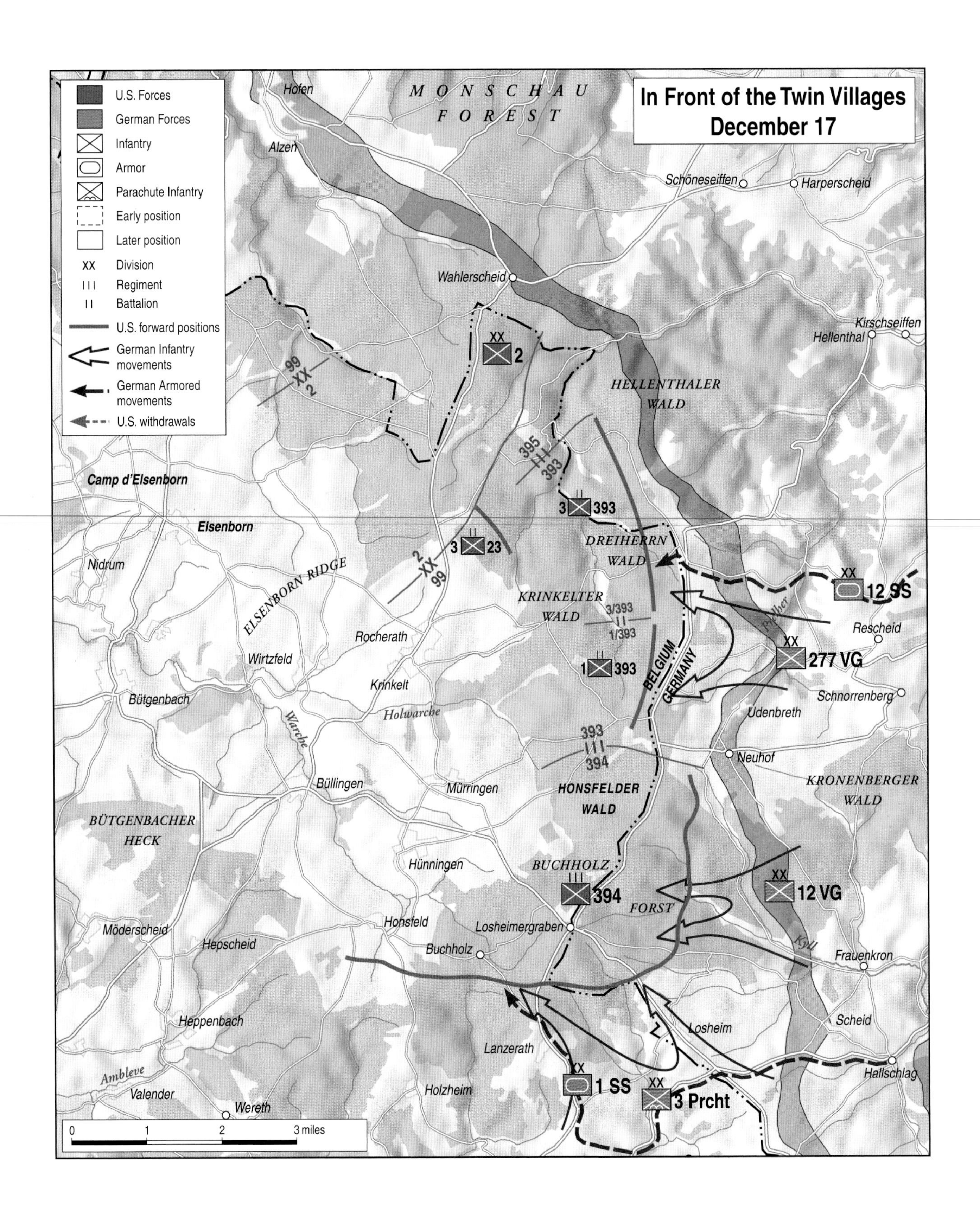

In Front of the Twin Villages
December 17
U.S. Forces
German Forces
Infantry
Armor
Parachute Infantry
Early position
Later position
XX Division
III Regiment
II Battalion
U.S. forward positions
German Infantry movements
German Armored movements
U.S. withdrawals
MONSCHAU FOREST
Hofen
Alzen
Schöneseiffen
Harperscheid
Wahlerscheid
Kirschseiffen
Hellenthal
HELLENTHALER WALD
Camp d'Elsenborn
Elsenborn
Nidrum
ELSENBORN RIDGE
DREIHERRN WALD
KRINKELTER WALD
Rocherath
Wirtzfeld
Krinkelt
Holwarche
Bütgenbach
Warche
Rescheid
Schnorrenberg
Udenbreth
Neuhof
BELGIUM
GERMANY
KRONENBERGER WALD
Büllingen
Mürringen
HONSFELDER WALD
BÜTGENBACHER HECK
Hünningen
BUCHHOLZ FORST
Honsfeld
Losheimergraben
Buchholz
Möderscheid
Hepscheid
Frauenkron
Kyll
Scheid
Heppenbach
Lanzerath
Losheim
Hallschlag
Ambleve
Valender
Wereth
Holzheim
2
99
395
393
3 393
3 23
3/393
1/393
1 393
394
394
12 SS
277 VG
12 VG
1 SS
3 Prcht
0 1 2 3 miles

Its survivors streamed through the 23rd Infantry's front and only a few turned to keep up the fight with Tuttle's men. The others, exhausted and hollow-eyed, staggered to the south and the crossroads at Rocherath and Krinkelt.

All morning long, artillery rained down on the 3rd Battalion, 23rd Infantry. Between barrages, the Germans came rushing at the battalion in screaming waves. On Company I's front, the men battled all morning long, throwing back seven attacks. The Germans ignored casualties and pressed their attacks to within a few meters of the American positions. Hand grenades, machine guns, and carbines stopped them cold, but they'd withdraw to a small gulley, reform, and attack again.

Ammunition ran low, and battalion had nothing to offer the line companies. Artillery support was in critically short supply as well. The guns on Elsenborn Ridge also lacked ammo. Full fire-for-effect missions consisted of three rounds. Instead of a protective curtain of high-explosive shells, the battalion's forward observers could only take potshots at concentrations of German troops and tanks.

The defenders began to crack. The company commanders asked for help. There was none. They asked to withdraw. Tuttle told them to hold fast. The men counted their remaining rounds and waited for the next German assault.

An American infantryman, armed with a Thompson submachine gun, examines a dead German who froze where he fell.

Heavy 155mm howitzers fire from concealed positions south of Monschau. The 2nd Infantry Division's stand in front of Elsenborn Ridge could not have succeeded without the massive assistance of U.S. field artillery battalions. Gerow's V Corps used concentrated bombardments to break up almost every German assault.

The 2nd Infantry Division concluded its illustrious combat career by driving deep into central Germany in the spring of 1945. Here, GIs from the 23rd Infantry Regiment move into Leipzig on April 18, 1945, supported by M24 Chaffee light tanks from the 612th Tank Destroyer Battalion.

Meanwhile, behind the 3rd Battalion's stand, General Robertson orchestrated one of the most impressive tactical movements in American military history. For him, the morning began with bad news. To the north, the 38th Cavalry got hit again at Monschau, and while its B Troop nearly got wiped out, the unit held on until elements of the 5th Armored Division swept in and threw the Germans back. But to the south, the news was not good. General Lauer, the 99th Division's commander, called Robertson at about 0700 to tell him that the 99th's center and right had been overrun by a combined infantry and tank assault. He himself was pulling out with his staff and relocating his divisional command post farther to the rear.

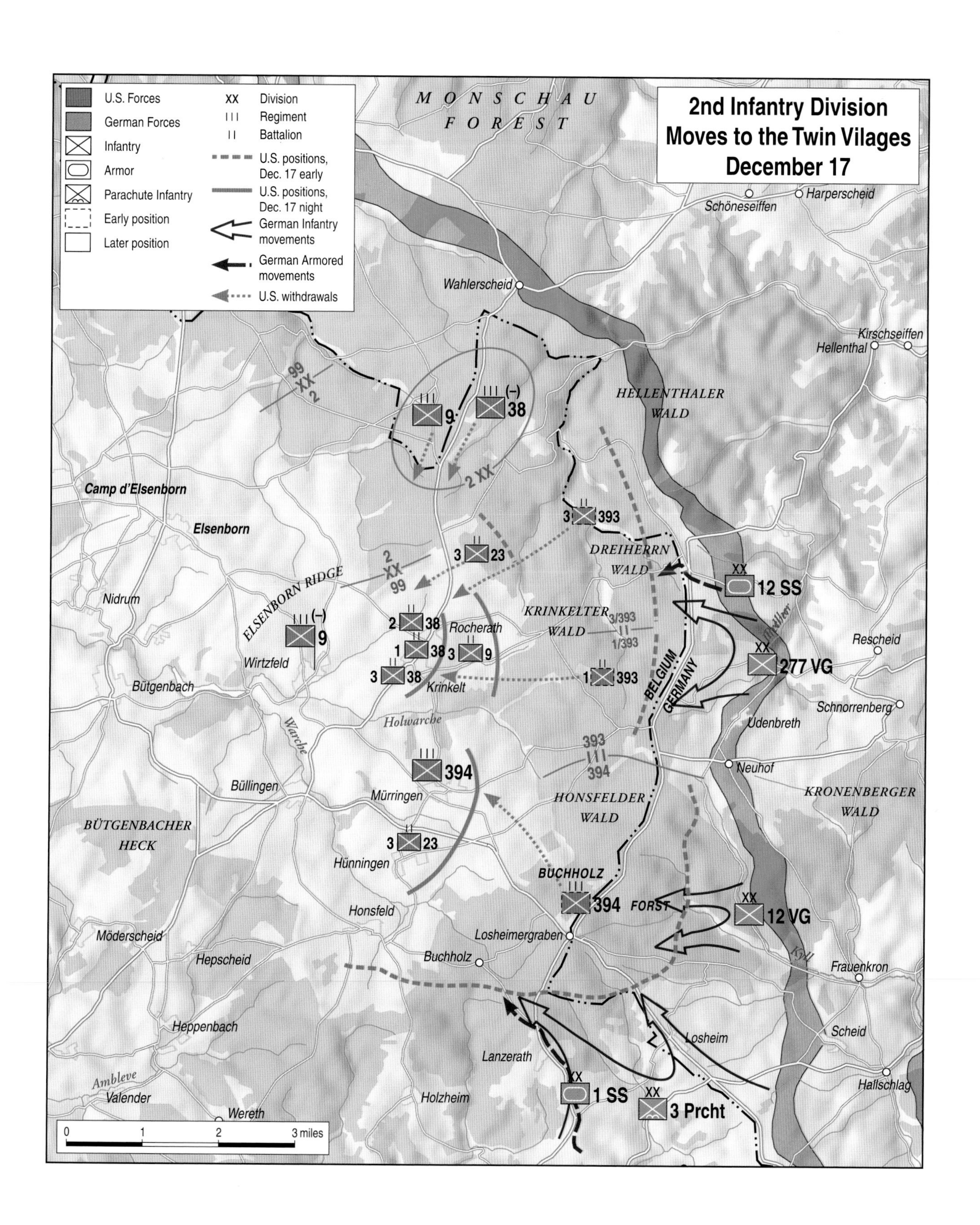
2nd Infantry Division
Moves to the Twin Vilages
December 17
U.S. Forces
German Forces
Infantry
Armor
Parachute Infantry
Early position
Later position
XX Division
III Regiment
II Battalion
U.S. positions, Dec. 17 early
U.S. positions, Dec. 17 night
German Infantry movements
German Armored movements
U.S. withdrawals
MONSCHAU FOREST
Schöneseiffen
Harperscheid
Wahlerscheid
Kirschseiffen
Hellenthal
HELLENTHALER WALD
Camp d'Elsenborn
Elsenborn
ELSENBORN RIDGE
Nidrum
Wirtzfeld
Bütgenbach
Rocherath
Krinkelt
DREIHERRN WALD
KRINKELTER WALD
12 SS
277 VG
Rescheid
Schnorrenberg
Udenbreth
Neuhof
BELGIUM
GERMANY
Holwarche
Warche
Büllingen
Mürringen
Hünningen
HONSFELDER WALD
KRONENBERGER WALD
BÜTGENBACHER HECK
BUCHHOLZ FORST
12 VG
Honsfeld
Losheimergraben
Buchholz
Möderscheid
Hepscheid
Frauenkron
Heppenbach
Lanzerath
Losheim
Scheid
Ambleve
Valender
Wereth
Holzheim
1 SS
3 Prcht
Hallschlag
0 1 2 3 miles

Maj. Gen. Robertson decorates 1st Lt. Harold Carlson, a chaplain who evacuated wounded GIs while under fire during the Normandy campaign. Robertson earned a reputation for being a soldier's general. During the first days of the Bulge, he led from the front, and his leadership and decision-making on the fly played a vital role in holding the north shoulder.

The men of the 2nd Infantry Division had little time to dig defensive positions during the chaotic first days of the German offensive. Their stand at the Twin Villages saved Elsenborn Ridge, the key terrain feature on the Bulge's north shoulder.

General Gerow had already authorized Robertson to withdraw from the Wahlerscheid Salient at 6:30 a.m., but now Lauer's news dimmed the 2nd Infantry Division's chances of getting out with all its vehicles and heavy equipment. For the men of the Indian Head Division, the only avenue of retreat lay on a road running southerly to the Twin Villages of Rocherath and Krinkelt. To get out of the trap, they would need to move right across the 277th Volksgrenadier and 12th SS Panzer Divisions' lines of advance. This at best was a perilous proposition.

Robertson pulled out of the Wahlerscheid Salient one battalion at a time, starting with his forwardmost units. They leapfrogged backwards and then assembled on the road to the Twin Villages. Gerow needed those two towns held at all costs for the next two days so that he could finish organizing the defense of Elsenborn Ridge. If the 12th SS managed to take the villages, they would have an open road ahead that would carry them right into the middle of the artillery battalions emplaced on the reverse slopes of the ridge.

The road between Wahlerscheid and the Twin Villages was protected by the last remnants of the 393rd Infantry and the hard-pressed men of Tuttle's 3rd Battalion, 23rd Infantry. Should they collapse, Robertson's men would be hit in the flank while in column of march, and a massacre would ensue.

GIs from A Company, 38th Infantry Regiment, 2nd Infantry Division, hike down the road to the Twin Villages on December 17. The Germans interdicted the road repeatedly that day with armor and infiltration teams, making the division's redeployment to the Twin Villages very nerve-wracking. Still, Robertson's regiments effected the movement south and arrived at their destinations just in time to hold off the Hitler Youth SS Panzer Division. The photo was taken by Pfc. Richard W. Crampton, who served with the 165th Signal Company.

A knocked-out, partially camouflaged Panther. With thick, sloped armor and a high-velocity, long-barreled 75mm cannon, the Panther ranked as one of the best medium tanks of World War II. They were very difficult targets to knock out, especially with the inferior antitank weapons the U.S. Army fielded in 1944.

The divisional reserve headed south first. This was the 3rd Battalion, 38th Infantry, Lt. Col. Olinto Barsanti's men. Barsanti actually drove out ahead of his marching men on a leader's recon. As his jeep approached Krinkelt, a German Panther tank rolled into view and took him under fire. His driver swerved and dodged and tried to escape. At the last second, an American tank destroyer from nearby Wirtzfeld caught the Panther by surprise and knocked it out.

Barsanti's recon proved the way into the Twin Villages was not clear. The 2nd Infantry Division would have to run a race for its life and fight a meeting engagement at its destination against one of the storied units in the German Army.

Barsanti changed his battalion's approach slightly, and by 10:30 a.m., the Heavy Weapons Company reached Krinkelt and started to dig in. The rest of the battalion got into town at 11:30 a.m. and covered the east and southeast approaches.

Meanwhile, Robertson climbed into his jeep and drove down the road to the Twin Villages to supervise the withdrawal and redeployment. All morning long he zipped around, exhorting his men to move faster, unsnarling traffic, barking orders, and keeping things moving. At one point, as the division's 1st Battalion, 38th Infantry, arrived in the Twin Villages, Robertson greeted the men and asked a young sergeant which outfit he was from. When the NCO told him, he gave him directions to his company's new position. The men obeyed, came around a corner and ran smack into a German tank. An M10 tank destroyer blasted it into burning wreckage, and the men took up positions inside nearby buildings.

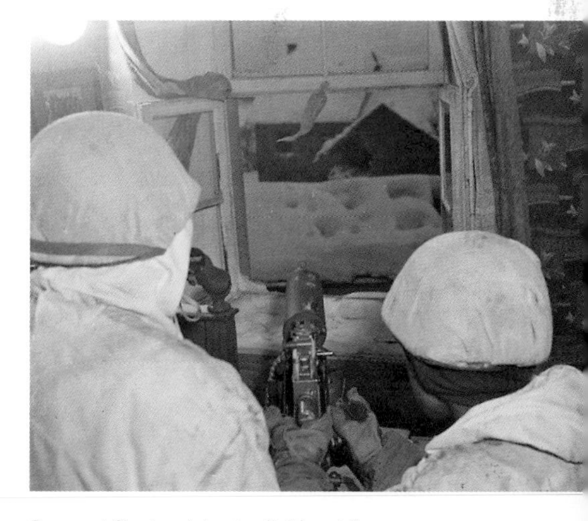

Sergeant Charles Johnston (left) and Sergeant Joe Ulibarri of the 38th Infantry Regiment man a .30-caliber medium machine gun and scan for targets from the safety of a Belgian farmhouse near Wirtzfeld.

While Robertson's men streamed south, the 12th SS Panzer Division battered away at the 393rd Infantry and the 3rd Battalion, 23rd Infantry. Around 4:30 p.m., a tank-infantry assault slammed into I Company of the 3rd Battalion. The men, lacking ammunition and bazookas, could not hold. They fell back, covered by Pfc. Richard Cowan, a Kansas native who had been attending Oberlin College when the war broke out. He stayed behind, manning a .30-caliber machine gun as a company-sized force of Germans advanced straight at him with a King Tiger in support. He held his fire until they were at point-blank range and then tore the company apart. Almost half of the eighty or so men in front of Cowan became casualties.

A truck-turned-snowplow clears the road to Krinkelt.

An infantry squad from the 23rd Infantry Regiment, 2nd Infantry Division, stays low and snakes through the Belgian snow.

The Germans poured fire into his machine gun nest. The King Tiger opened up on him. Three MG-42s unloaded on him. Somebody fired a rocket into his position, but he stayed in the fight, walking his fire back and forth, inflicting tremendous losses on the Germans. Ultimately, he picked up his weapon and withdrew to the 3rd Battalion's reformed lines to the west, and later made it into Krinkelt. He was killed in action the following day. Cowan's parents received his posthumous Medal of Honor from President Harry Truman on the White House lawn a few months later.

As the 3rd Battalion, 23rd Infantry, cracked and the Germans pressed hard to turn their retreat into a rout, another machine gunner played a vital role in giving the battalion a chance to break contact. Sergeant Jose Lopez manned another .30-caliber machine gun and stayed behind as the rest of his company fell back. Despite artillery and tank fire, he continued to fire his .30-caliber gun from a shallow foxhole that afforded little protection. When the Germans tried to envelope his retreating company, he scythed down both pincers and inflicted scores of casualties on them. He then carried his weapon back to his company and continued the fight. Lopez, a native of Mexico who grew up in Mission, Texas, received the Medal of Honor for his bravery on June 18, 1945.

The line had buckled, and then it broke. The Waffen-SS troops sensed victory and poured through the holes with scattered elements from the 277th Volksgrenadiers. The 2nd Infantry Division, still on the road to the Twin Villages, would surely be destroyed.

Pvt. Francis Lotito (left), a New Yorker, and Pfc. Paul Ronan, a Montanan, of the 2nd Infantry Division, move forward, rifles slung. Only their helmets are camouflaged, but that's better than nothing. The photo was taken by Sgt. Bill Augustine, 165th Signal Company.

9

THE PANTHER KILLERS

ROBERTSON DISCOVERED THE GERMAN BREAKTHROUGH during a visit to the 393rd Infantry Regiment's command post. Tuttle's men were streaming back for the Twin Villages, and now nothing stood between the Germans and the strung-out 2nd Infantry Division working its way south on the road to Rocherath.

Robertson jumped into his jeep and sped back to the road. There, he collared the first unit that he encountered and diverted it east. A company here, a platoon there, they started for the breach in the line. Finally, along came Lt. Col. William McKinley, a direct relative of former President William McKinley, and who also commanded Robertson's 1st Battalion, 9th Infantry. Robertson conferred with him and ordered McKinley to protect the road at all costs. "Hold until ordered to withdraw," Robertson told him in a scene very reminiscent of Hancock's conversation with Col. William Colvill, the commander of the 1st Minnesota Volunteers on Gettysburg's second day. Hancock, who had been all over the battlefield handling all manner of crises, just as Robertson did on December 17, had seen a gap open in the Union lines that an entire brigade of Confederates attacked into. To buy time and fill the gap, Hancock ordered Colvill to counterattack and buy time for reinforcements to come up and stem the Rebel assault.

Soldiers of the 2nd Infantry Division slog along a muddy road in wet, freezing weather. The misery quotient was high for the infantrymen in the field.

What Robertson and Hancock ordered in both cases seemed tantamount to a death sentence to the men under their commands. The 1st Minnesota lost 83 percent of its strength in fifteen minutes of furious combat. McKinley was looking at trying to stem an elite Waffen-SS panzer division's spearpoint with both his flanks in the air and no help of reinforcement.

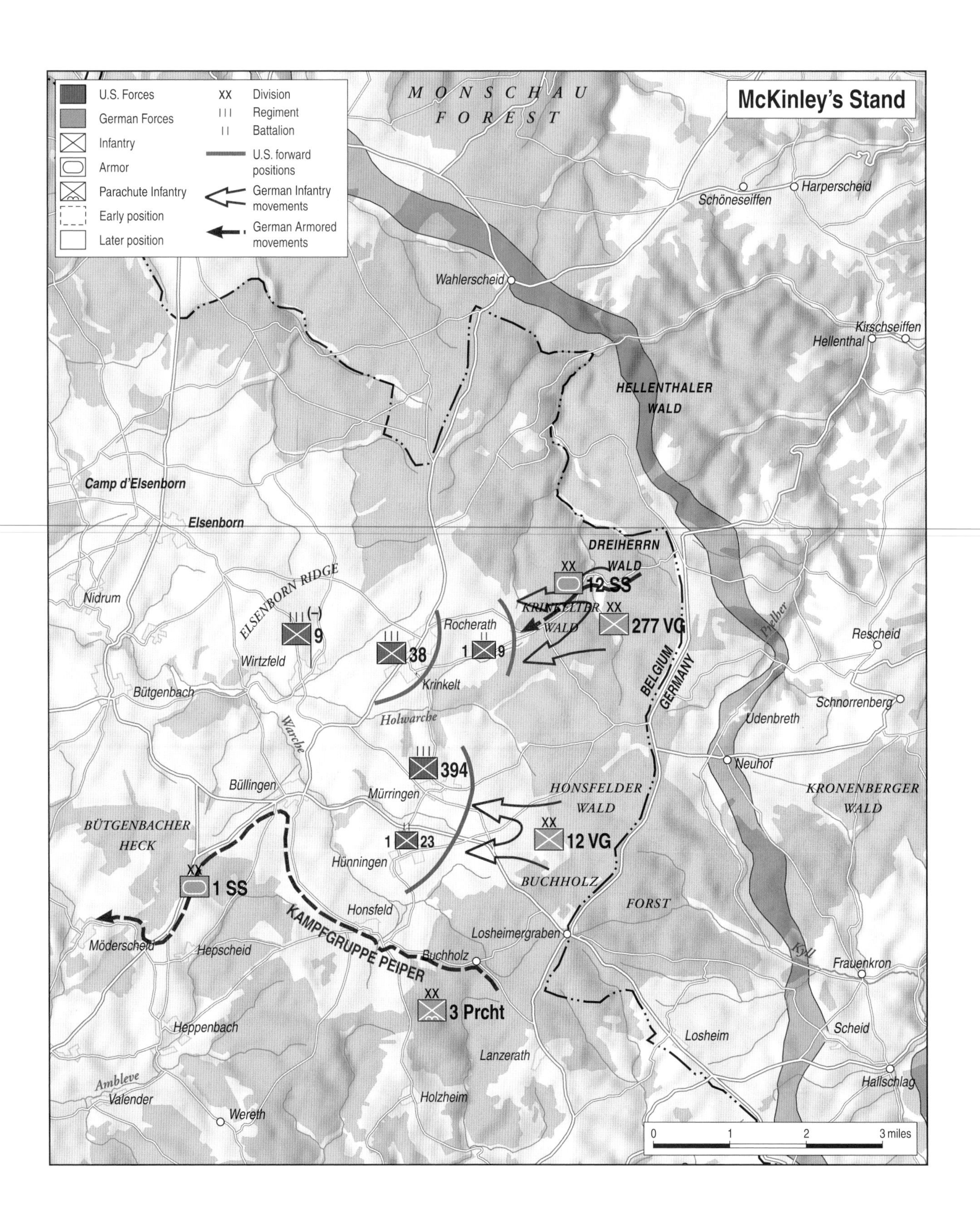
McKinley's Stand
U.S. Forces
German Forces
Infantry
Armor
Parachute Infantry
Early position
Later position
XX Division
III Regiment
II Battalion
U.S. forward positions
German Infantry movements
German Armored movements
MONSCHAU FOREST
Schöneseiffen
Harperscheid
Wahlerscheid
Kirschseiffen
Hellenthal
HELLENTHALER WALD
Camp d'Elsenborn
Elsenborn
DREIHERRN WALD
12 SS
ELSENBORN RIDGE
Nidrum
9
Rocherath
KRINKELTER WALD
277 VG
38
Wirtzfeld
Krinkelt
Bütgenbach
BELGIUM
GERMANY
Rescheid
Schnorrenberg
Udenbreth
Holwarche
Warche
394
Neuhof
Büllingen
Mürringen
HONSFELDER WALD
KRONENBERGER WALD
BÜTGENBACHER HECK
12 VG
23
Hünningen
1 SS
BUCHHOLZ FORST
Honsfeld
KAMPFGRUPPE PEIPER
Losheimergraben
Möderscheid
Hepscheid
Buchholz
Frauenkron
3 Prcht
Heppenbach
Losheim
Scheid
Lanzerath
Ambleve
Valender
Hallschlag
Holzheim
Wereth
0 1 2 3 miles

Forward observers were probably the most important men on the battlefield during the opening days of the Bulge. Their ability to call down curtains of steel at a moment's notice staved off defeat time and again. Their role has rarely been acknowledged by postwar historians.

McKinley, like Colvill, did not hesitate. Gathering his men, he led them posthaste down the most obvious axis of advance the Germans would use. At 6:30 p.m., three German tanks appeared and rolled right over McKinley's men, who had thought they might be American stragglers. They rumbled down the road toward the Twin Villages and then for some reason pulled off and paused. That gave McKinley's fire-support officer (FSO), Lt. John C. Granville, a chance to call fire down on them. A rain of 105mm howitzer and 81mm mortar shells erupted around the tanks, killing and wounding many of the infantry riding on their back decks and knocking one of the tanks out.

A few minutes later, four more tanks appeared on the road east of the battalion's position. Two struck mines, but the other two charged McKinley's lines. Fortunately, as they had pulled off the road earlier that day, the battalion had tumbled across an ammunition truck carrying fifteen bazookas. The men pulled them out and passed them around, stuffing the rockets into every available space in their packs. Now, the extra anti-armor capability served them well.

Tank-hunting teams went after the two surviving tanks and knocked them both out. But this turned out to be just the advanced party for Kampfgruppe Mueller, the 12th SS Panzer Division element that had achieved the breakthrough in the 393rd Infantry's lines earlier in the day. A half hour after the fourth tank took its fatal hit, the main body showed up and launched a concerted assault on the battalion's positions. Granville played a key role stopping the Waffen-SS troopers that evening. In the growing darkness, his well-placed fire missions scraped off the panzergrenadiers and left the tanks vulnerable to bazooka fire. The Germans withdrew, regrouped, and tried again an hour later.

A bazooka team from the 26th Infantry Division emerges from positions near Wiltz, Luxembourg, after three days of continuous combat. The physical and psychological effects are evident on the faces of these men. The M9 bazooka was the U.S. infantry's primary hand-held antitank weapon, but it wasn't terribly effective. Bazooka teams learned that the only way to stop a German panzer was to get in close and take a flank or rear shot. The photo was taken by Sergeant Gilbert, 166th Signal Company.

The M7 Priest provided mobile artillery support for the infantry. Armed with a 105mm howitzer, the Priest served as the mainstay of American self-propelled battalions during the war.

Through the black autumn night, sheathed in fog, the 12th SS charged again. This time they launched three columns of tank-infantry teams at the 1st Battalion, 9th Infantry. Granville got on the radio and orchestrated a massive artillery mission using all four of the division's 105mm artillery battalions, along with three V Corps' 155mm howitzer battalions. The barrage decimated the Germans, and only three panzerjägers (tank hunters) with about a platoon of infantry were able to slip past McKinley's right flank and drive into the Twin Villages.

On and off through the night, the 12th SS tried to batter its way past the stubborn American battalion. During the fighting, Pfc. William Soderman disabled three tanks with a bazooka, despite losing his loader to shrapnel wounds early in the fight. He knocked the third tank out with his last rocket, and seconds later suffered a serious wound in the shoulder. He still managed to get back to friendly lines with his empty weapon. For his actions, Private First Class Soderman received the Medal of Honor.

The fighting raged on in chaos and confusion. Rifles flashed and machine guns chattered. Bazooka men laid low in their trenches until the Panthers overran them. Then, they'd leap from

William Soderman receives the Congressional Medal of Honor from President Truman on the White House lawn during a ceremony immediately after the war. While with the 2nd Infantry Division, he disabled three tanks from the 12th SS Panzer Division with a bazooka during the fighting around the Twin Villages.

Knocking out a panzer with an M9 bazooka took consummate skill and serious guts. German infantry, when teamed with tanks, made American bazooka teams their primary targets.

the foxholes and chase the monstrous German panzers and take a flank or rear shot whenever the chance arose. Corporal Charles Roberts and Sgt. Otis Bone spotted an immobilized panzer that defied all attempts to kill it with bazookas. Proving they had more courage than sense, they drained some gasoline out of a wrecked vehicle and climbed atop the German tank, doused it with the fuel, and set it on fire with a Thermite grenade. That did the trick.

McKinley held. The 2nd Infantry Division survived its leapfrogged withdrawal from the Wahlerscheid Salient and had just enough time to get to the Twin Villages—but *just.*

In the darkness, the last elements from the division finally double-timed into Rocherath. For much of the day, the Germans had interdicted the road south by accurate artillery barrages,

A .50-caliber machine gun team hunkers down inside a building. American GIs learned to carve out firing positions from the walls of such buildings instead of relying on windows alone.

A GI holds a .45-caliber pistol on a crewman who escaped from a burning Panther of the 12th SS Panzer Division. It was part of a column that penetrated behind the 2nd Infantry Division's main line of resistance. GIs hunted it down and knocked it out.

and some of the 2nd Infantry Division's infantry companies suffered heavy losses as they force-marched through it.

In Rocherath, elements of the 38th Infantry arrived well past sundown. They stumbled right into a panzer and panzergrenadier unit, and part of the 1st Battalion collapsed and ran. The Germans wiped out two platoons from one company, and the fighting devolved into total chaos in the streets of both villages. Knives, grenades and bazookas were the order for the night, and the scene was punctuated with gruesome episodes of hand-to-hand combat. At the same time, tank-hunter teams prowled the darkened streets, creeping around corners and launching rockets at the panzers wherever they were found. Lieutenant Jess Morrow, the

SS troops wade through mud and snow during the first days of the offensive.

1st Battalion's communication officer, surprised and destroyed a tank with a well-placed rifle grenade shot.

The unit lines blurred and then broke down altogether. In the savagery of close-quarters urban combat at night, the men rallied to strong leaders. The commander of the 1st Battalion, 38th Infantry, Lt. Col. Frank Mildren, fought through the entire night with soldiers from sixteen different companies. Where a leader emerged, the men stood and fought.

Acts of gallantry abounded. Technician 4th Class Truman Kimbro helped stall a panzer attack by breaking cover and running in front of the big German tanks to place mines across a vital crossroad. As he sprinted across open terrain in front of at least one panzer and a platoon of German infantry, he was shot repeatedly and severely wounded. Nevertheless, he crawled forward, laid all his mines, and then was riddled with bullets as he tried to get away. He died in the snow on the outskirts of Rocherath and received a posthumous Medal of Honor a few months later.

Hastily placed mines took a toll on German armor and helped slow down the advance in its early stages.

Men of the 99th Infantry Division dig in at the base of Elsenborn Ridge.

Waffen-SS troops captured during the fighting are guarded by a GI armed with an M1 Garand and another carrying a Thompson submachine gun. The 12th SS Panzer Division suffered unsustainable losses during the fighting for the Twin Villages. The 2nd Infantry Division held long enough for Gerow to organize the defense of Elsenborn Ridge itself, ensuring that the north shoulder would hold.

By midnight, the last Germans had been hunted down and the last panzers knocked out. The villages, their buildings silhouetted by burning vehicles, grew silent. Sepp Dietrich's best chance of snatching the highest piece of real estate in Belgium had failed. Robertson's stand allowed the fragments of the 99th Division to tuck back into tighter positions around Elsenborn Ridge and prepare defensive emplacements. Later that night, the 395th Infantry Regiment, which had fought so well the day before at Hofen, bounded back through the 2nd Infantry Division and dug in along the base of Elsenborn Ridge.

In Krinkelt, the fighting raged street to street. Panthers, unsupported by infantry, rolled through the town and were overwhelmed by tank-hunting GIs and their supporting Shermans and M10 Wolverines. After the battle, Krinkelt was littered with burnt-out Panther carcasses. The 12th SS Panzer Division lost much of its armor trying to take the Twin Villages in the first two days of the offensive.

The fighting had been exceptionally brutal, with little quarter asked or given. Word had already spread through the American ranks that the SS troopers were shooting prisoners. The favor was returned, and the GIs often stood in place and died fighting, rather than run the risk of being shot while unarmed.

The next morning, the Germans massed their forces. Elements of the 12th SS Panzer Division and the 12th and 277th Volksgrenadier Divisions rammed headlong into the villages and their surroundings. The battle swelled, and once again units fragmented. The fighting fell to small groups of men here and there, young Americans who conquered fear to get in close for a killing bazooka shot on a tank, while machine gunners snapped out long bursts even though the chaos ebbed and flowed around them. When panzers appeared and the GIs had no antitank weapons, they improvised and stopped them with whatever they could cobble together.

In the end, Robertson's men held. The battle waned in the darkened hours of December 18. The next morning, the 2nd Infantry Division pulled back to positions along or below Elsenborn Ridge, while the 12th SS Panzer Division probed west toward Bütgenbach, looking for a way up onto the ridge.

The Indian Head Division's stand bought General Gerow the time he needed. Elsenborn was virtually impregnable by the time the Germans invested the village, and their chance to get up on the high ground, like Gen. Richard Ewell's at Cemetery Hill on the first day at Gettysburg, slipped away.

It did not come without a price. The 99th Infantry Division lost almost three thousand men, and some of its battalions, like the 1st of the 393rd Infantry, had been virtually wiped out. The 2nd Division suffered almost as badly. But the 12th SS Panzer Division left half of its 126 tanks on the shattered approaches to the Twin Villages. The direct approach was not going to work. The Germans would have to find another way onto Elsenborn Ridge.

Channeling their pioneer roots, men of the 196th Field Artillery Battalion build a log shelter south of Monschau. The photo was snapped on Christmas Eve by Pfc. John Weart of the 165th Signal Company.

10

BLUE SPADERS AT THE HOT CORNER

AFTER THE TWIN VILLAGES, the 2nd Infantry Division and the battered 99th tucked themselves tight against the base of Elsenborn Ridge and dug in deep. This presented no easy task. Frequently, the first foot of soil was frozen solid, and hacking through it required arduous labor from the perpetually exhausted and sleep-deprived GIs. Worse, once down past that frozen layer, the men frequently struck ground water. When they had time, they built their foxholes with steps on either side so the men could sit or sleep above the muck and water at the bottom of their holes. The best holes were three or four feet wide, six feet long, and four or five feet deep.

When there were engineers around, they made sure the infantry had an easier time at preparing their positions. Rifle shots into the ground would open a divot in the frozen ground that the engineers would stick explosives into, then set them off to blast a crater that the GIs could then flesh out into a foxhole.

As the two divisions prepared their positions, the men learned that they couldn't stay immobile in their foxholes for long. To do so invited frozen limbs. The weak sisters—and there were always a few—sometimes used this as an honorable way out of the front lines. They would deliberately stay in place for five or six hours at a stretch until their legs began to freeze. Then they'd be evacuated, much to the disgust of the rugged veterans who knew the score.

Four thousand five hundred yards from the anchor of the 2nd Infantry Division's southern flank stood the small Belgian town of Bütgenbach. Here, the battered 26th Infantry Regiment—part of the storied Big Red One (1st Infantry Division)—took up positions to protect the flank and rear of General Robertson's men.

The war had not been kind to the 26th Infantry Regiment. It had fought in North Africa and Sicily before landing at Omaha Beach on D-Day morning. Hard fighting in the Normandy hedgerows had followed, and even the breakout did not offer any relief. The regiment was flung into the Hürtgen Forest, then into the Roer dam offensive. By the start of

Pvt. Frank Lawrence (in the foxhole), of Trenton, New Jersey, talks with Pvt. Carl Williamson of Russellville, Ohio. The two GIs from the 38th Infantry are able to relax a bit after the battle for the Twin Villages. The 2nd Infantry Division pulled back to the base of Elsenborn Ridge, then dug in and awaited the next German attack.

In this famous image, the lead elements of the Big Red One roll into Bütgenbach on December 17, 1944. The 1st Infantry Division played a pivotal role in denying the Sixth SS Panzer Army any maneuvering room on the north shoulder.

An antitank crew with the 1st Battalion, 26th Infantry, push their 57mm cannon into position on December 17.

A medic works on an infantryman's foot. Trenchfoot and frostbite were two major issues GIs faced in the muddy, frozen foxholes of the Ardennes that December.

the Bulge, hardly any veterans remained in the regiment. Its infantry companies were under strength and about 90 percent green replacements. The 2nd Battalion could count on only seven officers who had been in the unit prior to December 1.

The Blue Spaders, as the 26th was known, were in for another epic and sanguine moment in a history full of both as they dug in and reinforced their foxholes with tree limbs and sandbags. The few veterans left in the regiment made sure the new guys dug deep and camouflaged their fighting positions well.

The 2nd Battalion gained the toughest defensive assignment. They were pushed out in front of the rest of the unit and deployed behind Dom Bütgenbach along the Malmedy

continued on page 109

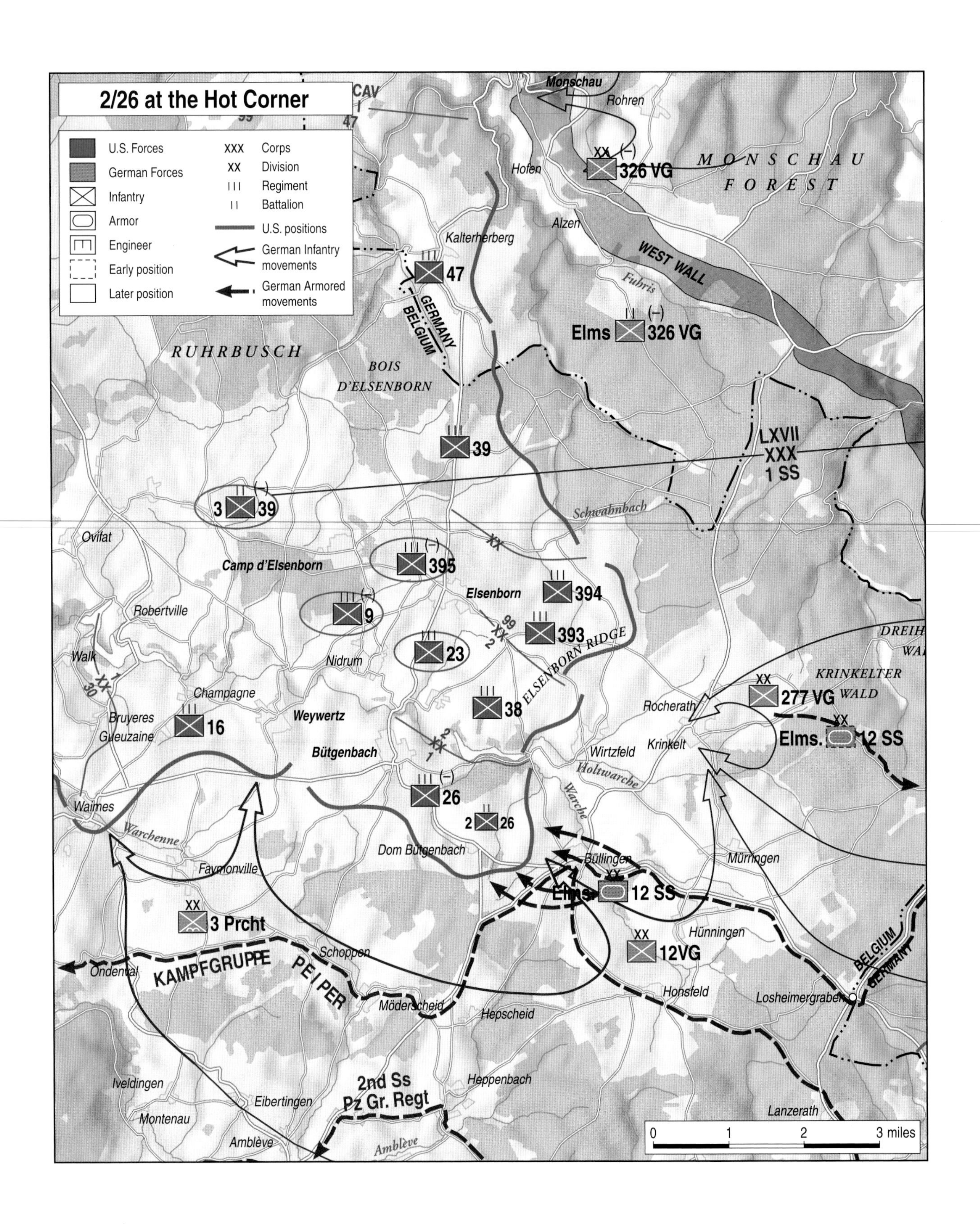
2/26 at the Hot Corner
U.S. Forces
German Forces
Infantry
Armor
Engineer
Early position
Later position
XXX Corps
XX Division
III Regiment
II Battalion
U.S. positions
German Infantry movements
German Armored movements
Monschau
Rohren
Hofen
326 VG
MONSCHAU FOREST
Alzen
Kalterherberg
47
WEST WALL
Fuhris
GERMANY
BELGIUM
Elms
326 VG
RUHRBUSCH
BOIS D'ELSENBORN
39
LXVII
XXX
1 SS
3 39
Schwalmbach
Ovifat
Camp d'Elsenborn
395
Elsenborn
394
Robertville
9
393
ELSENBORN RIDGE
Walk
Nidrum
23
KRINKELTER WALD
277 VG
Champagne
38
Rocherath
Bruyeres
Gueuzaine
16
Weywertz
Bütgenbach
Wirtzfeld
Krinkelt
Elms.
12 SS
Holtwarche
26
Waimes
2 26
Warche
Warchenne
Faymonville
Dom Bütgenbach
Büllingen
Mürringen
Elms.
12 SS
3 Prcht
Hünningen
12VG
Schoppen
KAMPFGRUPPE PEIPER
Ondenval
Honsfeld
Losheimergraben
Möderscheid
Hepscheid
Iveldingen
Heppenbach
2nd Ss Pz Gr. Regt
Eibertingen
Montenau
Lanzerath
Amblève
0 1 2 3 miles

The 1st Infantry Division joined the fight against Germany in November 1942 during the invasion of North Africa. For two years, the division had fought in some of the most significant campaigns of the war.

The 1st Infantry Division landed at Omaha Beach on D-Day, taking heavy losses on that first day of the campaign in Western Europe.

If North Africa, Sicily, Omaha Beach, the Normandy bocage, and the breakout were not enough, the 1st Infantry Division also saw heavy combat in the Hürtgen Forest. By the fall of 1944, hardly anyone who landed with the division during Operation Torch remained in the rifle companies.

Elements of the 1st Infantry Division spent the first day of the Bulge hunting German paratroops who had been dropped behind the lines. They were scattered all over the woods, and the operation had no effect on the fighting along the north shoulder. Most of the German parachutists were killed or captured.

A platoon from the 1st Infantry Division maneuvers on an isolated group of German airborne troops on December 16th.

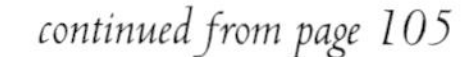

continued from page 105

Road—which in German terms was Rollbahn B and of critical importance to the success of any breakthrough. The battalion commander, a Ph.D. graduate from Clemson named Lt. Col. Derill Daniels, anchored his left flank on a small lake that stretched north to the edge of the 2nd Infantry Division's anchor point at Wirtzfeld. On the right, however, there was little effective terrain to use as an obstacle. As a result, the 2nd Battalion's flank dangled, exposed to any left-hook attacks coming from Büllingen, a few kilometers down the Malmedy Road.

Unknown to Daniels and his Blue Spaders, they'd dug in astride the 12th SS Panzer Division's axis of assault. They would be hit by everything the Hitlerjugend (Hitler Youth) Division had left, as the 12th SS made one last attempt to force its way through to the west.

After the failure to break through at the Twin Villages, the Germans shifted their focus to the west, sliding off the hard right shoulder of Gerow's V Corps in search of a way around all the American power now protecting Elsenborn Ridge and the two key

Well positioned astride a narrow, forested road, a bazooka-armed GI prepares to knock out an approaching German half-track.

rollbahns. The Waffen-SS soon discovered that Rollbahn B, the Malmedy Road, had its own problems. It was dirt and gravel, which meant in December 1944 it had devolved into mud and ice. When the 12th SS shifted its axis of advance and put its medium and heavy tanks on the road, they churned up the road and sank so deep some of them rumbled along with mud all the way to their decks. The support vehicles behind them suffered all manners of breakdowns and bog-downs as a result. In Hitler's mind, he saw a repeat of 1940 in the Ardennes. What he didn't see or factor into his plans were the conditions of the road and the weight of the tanks in 1944, which was at least four or five times greater than the Panzer Is and IIs of the 1940 campaign. That weight made a huge difference. Trying to cross bridges became problematical. The road network suffered, and the tracked vehicles ground the dirt ones into seas of frothy mud.

By midnight, December 20, the 12th SS Panzer Division had concentrated the remains of its panzer regiment, the 25th Panzer Grenadiers, and the 560th Panzerjäger Battalion in front of Dom Bütgenbach. The terrain on either side of the road proved to be too soft to support armor, so the armor would be restricted to a narrow front.

In pitch darkness, the panzers formed up on the road. Behind them, a battalion of dismounted infantry stumbled through the chilly night, checked their weapons, and prepared to advance.

Later that morning, they streamed up the road and ran headlong into F Company of the 2nd Battalion, 26th Infantry. A close-quarters tank-infantry skirmish quickly developed. The German gunners managed to kill three bazooka teams and take out a machine gun section, but Lieutenant Colonel Daniels had covered his front with well-placed 57mm antitank guns, which scored flank shots on a number of the panzers. At the same time, the battalion's forward observers called massive fire missions, and the German infantry faced a gauntlet of steel and high explosives.

A German Jagdpanzer IV rumbles forward. Based on the Panzer IV chassis, this tank hunter came armed with the same high-velocity Pak 42 L/70 75mm cannon the Panther used.

Forward observers played a vital role at the Hot Corner. The Germans recognized their phenomenal ability to dictate the flow of an engagement and made them high-priority targets.

The attack failed. The Germans fell back, reformed, and came again. This time, the panzerjägers—humpbacked Jagdpanzer IVs—joined in the attack. Artillery tore apart the infantry, and the bazooka men and 57mm antitank gunners knocked out at least eight tanks. During the fight, Sgt. Stanley Oldenski, who commanded a section of 57mm guns, sent most of his men out to hunt tanks with bazookas, keeping only Cpl. Henry "Red" Warner as his gunner. Together, the two GIs put four quick shots into a Jagdpanzer, setting it afire. Another one came in view, and they stopped it with two well-placed shots. Then their 57mm gun jammed. As they worked to clear it, another Jagdpanzer loomed before them. Rolling straight at the gun, with the intent to crush it and the two men manning it, the Jagdpanzer closed to less than thirty feet. Red Warner drew his pistol, swung out away from the gun, and

The 105mm howitzer served as the backbone of the U.S. Army's towed artillery units. These belonged to the 87th Infantry Division.

fired a single shot at the Jagdpanzer's commander, who had popped out of the commander's hatch to get a look around. The Waffen-SS NCO flopped forward, half in, half out of the turret, blood pouring from his fatal head wound.

The loss of their commander prompted the Jagdpanzer to reverse and break contact. Warner ultimately destroyed three panzers himself, but was killed by tank machine gun fire a few days later. He received a posthumous Medal of Honor for his actions.

Once again, as the Germans struggled through the snow to their objectives, American artillery came into its own. The flexibility of the fire-direction system, the ability of the gunners to launch time-on-target missions—where every shell fired from multiple battalions landed on the Germans at the same instant—and the skill of the forward observers all combined to make American artillerists the best on the planet in 1944.

Here, around Dom Bütgenbach, they more than demonstrated their skill again. Time after time, the 2nd Battalion, 26th Infantry, was shielded with a ring of high explosives, protecting the undermanned and hard-pressed infantry platoons from the full weight of the German assault. It allowed one battalion of Blue Spaders to stop the better part of an SS panzer division for two days.

Their positions, known among the men as "The Hot Corner," were littered with dead and dying SS troopers. About a hundred and eighty died in the second attack and over two hundred by the end of the 20th. Twenty-four panzers, squat and menacing, burned or smoldered in the battlefield. This represented half the division's remaining armor assets.

Night brought no reprieve. At 1:30 a.m. on December 21, three battalions of panzer grenadiers, supported by the remaining tanks in the division, charged forward through the black, foggy night. The Blue Spaders waited until they came within point-blank range. Then, machine guns barked. Bazooka men fired at the blue-red exhaust signatures of passing Panthers and Jagdpanzers. The 57mm crews, hard hit from the past few days, laid perfect ambushes and scored devastating flank shots.

The 1st Division's fire-control center gained access to no fewer than 348 guns from 23 battalions of artillery, all emplaced around Elsenborn Ridge. This highest piece of real state in Belgium had become the summit of American firepower on the north shoulder, and it was turned on the Germans like a fist of God.

The curtain became a wall. The wall became a divide. The battlefield in front of the 2nd Battalion, 26th Infantry's foxholes churned white and black as the 105s and 155s demolished the landscape.

A Panzer IV knocked out at Butgenbach, a victim of a 26th Infantry Regiment antitank team.

An American 57mm antitank gun, well concealed on a snowy forest slope, awaits a target.

A 155mm "Long Tom" pounds German troops at night. During the fighting around Bütgenbach, the forward observers in the 1st Infantry Division could call upon almost 350 pieces of artillery. Such firepower tipped the battle in favor of the outnumbered defenders.

This M4 Sherman was attached to the 16th Infantry Regiment, 1st Infantry Division. Tank support for the Big Red One was severely limited during the opening days of the German offensive. This photo was taken by Sgt. Bill Augustine of the 165th Signal Corps Company.

A scratchy German photo depicts self-propelled artillery pieces firing on American positions. While deadly effective at times, German artillery never achieved the effectiveness of the U.S. Army's artillery branch.

No army could stand such an onslaught. The SS troopers melted away. The Germans switched tactics. At 3:00 a.m., they laid their own steel curtain down on Lieutenant Colonel Daniels' men. Nebelwerfers formed part of this artillery assault. They wailed out of the black sky and exploded throughout the battalion's lines. Heavy and light guns joined with mortars to tear up all the communication wires between the companies and the battalion command post. The men went to ground and hid deep in the protective sanctuary of their snow-lipped foxholes. The German shellfire knocked out heavy weapons, took out machine gun nests and 57mm antitank guns, and demolished sections of the 2nd Battalion's main line of resistance.

The barrage continued almost until dawn. The GIs in it could only pray that the random nature of this means of death would spare them.

At 5:00 a.m. the Germans tried again. Supported once more by tanks and panzerjägers, the Hitler Youth Division charged to its doom. The American forward observers quickly called in every available gun. The 1st Infantry Division's fire-control center coordinated twenty-three battalions at once. The fist of God fell upon the Nazis, and the morning's light saw carnage and chaos engulf their ranks.

A GI tries to untangle a mass of communication wire following a German bombardment on the north shoulder. During a barrage, the shells usually knocked out telephone communications between the frontlines and the headquarters elements in the rear. Reestablishing that connection became an utmost priority, as it allowed the forward observers the best means of calling in fire missions.

In places, determined SS men followed a few courageous tankers, and they succeeded in reaching the 2nd Battalion, 26th Infantry's right flank. The tanks rumbled down parallel to the American lines, shooting down the BAR teams, killing the machine gun crews, and causing havoc. In their wake, the SS troopers followed, submachine guns chattering.

The battalion mortar platoon frantically laid down fire. Some of the tubes launched 750 rounds each that morning. Elsewhere, the forward observers (FOs) saw the collapsing right flank and focused their wrath on the Germans there. Nevertheless, about a company-sized armor element managed to break through and push toward their American rear. They were met by a track from the 634th Tank Destroyer Battalion, which killed seven German

An 81mm mortar crew loads and fires its tube. Mortars provided excellent indirect fire support to the infantrymen, even when communication with rear-echelon units went down. Each American infantry battalion included a platoon of 81mm mortars as the unit's organic indirect fire support. Each infantry company also had a section of 60mm light mortars it could rely on for short-range missions.

A bazooka team watches a German panzer burn.

The M36 Jackson, which had just reached frontline units in Europe, carried a modified version of the army's 90mm antiaircraft gun and stood a much better chance of knocking out a Panther than the 76mm-armed M10 tank destroyer.

A Geman half-track burns in the snow. The Waffen-SS units that attacked the 1st Infantry Division suffered grievous losses for little gain.

panzers as they rumbled over a ridge. Two Shermans from also joined in the fight, each taking out a panzer before they were blown to pieces by the superior German guns.

The armored thrust reached Lieutenant Colonel Daniels' command post, but the battalion's mortar teams pummeled the approaching German tanks. Then a pair of M36 Jacksons—90mm-armed tank destroyers—rolled into the battle and polished off the last elements that achieved the breakthrough.

It had been a near-run thing. Colonel Daniels later wrote, "We wouldn't be here now without them (the artillery support)." For eight hours, the battle ebbed and flowed. A quarter of the Blue Spaders fell. The American guns dropped no fewer than ten thousand shells on the Hitler Youth Division. The men in the foxholes repelled assault after assault. In one case, a full company of panzer grenadiers attacked a dug-in platoon from the 2nd Battalion, 26th Infantry. A furious artillery fire mission, perfectly timed, shattered their attack and saved the desperate GIs.

Finally, as the sky darkened once again, the 12th SS threw in the towel. The SS men had suffered almost a thousand casualties and had lost forty-seven tanks and AFVs.

Elsenborn Ridge would never fall to the Germans.

Part III

THE CENTER FAILS

★ ★ ★ ★ ★

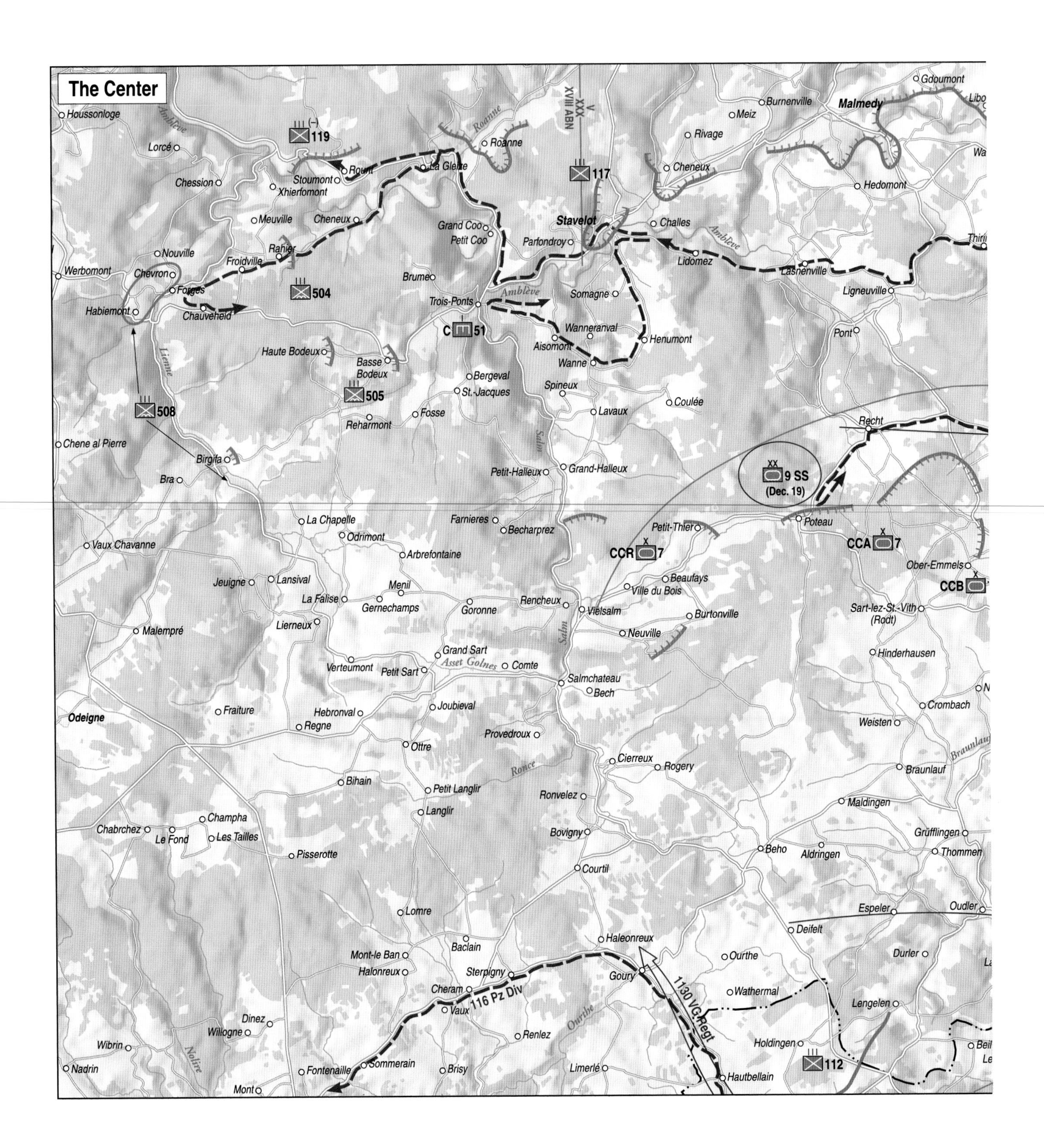
The Center
Houssonloge
Lorcé
Chession
Xhierfomont
Stoumont
Rouvit
La Gleize
Roanne
Roanne
119
117
V
XXX
XVIII ABN
Meiz
Burnenville
Malmedy
Gdoumont
Rivage
Cheneux
Hedomont
Meuville
Cheneux
Grand Coo
Petit Coo
Stavelot
Parfondroy
Challes
Amblève
Lidomez
Lasnenville
Ligneuville
Nouville
Froidville
Rahier
Werbomont
Chevron
Forges
Habiemont
Chauveheid
504
Brume
Trois-Ponts
Amblève
Somagne
C 51
Wanneranval
Aisomont
Henumont
Wanne
Pont
Haute Bodeux
Basse Bodeux
Bergeval
St.-Jacques
Spineux
505
508
Lienne
Fosse
Reharmont
Lavaux
Coulée
Recht
Chene al Pierre
Birgifa
Bra
Salm
Petit-Halleux
Grand-Halleux
9 SS
(Dec. 19)
La Chapelle
Odrimont
Farnieres
Becharprez
Petit-Thier
Poteau
Vaux Chavanne
Arbrefontaine
CCR 7
CCA 7
Ober-Emmels
CCB
Jeuigne
Lansival
Menil
La Falise
Gernechamps
Goronne
Rencheux
Beaufays
Ville du Bois
Vielsalm
Burtonville
Sart-lez-St.-Vith
(Rodt)
Malempré
Lierneux
Neuville
Hinderhausen
Grand Sart
Verteumont
Petit Sart
Asset Golnes
Comte
Salmchateau
Bech
Crombach
Odeigne
Fraiture
Hebronval
Regne
Joubieval
Weisten
Provedroux
Ottre
Cierreux
Rogery
Braunlauf
Ronce
Bihain
Petit Langlir
Langlir
Ronvelez
Maldingen
Champha
Chabrchez
Le Fond
Les Tailles
Bovigny
Grüfflingen
Pisserotte
Beho
Aldringen
Thommen
Courtil
Lomre
Espeler
Oudler
Deifelt
Baclain
Haleonreux
Mont-le Ban
Halonreux
Ourthe
Durler
Sterpigny
Goury
Cheram
116 Pz Div
1130 VG Regt
Wathermal
Vaux
Lengelen
Dinez
Willogne
Renlez
Ourthe
Wibrin
Holdingen
Nadrin
Noliire
Fontenaille
Sommerain
Brisy
Limerlé
Hautbellain
112
Mont

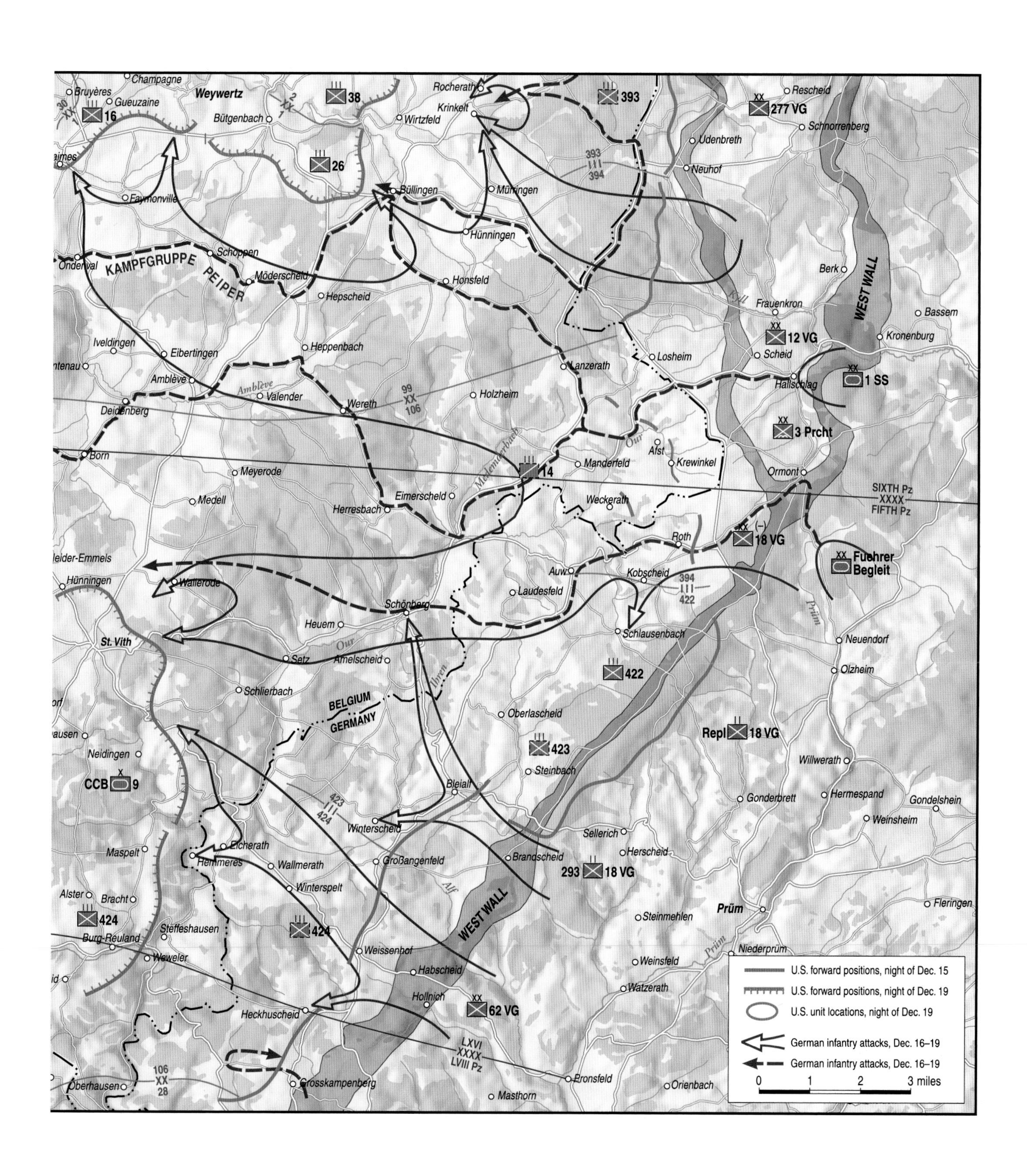
U.S. forward positions, night of Dec. 15
U.S. forward positions, night of Dec. 19
U.S. unit locations, night of Dec. 19
German infantry attacks, Dec. 16–19
German infantry attacks, Dec. 16–19
0 1 2 3 miles
KAMPFGRUPPE PEIPER
WEST WALL
BELGIUM
GERMANY
SIXTH Pz
XXXX
FIFTH Pz
St. Vith
Prüm

Waffen-SS panzergrenadiers in action on the Eastern Front.

11

A NOOSE FOR A WAR CRIMINAL

JOACHIM "JOCHEN" PEIPER OOZED ARROGANCE AND POWER. He also looked like a recruiting image poster child for the Waffen-SS—tall, Aryan features, blond hair, and blue eyes. He was a Nazi quintessential Germanic warrior.

He had joined the SS in 1933 and later applied to join Sepp Dietrich's Liebstandarte Adolf Hilter unit, which would ultimately become the 1st SS Panzer Division. In 1938, Peiper became Heinrich Himmler's personal adjutant, a role he filled until August of 1941. This meant he was present with Himmler when he issued the initial orders to begin executing Jews in Eastern Europe, which began in July 1941.

He rejoined the Leibstandarte Adolf Hitler and fought with it throughout the Eastern Front campaigns. He gained a reputation as a brilliant tactical officer, dedicated and willing to do whatever it took to accomplish his mission. He also left a trail of war crimes allegations wherever he went. Over the course of a four-year combat career, Peiper served in some of the key battles in Russia, Italy, and France. In the fall of 1944, in Germany's greatest hour of need, he was entrusted with the most important role in the Sixth Panzer Army: He would lead the Leibstandarte to the Meuse River with his reinforced kampfgruppe.

Joachim Peiper, nicknamed "Jochen" by his SS comrades, showed little mercy to his enemies. He served as Heinrich Himmler's personal adjutant earlier in the war. He would become a figure of great controversy during the Battle of the Bulge.

Kampfgruppe Peiper consisted of about 4,500 men, 149 half-tracks, two companies of Panthers totaling thirty-five tracks, another thirty-five Panzer IVs, and twenty King Tigers, which belonged to the 501st Heavy Panzer Battalion. Peiper also had his own engineers, artillery, and motorized antiaircraft vehicles. Altogether, including trucks and staff vehicles, Kampfgruppe Peiper included over eight hundred vehicles.

That required an awful lot of fuel, especially the Tiger II's, which sucked gas at a furious rate. With the fuel depots still on the east bank of the Rhine

The German SdKfz 250 reconnaissance half-track was light and agile, and saw heavy use in German panzer reconnaissance battalions.

Waffen-SS troops pause to smoke captured American cigarettes. These men belonged to the 1st SS Panzergrenadier Regiment. The photo was taken on the first or second day of the Bulge.

River—Hitler refused to move them closer to the Ardennes for fear they would be overrun—Peiper would not have ready access to resupply as he drove to the Meuse. As a result, part of his mission included finding and capturing American gas dumps.

On December 16, Peiper waited and fumed as the 3rd Fallschirmjäger Division fumbled its initial assault against Lt. Bouck's I&R Platoon outside of Lanzerath. By midnight, the SS officer was in full rage mode. A day had been wasted waiting around for the paratroops to do their job. He stormed into the 3rd Fallschirmjäger's headquarters and confronted the division's commander. When his answers didn't satisfy him, Peiper basically appropriated a battalion of paratroopers, put them atop his vehicles, and drove west.

The useless behemoth, a Tiger II, gets a look-over by a curious GI after its crew bailed out and abandoned it. A product of the gun-armor race on the Eastern Front, the Tiger II represented a totally unbalanced weapon of war. Though almost impervious to American antitank weapons and possessing a powerful 88mm cannon, its weight and fuel consumption made it a difficult panzer to employ. Many bridges could not handle its seventy metric tons. It couldn't operate effectively on soft surfaces or in muddy terrain, making its employment in battle problematical. The Tiger IIs also had mechanical troubles, and they frequently broke down while on the move.

A Tiger II loaded with fallschirmjägers dragooned into Kampfgruppe Peiper rolls through Ligneuville. The Tiger II was the exact wrong tank to employ in the Ardennes. With its already limited mobility, the weather and the inadequate roads and bridges slowed the heavy tank battalions to a crawl and hindered Peiper's advance. The nature of the terrain also precluded the Tiger II crews from using their greatest asset—the long-range killing power of the tank's 88mm gun.

When the Germans poured through the Ardennes in 1940, they did so with lighter tanks, such as the Panzer III seen here. For its time, the Panzer III was one of Germany's heaviest armored vehicles, tipping the scales at twenty-three tons. When Hitler conceived the 1944 Ardennes counteroffensive, he didn't take into consideration the problems the heavier Panthers and Tigers would have with the infrastructure and terrain in the region.

It took all day on the 17th for the full kampfgruppe to pass through Lanzerath. By the time the last vehicle got through town after dark, Peiper's forward elements had reached Stavelot and the Amblève River.

The Tiger IIs and the heavier German panzers turned out to be more of an impediment than anything else to Peiper. They contributed little to the fighting that day, and in subsequent days they broke down and became scattered along Peiper's narrow corridor. The terrain was totally unsuited for their use, most of the roads could not support them, and the amount of fuel they consumed was far too costly.

Had the kampfgruppe been built around Panzer IVs and a small core of Panthers, it would have been more mobile and required less fuel. Instead, Peiper's column lagged and splintered as more and more vehicles broke down.

The van of Peiper's massive column reached Buchholz Station early on the 17th. After sweeping aside minor opposition, the lead elements rolled into Honsfeld, which served as a rest center for the 99th Infantry Division. It was also supposed to be well defended with elements of the 32nd Cavalry Reconnaissance Squadron, two battalions of 90mm antiaircraft guns, part of the 512th and 801st Tank Destroyer Battalions, and units from the 99th Infantry Division. The first German vehicles showed up just before 6:00 a.m. and blended into a convoy of American vehicles. By the time Honsfeld's defenders realized there were Germans in their midst, it was too late. Peiper's half-tracks and tanks raked the streets and buildings as the fallschirmjägers dismounted and began clearing the town. In the confusion, most of the Americans fled.

Wanting to stay on a paved road for as long as possible, Peiper turned north for Büllingen. Capturing that town would give him good access to a major east-west road, but

The Panzer IV was much better suited for offensive operations in the Ardennes than its heavier stable mates. It consumed significantly less fuel than the Panther and Tiger I and II, plus its lighter weight allowed it to negotiate roads and bridges the other vehicles could not traverse.

The M8 Greyhound armored car served as the primary fast-moving armored fighting vehicle in the U.S. Army's cavalry troops. While it could be a useful infantry-support weapon, against tanks it stood no chance.

Kampfgruppe Peiper rolls through Honsfeld, en route to Büllingen.

Luftwaffe troops loot American dead in Honsfeld.

Dead American GIs killed by Kampfgruppe Peiper lie beside a 76mm antitank gun at Honsfeld.

it was defended by three companies from the 254th Engineers, supported by antitank guns. Sometime about 7:30 a.m., Peiper's spearhead struck the engineers, who knocked out a Panzer IV and repelled three separate assaults. Finally, the Germans broke through and pushed into the town, where engineers took potshots at their passing half-tracks from second- and third-story windows. Such sniping paid off: Peiper lost two platoon leaders in this fashion.

The engineers refused to break, even as an overwhelming panzergrenadier force, supported by Panthers and Mark IVs, swarmed into the town. Instead, the plucky Americans executed a fighting withdrawal and pulled out of Büllingen in good order. They reestablished a defensive line about 1,500 meters north of the town. When a few Panzer IVs probed the new positions, the Americans seriously damaged the lead track and killed its commander. The Germans turned around and returned to Büllingen.

What happened next has been discussed for decades. Peiper had his orders: Go west with all possible speed. Hold nothing back, and get across the Meuse River so the rest of the 1st SS Panzer Division following in his wake could exploit his breakthrough. However, with his capture of Büllingen, Peiper had the chance to hit the 99th and 2nd Infantry Divisions in the flank at a time when they were still heavily engaged holding Elsenborn Ridge. Had he disregarded his orders, he could have unseated the entire First Army's effort on the north shoulder and uncorked the rest of the Sixth Panzer Army.

Of course, at the time Peiper didn't know that, but American commanders on the scene never understood why Peiper didn't keep going north. But orders were orders, and Peiper was of singular purpose: get to the Meuse at all costs. Instead of heading north, he followed the road southwest out of Büllingen and missed a golden opportunity to deal a devastating blow to the American defenses in the Ardennes.

At Büllingen, American engineers sniped at Peiper's passing vehicles from rooftops and other elevated positions. Their pluck paid off: two of his platoon leaders fell victim to such attacks while riding in half-tracks.

American survivors of the Malmedy Massacre. Front row: Cpl. George Bishop, Disputanta, Virginia; Pfc. William Portell, Kalamazoo, Michigan. Back row: Pvt. Louis Bristen, Akron, Ohio; Pvt. Eugene Campbell, Cincinnati, Ohio; and Pfc. Roy Stratton, Leesburg, Florida. This photo was snapped by Sergeant Taylor of the 165th Signal Company on December 17, 1944.

The wreckage of Malmedy itself. The Germans shelled the town and inflicted considerable damage.

Cataloging the dead of the Malmedy Massacre.

An American antitank gun at a roadblock in the Ardennes. While such positions could not stop the lead elements of the 1st SS Panzer Division, they slowed Peiper down. And for the Germans, losing time meant losing the battle.

Not long after the spearhead departed Büllingen, Peiper's men ran into a column of about 140 men from Battery B, 285th Field Artillery Observation Battalion. Their soft-skinned vehicles came under heavy fire from Peiper's tanks and half-tracks, and the unit surrendered en masse. Exactly what happened next has been a matter of some dispute. Whether ordered or not, the Waffen-SS men opened fire on the unarmed American prisoners and massacred all but a handful. A few men managed to escape back to U.S. lines, where their story spread like wildfire.

This wasn't the first time Peiper's men killed unarmed prisoners of war. Through the Ardennes Campaign, his kampfgruppe was later accused of slaughtering hundreds of Belgian civilians and POWs. There would be a reckoning for these actions after the war.

Peiper pushed his SS men on with a ruthless sense of purpose. He was running far behind schedule, and he flogged his units to try to make up the time. Trouble was, at every town and intersection he encountered a delaying force of antitank guns and engineers. They slowed his progress and then pulled out before the kampfgruppe could deal them a decisive blow.

At Ligneuville, Peiper ran into American armor. There was a repair facility in town, as well as the headquarters element for the 49th Antiaircraft Brigade, and Peiper just missed capturing its commanding officer, Brigadier General Timberlake. As German tanks pressed into town, a Sherman dozer opened fire from a concealed position and knocked out a Panther with a well-placed flanking shot. Unfortunately, the American tank was under repair and not mobile, and the remaining panzers made short work of it.

American resistance at Ligneuville soon collapsed, and Peiper drove straight northwest for the sleepy Belgian town of Stavelot. With a population of about 7,500, Stavelot held significant strategic importance for the Sixth Panzer Army. First, it was a major crossroads town in the area, with roads running north, south, east, and west out of the town. Second, in the heart of the town stood a robust stone bridge over the Amblève River that could bear the weight of Peiper's panzers.

The Waffen-SS men reached the outskirts of Stavelot just after sunset on December 17. Winding their way along a treacherous mountain road, the head of Peiper's column ran into an American roadblock just a few thousand meters from the Amblève River bridge. Manned by only thirteen men from an engineer unit, the roadblock had been established

At Ligneuville, Peiper's spearhead ran into an ambush laid by a Sherman dozer that had been under repair in the town. The dozer's crew manned their track, even though it wasn't mobile, and knocked out a Panther with a masterful flank shot. The Panther's platoon mates quickly destroyed the Sherman dozer.

A Panther burns after trying to engage Americans to its rear. U.S. tankers and bazooka teams learned to be patient and work their way around and behind German panzers to hit their less-armored rears. This particular Panther was knocked out at Krinkelt on December 18 and belonged to the 12th SS Panzer Division.

The ruins of Stavelot, Belgium. This town, with its strategically important stone bridge over the Amblève River, played a key role in the destruction of Peiper's command.

The bridge over the Amblève River at Stavelot.

A bazooka-armed GI sits in his foxhole and overwatches a road. Such delaying positions like this one hampered Peiper's advance and utterly frustrated him.

Peiper's SS men not only shot American POWs, but Belgian civilians as well. As one group of civilians was about to be executed, one of the Belgians asked why. An SS trooper replied, "The innocent must pay for the crimes of the guilty." These victims were shot at Stavelot.

along a perfect bottleneck. A steep cliff going straight up dominated one side of the road. A precipitous hundred-foot drop to a valley below dominated the other side. As the first German panzer reached the roadblock, Pvt. Bernie Goldstein stepped in front of the SS column and shouted, "Halt!"

His challenge was met by machine gun fire, and he dove for cover as his buddies responded with their M1s and a bazooka. When a panzer took a bazooka hit, the Germans pulled back. Peiper, convinced that Stavelot was heavily defended, decided to call it a day. His men had been up and operating for thirty-six straight hours and needed rest.

In fact, Goldstein's squad was the only fighting force standing between the kampfgruppe and the bridge over the Amblève River. It wasn't until early the next morning that American reinforcements streamed into Stavelot, hoping to delay Peiper yet again. Peiper wasted a golden opportunity to get across the Amblève River on December 17.

Nevertheless, on the morning of the 18th, his panzer grenadiers and paratroops dismounted and moved down the road toward the Amblève River bridge. They ran into two platoons of American antitank guns, which had been unwisely pushed across the river and set

A German soldier lies dead in the streets of Stavelot.

into hasty defensive positions not far from the original road block. The Waffen-SS troopers overran both platoons, sending the survivors scurrying back across the bridge

The bridge itself was supposed to have been blown up the night before, but for some reason the lieutenant in charge of its demolition decided to mine it instead. In the confusion of the pre-dawn German assault, the bridge remained intact, giving a canny Panther crew the opportunity to charge across it and seize ground on the north bank. More vehicles soon followed. By this time, Stavelot was defended by a mixed lot of engineers, American armored infantry, antitank guns, and two M10 tank destroyers. They didn't have the power to resist the German assault. The M10 crews received the target of a lifetime at one point when Peiper's column was backed up at the bridge. From atop a hill on the north side of the river, the pair of American armored vehicles sniped at the traffic jam below, knocking out several German tracks. But it was simply not enough to stop the Waffen-SS from seizing the town. The Americans, under the command of Maj. Paul Solis, withdrew north to an enormous First Army fuel depot a few kilometers out of town. To prevent the Germans from following, Solis created antitank barriers by setting fire to some of the depot's gasoline, something that was later used as the climactic scene in the movie *The Battle of the Bulge.*

A knocked-out 3-inch tank destroyer.

An M10 after taking two direct hits on the glacis.

Peiper rushed onward, racing for the Meuse. The next major bottleneck was at a town called Trois Ponts. Here, the Salm River flows into the Amblève. Trois Ponts, which means "Three Bridges," grew up around this confluence and became another significant communication hub. To capture it, Peiper split his force and sent part of his panzers down the south bank of the Amblève. The rest crossed the bridge at Stavelot and then followed the north bank to Trois Ponts.

continued on page 141

One of the three bridges at Trois Ponts. When the engineers blew these vital crossing points, they denied Peiper much of his freedom of movement and forced him to turn northwest to find another way to the Meuse River.

Part of Peiper's force came across an American liaison squadron parked in a field. The passing German column shot up the L4 light observation planes and destroyed most of them. Later, the L4s struck back and detected Peiper's vanguard outside of Cheneux.

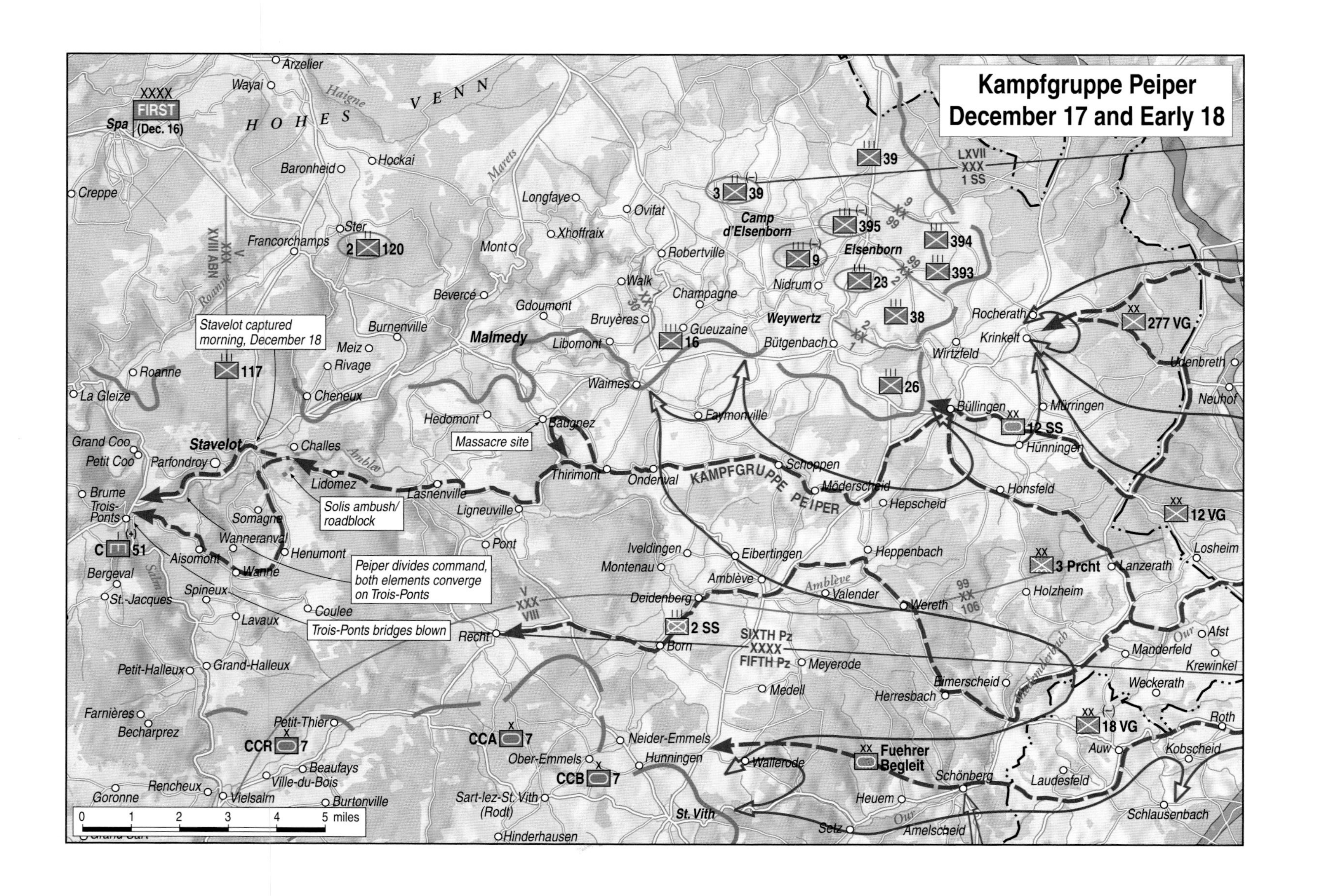
Kampfgruppe Peiper
December 17 and Early 18
Stavelot captured morning, December 18
Solis ambush/ roadblock
Peiper divides command, both elements converge on Trois-Ponts
Trois-Ponts bridges blown
Massacre site
KAMPFGRUPPE PEIPER
HOHES VENN
XXXX FIRST (Dec. 16)
V XXX XVIII ABN
LXVII XXX 1 SS
V XXX VIII
SIXTH Pz XXXX FIFTH Pz
277 VG
12 VG
18 VG
12 SS
3 Prcht
2 SS
Fuehrer Begleit
CCA 7
CCB 7
CCR 7
Spa
Arzelier
Wayai
Creppe
Baronheid
Hockai
Francorchamps
Ster
Roanne
La Gleize
Stavelot
Grand Coo
Petit Coo
Parfondroy
Brume
Trois-Ponts
Bergeval
St.-Jacques
Aisomont
Wanne
Wanneranval
Somagne
Henumont
Spineux
Lavaux
Coulee
Challes
Lidomez
Lasnenville
Ligneuville
Pont
Cheneux
Rivage
Meiz
Burnenville
Bevercé
Mont
Longfaye
Xhoffraix
Ovifat
Robertville
Walk
Champagne
Gdoumont
Malmedy
Libomont
Bruyères
Gueuzaine
Waimes
Hedomont
Baugnez
Thirimont
Ondenval
Faymonville
Schoppen
Möderscheid
Hepscheid
Camp d'Elsenborn
Elsenborn
Nidrum
Weywertz
Bütgenbach
Rocherath
Krinkelt
Wirtzfeld
Büllingen
Mürringen
Hünningen
Honsfeld
Udenbreth
Neuhof
Losheim
Lanzerath
Holzheim
Heppenbach
Eibertingen
Iveldingen
Montenau
Amblève
Valender
Deidenberg
Wereth
Recht
Born
Meyerode
Medell
Herresbach
Eimerscheid
Manderfeld
Afst
Krewinkel
Weckerath
Roth
Auw
Kobscheid
Laudesfeld
Schlausenbach
Schönberg
Heuem
Setz
Amelscheid
St. Vith
Wallerode
Neider-Emmels
Hunningen
Ober-Emmels
Sart-lez-St. Vith (Rodt)
Hinderhausen
Petit-Thier
Beaufays
Ville-du-Bois
Vielsalm
Burtonville
Rencheux
Goronne
Farnières
Becharprez
Petit-Halleux
Grand-Halleux
Amblève
Salm
Our
Roanne
Haigne
Marets
0 1 2 3 4 5 miles

Colonel Ray J. Stecker, commander of the 365th Fighter Group (the "Hellhawks"), gives a quick briefing to his three squadron leaders, Majs. George Brooking, John Motzenbecker, and Robert Fry. The 365th shot up Peiper's vehicles outside Cheneux on December 23.

continued from page 137

The engineers were waiting for them. Again. This time, they blew the Amblève River bridge just as Peiper arrived. Not long after, when the rest of the kampfgruppe reached the area, the engineers blew the remaining two bridges, both over the Salm.

His force now divided, Peiper checked his map. Without bridging equipment, he faced a serious dilemma. The Amblève winds all over this section of the Ardennes, and he would need to get over it again in order to reach his objective. How to get to the Meuse now? The only way left was to turn north, follow the Amblève to La Gleize, then either press on via Stoumont or cross the Amblève again at Cheneux.

Peiper put his tracks on the road. His panzers took La Gleize and then sped on for Cheneux. He had not been resupplied, and all his vehicles were now starting to run low on fuel.

Just short of Cheneux, the overcast skies began to clear up. Patches of sunlight shone through across the snowy landscape. An American liaison plane, out looking for Peiper, discovered the SS column and called it up the chain of command.

A 365th Fighter Group P-47 warms up before a mission over the Ardennes.

A P-47 ranges across the battlefield.

GIs examine two Flakpanzer IV Wirbelwind (Whirlwind) quad 20mm tracks. Against low-firing aircraft, the Whirlwind could be deadly. Against infantry, the four 20s could inflict utter carnage. They were based on the Panzer IV chassis, and fewer than a hundred were produced. German AA units were well-armed and well-trained.

Capable of carrying two 1,000-pound bombs or eight rockets, the P-47's rugged construction and eight .50-caliber machine guns made it the quintessential fighter-bomber platform of World War II. These particular P-47s belonged to the 350th Fighter Group.

Ninth Air Force Republic P-47 Thunderbolts descended on Peiper's vehicles. For two hours, the Waffen-SS men faced strafing and bombing runs, which caused a lot of casualties and destroyed five Panthers and three half-tracks. Even worse for Peiper's orders, the attack had delayed his progress by almost two hours. It turned out to be a fatal delay.

Peiper's head was in a noose. And a National Guard division was about to serve as his executioner.

The 30th Infantry Division liberates Louviers, France, in August 1944. By the time it joined the Battle of the Bulge, the 30th had secured its reputation as one of the best infantry divisions under Eisenhower's command.

12

THE GUARDSMEN AND THE SS

AS SOON AS THE WRECKED TANKS AND SELF-PROPELLED WEAPONS could be pushed off the road, Peiper's column got moving again. They reached Cheneux, captured the vital bridge there, and continued westward. Perhaps the way to the Meuse was open after all.

Then the panzers reached the bridge across Lienne Creek. It was wired with 2,500 pounds of TNT. The engineers who planted those demolitions waited until the first German tanks were practically on the bridge before blowing it. Peiper had been blocked yet again.

He sent a small reconnaissance party north, looking for another bridge across this creek. If he had only brought his own bridging gear, this would not have been an issue. A few engineers could never stand for long against an SS kampfgruppe. Instead, his reconnaissance force discovered another bridge, but it was too fragile to bear the weight of Peiper's armor.

He had no choice now but to double back to La Gleize and try to advance via Stoumont in the morning. The kampfgruppe turned around and wasted much of its remaining fuel retracing its route.

That night, the first nail in Peiper's coffin was hammered home. Back in Stavelot, the Germans came under sudden attack by a strong and experienced force of Americans. This was a battalion from the 30th "Old Hickory" Infantry Division. Composed of National Guardsmen from Tennessee and North and South Carolina, the 30th had seen hard fighting in the bocage during the summer, and its men were steady veterans, unafraid of tackling the best the Third Reich had left to field. Later, the division would be called "Eisenhower's Praetorian Guard." Without a doubt, it was one of the best infantry units the United States produced during World War II.

The division's 117th Infantry Regiment was tasked with retaking Stavelot. Launching a night attack on December 18–19, the National Guardsmen advanced all the way to the bridge over the Amblève River, effectively cutting off Peiper from the rest of the 1st SS Panzer Division.

continued on page 148

One of the Peiper's knocked-out Panthers was pushed off the road so the advance could continue.

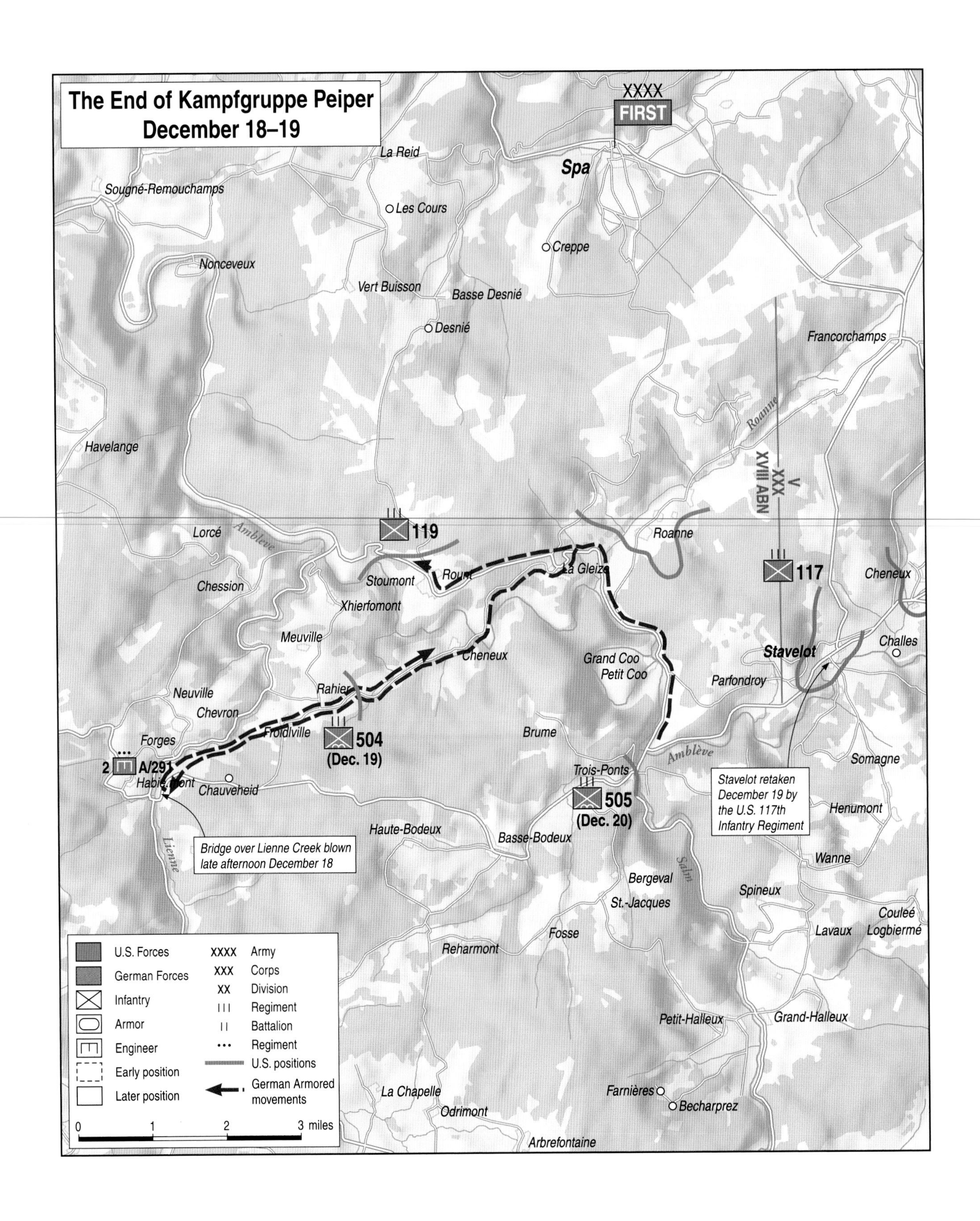
The End of Kampfgruppe Peiper
December 18–19
XXXX
FIRST
Spa
La Reid
Sougné-Remouchamps
Les Cours
Creppe
Nonceveux
Vert Buisson
Basse Desnié
Desnié
Francorchamps
Roanne
Havelange
V
XXX
XVIII ABN
119
Lorcé
Amblève
Roanne
117
Cheneux
Stoumont
Rouat
La Gleize
Chession
Xhierfomont
Meuville
Cheneux
Grand Coo
Petit Coo
Stavelot
Challes
Parfondroy
Neuville
Rahier
Chevron
Forges
Froidville
504
(Dec. 19)
Brume
2
A/291
Habiémont
Chauveheid
Trois-Ponts
505
(Dec. 20)
Amblève
Somagne
Stavelot retaken December 19 by the U.S. 117th Infantry Regiment
Henumont
Haute-Bodeux
Basse-Bodeux
Bridge over Lienne Creek blown late afternoon December 18
Lienne
Salm
Wanne
Bergeval
St.-Jacques
Spineux
Couleé
Lavaux
Logbiermé
Fosse
Reharmont
U.S. Forces
German Forces
Infantry
Armor
Engineer
Early position
Later position
XXXX Army
XXX Corps
XX Division
III Regiment
II Battalion
••• Regiment
U.S. positions
German Armored movements
Petit-Halleux
Grand-Halleux
La Chapelle
Odrimont
Farnières
Becharprez
Arbrefontaine
0 1 2 3 miles

In a region full of rivers and swollen creeks, any German offensive needed bridging equipment to be successful. But in December 1944, there wasn't much bridging gear left in the German Army, and Peiper led the way to the Meuse without any ability to make his own crossing points over the Amblève and Salm rivers. The lack of this vital equipment in the 1st SS Panzer Division's spearhead formation played a major role in getting Peiper's kampfgruppe cut off and destroyed. This Type J bridge, which was used outside of Malmedy, was one of the few available to Dietrich's frontline units during the opening days of the offensive.

An M4 Sherman of the 30th Infantry Division smolders after dueling with a Sturmgeschütz III in the bocage country outside Tampone, France, on August 2, 1944.

A flamethrower team from the 30th Infantry Division burns out an old pillbox during a training exercise designed to prepare the men for attacking the Siegfried Line in the fall of 1944. The 30th stopped the German counteroffensive at Mortain, then took part in the drive across France.

Armed with rifle grenades, a fire team from the 30th Infantry Division prepares to enter and clear a house from which they had taken sniper fire during the recapture of Stavelot.

continued from page 145

Simultaneously, the 30th Division's 119th Infantry Regiment deployed around Stoumont. Peiper now faced two crack regiments—one to the west and north, the other in his rear. To finish the trap, the 82nd Airborne Division arrived and deployed the 504th Parachute Infantry Regiment (PIR) in front of Cheneux. The 505th PIR swung south and east and dug in at Trois Ponts.

The next morning, Peiper threw the full weight of his kampfgruppe at Stoumont. They attacked the 119th through dense fog that allowed the dismounted fallschirmjägers and Waffen-SS pioneers leading the assault to get to within point-blank range before being detected. The first wave overran the 119th's outposts and captured a few antitank guns. Then a wall of American firepower stopped the attack cold and knocked out several

An M10 Tank Destroyer crew from the 823rd Tank Destroyer Battalion gained credit for knocking out four German Tiger IIs during the fighting at Stavelot. The crew includes (left to right) Pvt. Robert Crout, Columbia, South Carolina; Pfc. Raymond Clements, Indiantown, Florida; Technician 5th Class Clarence West, Lilly, Louisiana; Cpl. Buel Sheridan, Sheridan, Texas; Sgt. Clyde Gentry, Tucson, Arizona; and Staff Sgt. Oron Revis, Klamath Falls, Oregon. The photo was taken by Technician 3rd Class V. C. Calvano from the 167th Signal Company.

A derelict Tiger II lies abandoned in the wreckage of Stavelot.

The 82nd Airborne Division arrived just in time to put the stopper in the bottle. Deployed initially around Cheneux and Trois Ponts, the 82nd soon faced hard fighting in both towns.

Men of the 325th Glider Infantry Regiment, 82nd Airborne Division, lay antitank mines at a roadblock near Vaux Chavanne, Belgium. Technician 5th Class Don Cunningham of the 165th Signal Company took the photo.

Panthers. The Germans fell back, reformed, and attacked again. As they did, ten Shermans from the 743rd Tank Battalion showed up to reinforce the 119th and joined the battle.

The fighting in Stoumont raged all morning. Finally, by noon Peiper gained the upper hand. The National Guardsmen pulled out of the town and reformed to the west near a railroad station. There, the line was solidified with a 90mm antiaircraft gun and C Company, 740th Tank Battalion. The 740th was the last armored reserve in the First Army, and it had no tanks at the start of the Ardennes offensive. It had been waiting for a fresh resupply of Shermans, but the situation became so desperate that its crews were sent to a nearby depot to grab anything with tracks and a working motor. They rolled into battle with four Sherman DDs that had landed at Normandy on D-Day, ten regular M4s, and a single M36 Jackson tank destroyer.

As the guardsmen tried to hold on to the station against increasing pressure from Peiper, Lt. Col. Robert Herlong's 1st Battalion of the 119th Infantry arrived to stabilize the situation. He set up a defensive line behind the railroad station, grabbed the 740th Tank Battalion's motley collection of armor and decided to counterattack. The battalion drove headlong into Peiper's assault elements and chopped them up. They reeled backwards, leaving several burning tanks behind while fighting furiously as Herlong's men pursued them.

Private First Class Ed Nobles, a North Carolinian from Chadbourn, watches his assigned field of fire from a prepared position. Nobles belonged to D Company, 1st Battalion, 119th Infantry, 30th Infantry Division.

The remains of another of Peiper's precious Panthers.

Men of the 30th Infantry Division inch forward on their bellies.

By mid-afternoon, Kampfgruppe Peiper was all but out of fuel. The race to the Meuse was over. Now Peiper could only hold on and hope that another element of the 1st SS Panzer Division would come and rescue him. That night, engineers with the 117th Infantry in Stavelot finally blew the Amblève River bridge. With it went all of Peiper's hopes for salvation.

The next day, the Americans closed in. Peiper had broken up his kampfgruppe to garrison Stoumont, La Gleize, and Cheneux. He also sent his reconnaissance element back east toward Stavelot, hoping to open up the way to the Amblève River bridge. Instead, his recon battalion was virtually wiped out.

continued on page 156

This is one of four Sherman DDs scrounged up to equip the 740th Tank Battalion in the Ardennes. All four were battle-weary veterans of the D-Day landing.

An M36 Jackson in action in France. The M36 finally gave the American tank crews the firepower they needed to crack the thick-skinned Panther and Tiger tanks.

A First Army Sherman rolls into the fight.

A self-propelled M7 Priest rains down support fire from a position behind the American lines.

Sturmbannführer Gustav Knittle (right), who commanded the 1st SS Panzer Division's reconnaissance battalion, checks in with one of his staff members, Heinrich Golz, during a short pause on December 18 just outside of La Gleize. A short time later, Knittle's lightly equipped battle group was thrashed hard by the 30th Infantry Division when Peiper sent him east to reopen Stavelot.

Under mortar fire, medics rush to the aid of wounded GIs. The U.S. Army's medics were among the most courageous men on the battlefield.

continued from page 152

At Stoumont, the 119th Infantry fought a close-quarters battle for a thick-walled sanatorium on the outskirts of Stoumont. Possession of it would determine who controlled the town. At first, the 119th managed to take it, but the Waffen-SS rallied, counterattacked, and drove the Americans back.

While that fight raged, the 1st Battalion, 504th PIR, with minimal armor and artillery support, launched a fierce assault on Cheneux. Equipped with panzerfausts and panzerschrecks, handheld antitank rocket launchers, captured in Holland a few months before, the 504th

The 82nd loads up on a Sicilian airfield for the air drop into the Salerno beachhead, September 1943. The 82nd carried out more airborne operations than any other Allied unit during the war.

The 2nd Battalion, 505th PIR enters Naples in the fall of 1943. The 82nd Airborne saw extensive combat in Sicily and Italy prior to moving to England in preparation for Normandy.

Men of the 82nd clear the church at Sainte-Mère-Église on D-Day morning.

Troops from the 325th Glider Infantry Regiment receive a final briefing before the 82nd air-assaults into Nijmegen, Holland, as part of Operation Market-Garden.

Troopers en route to Nijmegen inside the cloistered interior of a C-47 Skytrain.

Paratroopers of the 82nd Airborne pose in Munich right as the war is ending. After the Bulge, the 82nd remained in the front lines and drove into Germany.

One of Peiper's Panthers after the battle at Cheneux. The 504th PIR's desperate assault on Cheneux ranks as one of the most courageous small-unit actions in the campaign in Western Europe. A regiment of paratroops successfully captured an objective held by a significant force of Waffen-SS panzergrenadiers, heavily supported by armored vehicles. It was a remarkable feat of arms, one that was paid for with the blood of over two hundred paratroopers.

took on the best German armored formation on the Western Front. The battle spilled into Cheneux, where the paratroopers clashed hand to hand with Peiper's panzer grenadiers. They overcame tanks, 20mm flak wagons, and armed half-tracks as they cleared Cheneux, street by street. In at least one case, men of the 504th clambered onto flak wagons and knifed the German antiaircraft crews. The 1st Battalion of the 504th suffered heavily for its courageous attack: 225 paratroopers died or suffered wounds. One company was left without a single officer and only eighteen men.

The pressure intensified. From north of La Gleize, the 3rd Battalion, 117th Infantry, drove south on Peiper, supported by Combat Command B of the 3rd Armored Division. By December 21 it was clear the kampfgruppe was finished. With the 82nd Airborne closing in

continued on page 162

Major Gen. James Gavin carries a rifle while visiting G Company, 3rd Battalion, 508th Parachute Infantry Regiment. As commander of the 82nd Airborne, he helped trap Peiper's kampfgruppe at La Gleize.

An SS flak track on the Eastern Front. These dual-purpose weapons played havoc on P-47s and infantry alike.

An American paratrooper hefts a German panzerschreck. With a bigger projectile, the panzerschreck could penetrate thicker armor than the bazooka, making it a favorite weapon to pick up and use against its former owners. The 504th Parachute Infantry Regiment carried a supply of panzerschrecks with them from Holland when the regiment went into battle against Kampfgruppe Peiper.

Another view of a German flak track, this one armed with a rapid-fire 37mm cannon, another deadly weapon.

At Cheneux, the 504th PIR faced multiple SS flak tracks. Their rapid-fire 20mm cannon cut down the attacking paratroopers in fearful numbers. The surviving Americans closed with the vehicles, climbed aboard, and knifed the crews.

A pair of 82nd Airborne troopers pose with a young SS captive.

A team from the 325th Glider Infantry Regiment, of the 82nd Airborne, loads an M9 bazooka and awaits Peiper's panzers on December 20, 1944. The photo was taken by Pfc. F. G. Poinsett of the 165th Signal Company.

The aftermath: a GI looks at the wreckage of snow-covered German armored vehicles. Peiper lost most of his eight hundred vehicles in his reckless, single-minded drive to the Meuse.

Peiper's fate: convicted war criminal. After the war, he was a lightning rod of controversy. He spent time in prison, and after his release, unknown assailants firebombed his house in 1976, and he was burned alive inside while shooting at his attackers.

The Tiger IIs that accompanied Peiper did not fare well. American antitank crews accounted for a few of them, but most either broke down or simply ran out of fuel and had to be abandoned.

The 82nd Airborne Division lines up about a company's worth of POWs. Though it took heavy losses, the 82nd demonstrated that paratroops with minimal armor support could successfully stand against an SS panzer formation.

A National Guardsman from the 117th Infantry moves past a wrecked panzer during the fighting for La Gleize.

The blasted remains of a Whirlwind antiaircraft track sit on the road outside Stoumont.

continued from page 159

from the south and the 30th Infantry Division squeezing them from north and west, the SS troops could surrender, die in place, or try to make a run for it.

Peiper made a run for it. Abandoning all his equipment and vehicles, he led his last eight hundred men on a desperate, sixty-kilometer hike through the snow-covered mountains. When he finally reached German lines again shortly before Christmas, he had 770 men left out of the 3,000 he had started with only a week before. Kampfgruppe Hansen, another element of the 1st SS Panzer Division, suffered five hundred casualties at Stavelot trying to get through to rescue Peiper and his men. The swift stroke to capture the Meuse, upon which all of Hitler's hopes rested, had ended in utter disaster. The north shoulder had held.

Part IV

BREAKTHROUGH

★ ★ ★ ★ ★

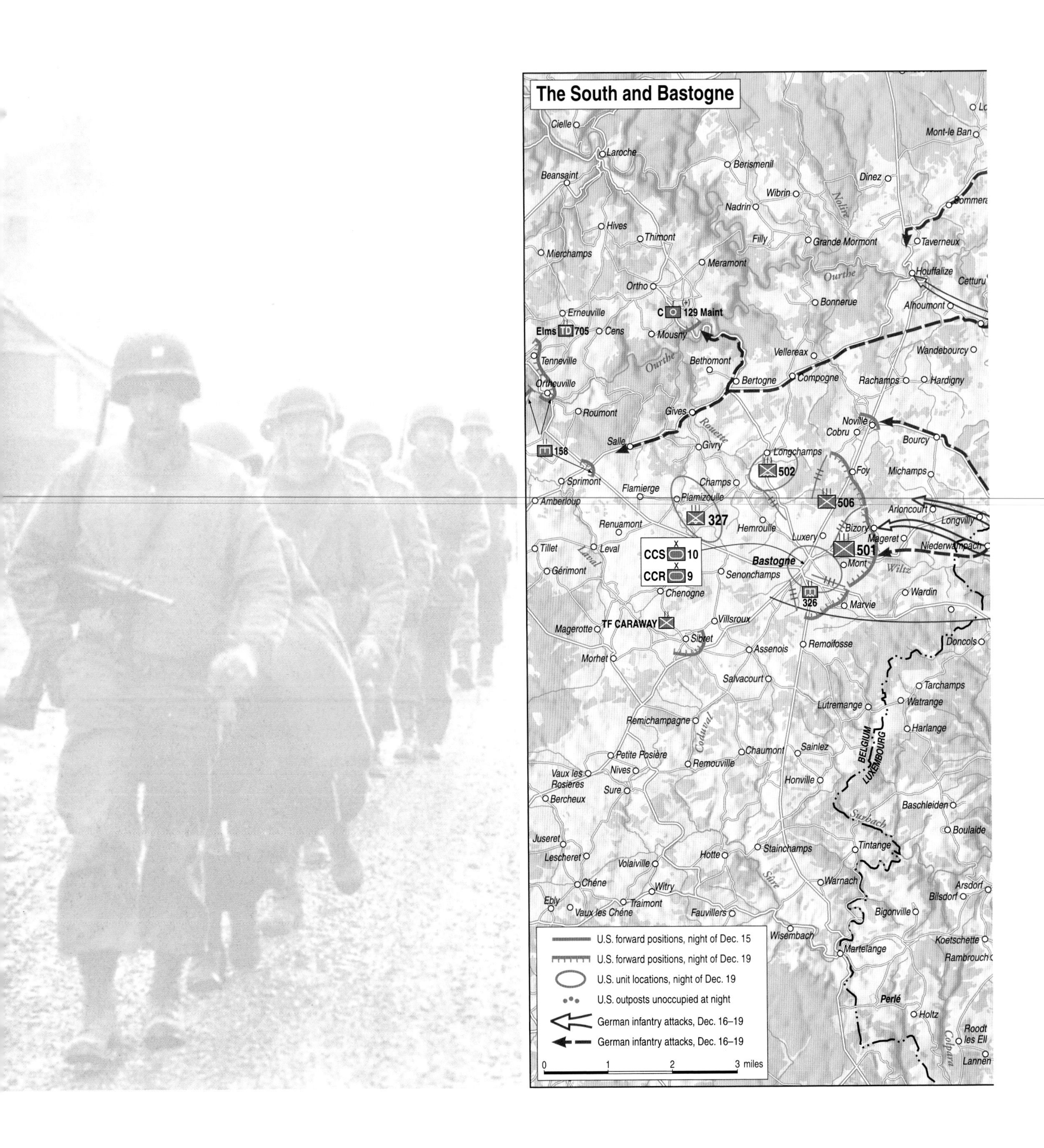

The South and Bastogne
Cielle
Laroche
Mont-le Ban
Berismenil
Beansaint
Dinez
Wibrin
Nolire
Nadrin
Hives
Thimont
Filly
Grande Mormont
Taverneux
Mierchamps
Meramont
Houffalize
Ourthe
Ortho
Bonnerue
Alhoumont
C 129 Maint
Erneuville
Elms TD 705
Cens
Mousny
Vellereax
Wandebourcy
Tenneville
Ourthe
Bethomont
Bertogne
Compogne
Rachamps
Hardigny
Orthéuville
Roumont
Gives
Noville
Cobru
Bourcy
Salle
Givry
Rouette
158
Longchamps
502
Foy
Michamps
Sprimont
Flamierge
Champs
Amberloup
Plamizoulle
506
Arloncourt
Longvilly
327
Renuamont
Hemroulle
Luxery
Bizory
Mageret
Niederwampach
Tillet
Leval
Laval
CCS 10
CCR 9
Bastogne
501
Mont
Wiltz
Gérimont
Senonchamps
Chenogne
326
Wardin
Marvie
Magerotte
TF CARAWAY
Villsroux
Sibret
Doncols
Assenois
Remoifosse
Morhet
Salvacourt
Tarchamps
Lutremange
Watrange
Remichampagne
Harlange
Codival
Chaumont
Sainlez
BELGIUM
LUXEMBOURG
Petite Posière
Remouville
Vaux les Rosières
Nives
Honville
Sure
Bercheux
Baschleiden
Surbach
Boulaide
Juseret
Tintange
Lescheret
Volaiville
Hotte
Stainchamps
Chéne
Witry
Sûre
Warnach
Arsdorf
Bilsdorf
Ebly
Traimont
Vaux les Chéne
Fauvillers
Bigonville
Wisembach
Koetschette
Martelange
Rambrouch
Perlé
Holtz
Roodt les Ell
Colpach
Lannen
U.S. forward positions, night of Dec. 15
U.S. forward positions, night of Dec. 19
U.S. unit locations, night of Dec. 19
U.S. outposts unoccupied at night
German infantry attacks, Dec. 16–19
German infantry attacks, Dec. 16–19
0
1
2
3 miles

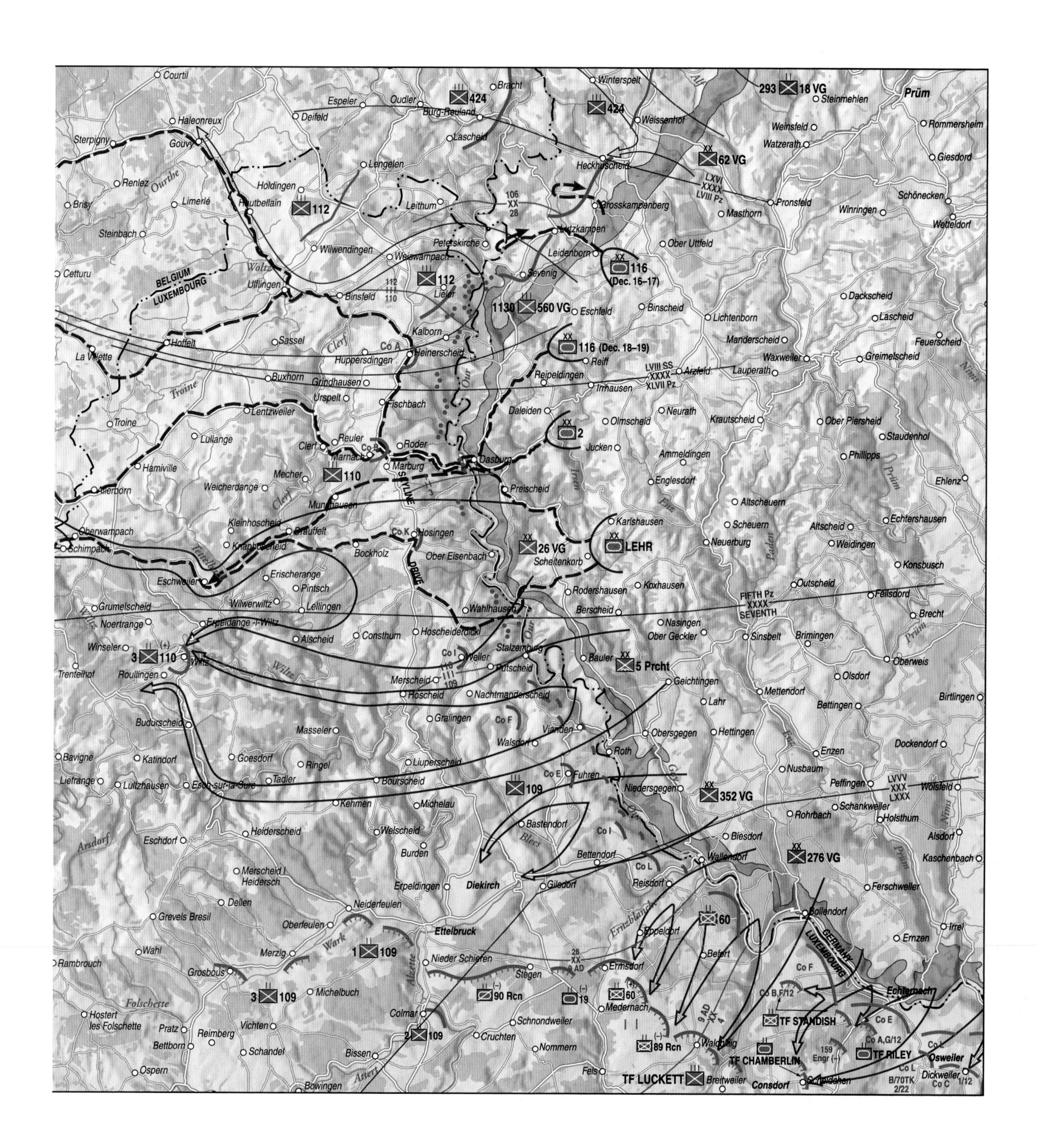

Courtil
Bracht
Winterspelt
Alf
293
18 VG
Prüm
Steinmehlen
Espeler
Oudler
424
424
Deifeld
Burg-Reuland
Weissenhof
Rommersheim
Haleonreux
Lascheid
Weinsfeld
Sterpigny
Gouvy
Watzerath
Giesdorf
Ourthe
Lengelen
Heckhuscheid
62 VG
Renlez
Holdingen
LXVI
XXXX
LVIII Pz
Brisy
Limerlé
Hautbellain
112
Leithum
106
XX
28
Grosskampenberg
Pronsfeld
Schönecken
Masthorn
Winringen
Steinbach
Lutzkampen
Wetteldorf
Peterskirche
Ober Uttfeld
Wilwendingen
Leidenborn
Weiswampach
116
(Dec. 16–17)
Cetturu
Woltz
112
Sevenig
BELGIUM
LUXEMBOURG
Ulflingen
112
110
Lieler
Binsfeld
1130
560 VG
Eschfeld
Binscheid
Dackscheid
Lichtenborn
Lascheid
Kalborn
Hoffelt
Sassel
Clerf
Co A
116 (Dec. 18–19)
Manderscheid
Feuerscheid
La Villette
Huppersdingen
Heinerscheid
Reiff
Waxweiler
Greimelscheid
Buxhorn
Grindhausen
Reipeldingen
LVIII SS
XXXX
XLVII Pz
Arzfeld
Lauperath
Nims
Troine
Urspelt
Irrhausen
Our
Lentzweiler
Fischbach
Daleiden
Neurath
Krautscheid
Ober Plersheid
Troine
Olmscheid
2
Staudenhof
Lullange
Reuler
Clerf
Co B
Roder
Jucken
Ammeldingen
Phillipps
Marnach
Hamiville
Marburg
Dasburg
110
Mecher
Englesdorf
Prüm
Ehlenz
Weicherdange
SKYLINE
Preischeid
Allerborn
Irsen
Munshausen
Enz
Altscheuern
Clerf
Kleinhoscheid
Karlshausen
Altscheid
Echtershausen
Oberwampach
Drauffelt
Co K
Hosingen
Scheuern
Knaphoscheid
LEHR
Neuerburg
Weidingen
Schimpach
Bockholz
26 VG
Ober Eisenbach
Scheitenkorb
Paden
DRIVE
Konsbusch
Erischerange
Eschweiler
Pintsch
Koxhausen
Rodershausen
Ütscheid
Wilwerwiltz
FIFTH Pz
XXXX
SEVENTH
Feilsdorf
Grumelscheid
Lellingen
Wahlhausen
Berscheid
Brecht
Noertrange
Erpeldange-l-Wiltz
Nasingen
Ober Geckler
Wiltz
Sinsbelt
Briminger
Prüm
Consthum
Hoscheiderdickt
Alscheid
Winseler
Stalzemburg
3
110
(+)
Co I
Weiler
Bauler
5 Prcht
Oberweis
Trenteihof
Roullingen
Wiltz
Putscheid
Geichtingen
Merscheid
109
Olsdorf
Hoscheid
Nachtmanderscheid
Mettendorf
Birtlingen
Lahr
Bettingen
Budurscheid
Gralingen
Masseler
Co F
Vianden
Obersgegen
Hettingen
Walsdorf
Roth
Enzen
Dockendorf
Bavigne
Katindorf
Goesdorf
Ringel
Liuperscheid
Nusbaum
Liefrange
Lultzhausen
Esch-sur-la-Sûre
Tadler
Bourscheid
Co E
Fuhren
Peffingen
LVVV
XXX
LXXX
Wolsfeld
109
Niedersgegen
352 VG
Kehmen
Michelau
Schankweiler
Rohrbach
Holsthum
Bastendorf
Heiderscheid
Welscheid
Co I
Biesdorf
Eschdorf
Alsdorf
Arsdorf
Blees
Burden
Bettendorf
Wallendorf
276 VG
Kaschenbach
Co L
Merscheid / Heiderscheid
Erpeldingen
Diekirch
Gilsdorf
Reisdorf
Ferschweiler
Dellen
Niederfeulen
Bollendorf
Grevels Bresil
60
Oberfeulen
Ettelbruck
Ernz Blanche
Eppeldorf
GERMANY
LUXEMBOURG
Irrel
Ernzen
Wark
1
109
Wahl
Merzig
Befort
Co F
Rambrouch
Nieder Schieren
28
XX
9 AD
Grosbous
Stegen
Ermsdorf
Echternach
Alzette
3
109
Michelbuch
90 Rcn
19
60
Co B,F/12
Folschette
Medernach
Hostert les Folschette
Colmar
9 AD
XX
4
TF STANDISH
Co E
Pratz
Vichten
Schnondweiler
Reimberg
Co A,G/12
2
109
Cruchten
89 Rcn
Waldbillig
159 Engr (–)
TF RILEY
Bettborn
Schandel
Nommern
TF CHAMBERLIN
Co L
Osweiler
Bissen
Ospern
Fels
Co L
Dickweiler
B/70TK
Co C
1/12
TF LUCKETT
Breitweiler
Consdorf
Scheidgen
2/22
Attert
Bowingen

American troops run for cover while under mortar fire.

13

THE ROAD TO SCHÖNBERG

THE GOLDEN LIONS—THE 106TH INFANTRY DIVISION—joined the war against the Third Reich on December 10, 1944. That day, they arrived and executed a relief in place for the 2nd Infantry Division along a forested series of hills and ridges known as the Schnee Eifel. The division, under Maj. Gen. Alan W. Jones, received little information on this quiet sector other than the fact that the Germans generally had left the 2nd Infantry Division alone.

The divisional front stretched fifteen miles through the Schnee Eifel and its southern approaches. Few roads cut through the area's hills and woods, but to the north the Losheim Gap offered an easy route into the division's rear via a paved road running southwest to Schönberg, a town directly behind two of the 106th Division's regiments. To the south, another road flanked the edge of the Schnee Eifel, running through Bleialf and on up to Schönberg. Here, General Jones had placed the left flank of his third regiment, the 424th Infantry.

To the north of the 106th Division's 422nd and 423rd Regiments, a thin screen from the 14th Cavalry Group defended the Losheim Gap. Two of its squadrons, under Lt. Col. Mark Devine, had garrisoned several of the most important towns in the gap, building roadblocks at key intersections.

On the other side of the lines, the 18th and 62nd Volksgrenadier Divisions prepared to destroy the Golden Lion division. As part of the Fifth Panzer Army, these two divisions fell under the overall command of Gen. Hasso von Manteuffel. He had ignored Hitler's order prohibiting any patrolling or pre-offensive reconnaissance. Instead, Manteuffel's divisions spent the early part of December sneaking and peeking around the American lines. In the Losheim Gap, one such patrol discovered a hole in the 14th Cavalry Group's screen that stretched some two kilometers. That American oversight would prove supremely costly.

General Hasso von Manteuffel, left, ignored Hitler's express order to cease all patrol activity in the Ardennes prior to the offensive. Disobeying the führer paid dividends, as Manteuffel's pre-offensive scouting uncovered key weaknesses in the American defenses in the Losheim Gap.

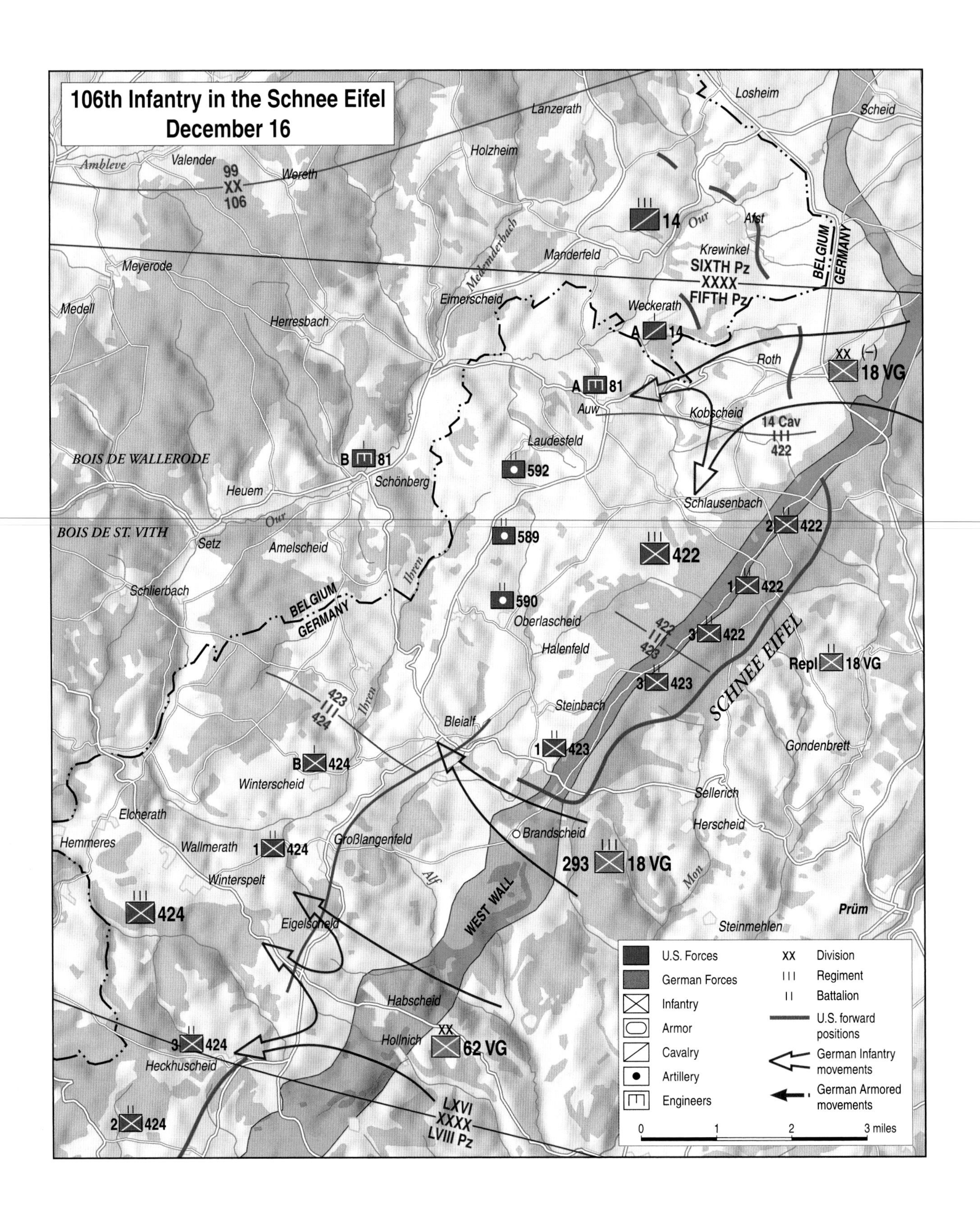
106th Infantry in the Schnee Eifel
December 16
Losheim
Lanzerath
Scheid
Holzheim
Valender
Ambleve
99
XX
106
Wereth
14
Our
Afst
Medemderbach
Manderfeld
Krewinkel
SIXTH Pz
XXXX
FIFTH Pz
BELGIUM
GERMANY
Meyerode
Eimerscheid
Weckerath
Medell
Herresbach
A 14
Roth
XX (–)
18 VG
A 81
Auw
Kobscheid
14 Cav
422
Laudesfeld
BOIS DE WALLERODE
B 81
592
Schönberg
Heuem
Schlausenbach
BOIS DE ST. VITH
Setz
Amelscheid
589
2 422
422
Ihren
Schlierbach
BELGIUM
GERMANY
590
1 422
Oberlascheid
422
423
3 422
Halenfeld
SCHNEE EIFEL
Repl 18 VG
3 423
423
424
Steinbach
Bleialf
Gondenbrett
1 423
B 424
Winterscheid
Sellerich
Elcherath
Herscheid
Brandscheid
Hemmeres
Wallmerath
1 424
Großlangenfeld
293 18 VG
Alf
Mon
Winterspelt
WEST WALL
424
Eigelscheid
Prüm
Steinmehlen
Habscheid
XX
Hollnich
62 VG
3 424
Heckhuscheid
LXVI
XXXX
LVIII Pz
2 424
U.S. Forces
German Forces
Infantry
Armor
Cavalry
Artillery
Engineers
XX Division
III Regiment
II Battalion
U.S. forward positions
German Infantry movements
German Armored movements
0
1
2
3 miles

A patrol from the 28th Cavalry Squadron tries to gain fire superiority in a small-arms ambush on the German border on September 30, 1944. The 28th fought its way across France after the breakout, usually as the tip of an American offensive drive. With light, maneuverable vehicles, they could dash ahead of the main armored units to scout the roads ahead or temporarily seize a key position. The cavalry units were not designed for static defensive operations, yet the 28th found itself in just such a situation in the Losheim Gap.

Manteuffel had no interest in hitting the 106th Infantry Division directly on the Schnee Eifel. He studied the division's dispositions and concluded the Golden Lions could be cut off with a double envelopment.

At 4:00 a.m., December 16, ahead of the main bombardment that started the Ardennes offensive elsewhere, two regiments from the 18th Volksgrenadiers Division crept through the fog and rain and passed between the 14th Cavalry Group's outposts at Roth and Weckerath. Supported by some forty Sturmgeschütz III assault guns, the volksgrenadiers got almost all the way to Auw before the Americans detected them.

German infantry advance past burning U.S. Cavalry vehicles in the Losheim Gap.

At Roth and Weckerath, the American garrisons held out until the afternoon, but they were surrounded and had no hope of relief. Both surrendered before sunset. Around Auw, an intense battle developed. Fragments of the 14th Cavalry Group stayed and fought in place, supported by the 105mm howitzers of the 592nd Field Artillery Battalion, whose gunners blazed away at attacking Sturmgeschütz IIIs

A Sturmgeschütz III sits derelict in the snow, a victim of an 82nd Airborne Division antitank team. The StuG served as the standard German armored infantry support vehicle. Cheap and easily produced, they also equipped panzer units to make up the shortfall in tanks those units were receiving.

A German soldier takes a look around the 14th Cavalry Group's living quarters at Roth, probably in search of something to loot.

The Americans at the 14th Cavalry Group's quarters were surrounded and cut off virtually before they knew they'd been attacked.

A 3-inch tank destroyer crew is in action. These guns were the best defense the 14th Cavalry Group had against German armor in the Losheim Gap. They were essentially 90mm antiaircraft guns set on a different chassis.

over open sights. It was only this point-blank direct fire that stopped the attack for the day. Nevertheless, by dark the Germans had pushed around the 106th Division's left flank and now threatened to get into its rear area.

To the south, the 18th Volksgrenadiers deployed a single regiment, supported by a self-propelled artillery battalion, to assault northwest toward Schönberg. Here, the Germans ran into heavy opposition at Bleialf. Just to the south, the 62nd Volksgrenadiers slammed into the 424th Infantry. The regiment, despite its inexperience, held fast and inflicted heavy losses on the grenadiers. By nightfall, though, the Germans had captured Bleialf and driven a wedge between the 424th Infantry and the rest of the 106th Division on the Schnee Eifel.

A 105mm-armed Wespe sits in ruins after suffering payback in France. German self-propelled artillery units were among the most dangerous the Wehrmacht fielded. Tough, dedicated crews manned these weapons with consummate skill. They could be used as direct-fire weapons against Allied infantry or static positions and could take on Allied armor as well.

A GI from the 106th Infantry Division's 424th Regiment overwatches a snow-covered field. After the destruction of the 106th's other two regiments, the 424th fought on until the end of the battle. Few images exist of the 106th fighting on the Schnee Eiffel. This photo was taken in January, after the 424th was issued proper winter clothing.

A 76mm gun-armed M4 Sherman from the 9th Armored Division rolls forward to meet the German attack.

Major Gen. Troy Middleton, the steadfast commander of VII Corps, on the road during the Bulge. A native of Baton Rouge, Louisiana, at age twenty-nine he became the youngest colonel in the U.S. Army in France during World War I. He received the Distinguished Service Medal for his actions in the Meuse-Argonne Offensive. After the war, Middleton served as president of Louisiana State University.

The Golden Lions were in a jam. If the Germans could press on and take Schönberg on December 17, the 422nd and 423rd Regiments would be trapped on the Schnee Eifel. Given the weight of the attack in the Losheim Gap, it was clear that the 14th Cavalry Group could not hold. Reinforcements were needed or a disaster would unfold.

That evening, General Middleton's VIII Corps headquarters gave General Jones Combat Command B, 9th Armored Division. General Omar Bradley also released the 7th Armored Division. Jones put together a plan to use Combat Command B of the 9th Armored to buttress his southern flank and then use the 7th Armored when it arrived to counterattack in the Losheim Gap.

On the morning of the 17th, the 9th Armored Division's tanks rumbled east, intending to set up a defensive line at Winterspelt. But as they approached the town, they discovered the

Exhausted survivors of the 106th Infantry Division. The unit had arrived in the Ardennes sector on December 10. Fresh from the United States, it had seen almost no combat prior to the German offensive. About two-thirds of the division was lost on the Schnee Eiffel.

Germans had beat them to it. Instead of trying to fill the gap between the 424th and 423rd Infantry Regiments on Schnee Eifel, Combat Command B found itself having to defend the west bank of the Our River and the approaches to the key road and rail intersections at Saint-Vith. The 424th, which had pulled back across the Our during the night of the 16th–17th, covered the tankers' right flank.

At Bleialf, the German 293rd Volksgrenadier Regiment launched a dawn assault on the town and its defenders. By 5:30 a.m., the Germans held the town, and the 293rd was double-timing up the road to Schönberg.

Simultaneously, the north flank gave way as well. In the Losheim Gap, the 14th Cavalry Group gave way completely. Part of it ended up at Wallerode, while the 18th Cavalry

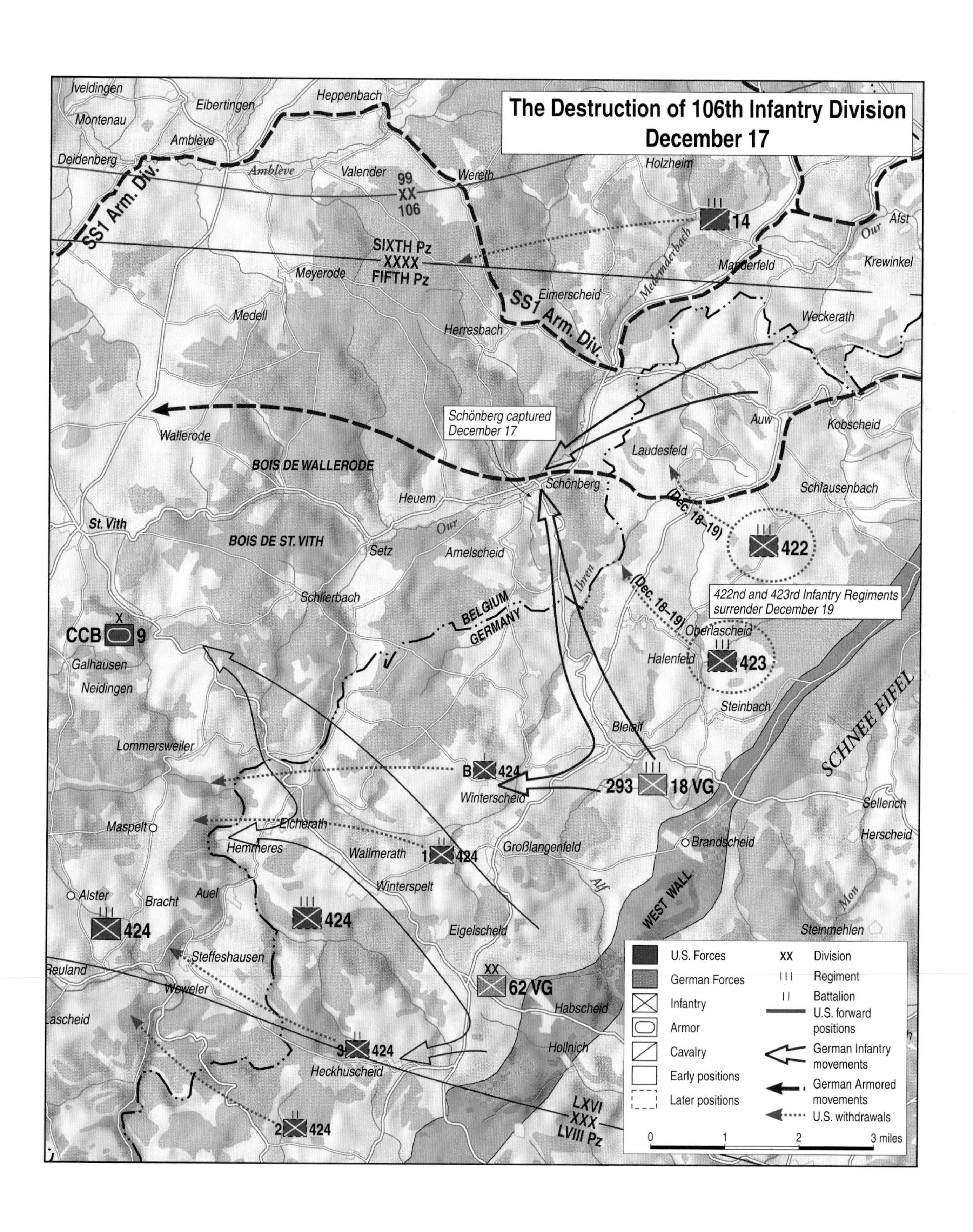
The Destruction of 106th Infantry Division
December 17
Iveldingen
Eibertingen
Heppenbach
Montenau
Amblève
Deidenberg
Amblève
Valender
99
XX
106
Wereth
Holzheim
SS1 Arm. Div.
SIXTH Pz
XXXX
FIFTH Pz
Meyerode
14
Afst
Our
Krewinkel
Manderfeld
Medell
Eimerscheid
SS1 Arm. Div.
Herresbach
Weckerath
Schönberg captured
December 17
Auw
Kobscheid
Wallerode
Laudesfeld
BOIS DE WALLERODE
Schönberg
Schlausenbach
Heuem
(Dec. 18–19)
St. Vith
Our
BOIS DE ST. VITH
422
Setz
Amelscheid
(Dec. 18–19)
422nd and 423rd Infantry Regiments
surrender December 19
Schlierbach
BELGIUM
GERMANY
CCB
9
Oberlascheid
Halenfeld
423
Galhausen
Neidingen
Steinbach
SCHNEE EIFEL
Bleialf
Lommersweiler
B
424
293
18 VG
Winterscheid
Sellerich
Maspelt
Eicherath
Hemmeres
Wallmerath
1
424
Großlangenfeld
Brandscheid
Herscheid
Winterspelt
Alf
WEST WALL
Mon
Alster
Bracht
Auel
424
424
Eigelscheid
Steinmehlen
Steffeshausen
Reuland
XX
62 VG
Weweler
Habscheid
Lascheid
3
424
Hollnich
Heckhuscheid
2
424
LXVI
XXX
LVIII Pz
U.S. Forces
German Forces
Infantry
Armor
Cavalry
Early positions
Later positions
XX Division
III Regiment
II Battalion
U.S. forward positions
German Infantry movements
German Armored movements
U.S. withdrawals
0
1
2
3 miles

A desperate attack to break out of their trap was the last option for the 422nd and 423rd Infantry Regiments. Elements of the 423rd actually made it to the outskirts of Schönberg, but they were chopped to pieces by German antiaircraft vehicles.

Reconnaissance Squadron limped northwest to Born, where it encountered elements of the 1st SS Panzer Division.

Aside from a few retreating American artillery units, there was nothing to stop the 18th Volksgrenadiers from taking Schönberg. By 9:00 a.m. on December 17, the two pincers met and cut off almost ten thousand American troops on the Schnee Eifel.

Refusing to panic, General Jones ordered the 422nd and 423rd to sit tight and establish all-round defensive perimeters while he worked to get them resupplied by air. He figured that the 7th Armored Division would arrive in the morning and could restore the situation.

But the resupply drops somehow got lost up the chain of command. A few C-47s were sent out from England and staged at airfields in Belgium, but they were never actually ordered to deliver their precious cargoes of food and ammunition.

Worse, as the day wore on, the 7th Armored Division's progress to Saint-Vith slowed to a crawl as its lead elements became ensnarled with traffic fleeing the area. By early afternoon, it was clear that the tankers wouldn't be ready to counterattack on the morning of the 18th as planned.

At 2:45 p.m., General Jones reversed himself and ordered the 422nd and 423rd to pull back to the Our River. With radio communication tenuous at best, the order didn't reach the regiments until after midnight—well after any chance of them getting out of the pocket had vanished.

The next morning, the two regiments moved out in battalion columns, pushing west. Jones amplified his orders at 7:30 a.m. His men were to break out by avoiding the concentration of German troops and armor around Schönberg. Not long after receipt of that message, the

2nd Battalion, 423rd Infantry, ran into German infantry on the Bleialf-Schönberg road. As the regiment deployed for a concentrated attack, Jones reversed himself again. This time, he ordered both regiments to redirect and attack Schönberg itself. The order was the death knell for almost two-thirds of the 106th Infantry Division.

All day long, the 423rd battered against the volksgrenadiers barring their path. Little progress was made. Finally, as dusk fell on December 18, the regiment formed a perimeter and settled in for the night. To its right, the 422nd had not encountered any serious German resistance during the day. Led by the I&R Platoon, the 422nd stopped for the night in some woods that the regimental staff thought were only about a mile from Schönberg. Truth was, the regiment had gotten lost and was actually more than three miles from its objective.

The 106th Infantry Division didn't have the time or experience to set up a robust radio network. When the land lines failed, communication became very difficult between General Jones and his isolated regiments. German jamming of American frequencies made the situation even more difficult.

General Alan Jones staked the fate of his two regiments in the Schnee Eifel on the ability to resupply them from the air, but the air drops never took place. The 422nd and 423rd soon ran out of ammunition, medical supplies, and food. Exactly why the C-47s never got the green light to carry out the resupply mission remains a mystery.

Exact numbers will never be known, but between seven thousand and ten thousand men from the 106th Infantry Division fell into German hands. (A wartime censor has scribbled out the faces of these American POWs.)

The wounded with the 423rd Infantry Regiment suffered enormously. Cut off from the normal medical pipeline, medics worked with almost no supplies to stabilize and save who they could.

On the morning of December 19, the 423rd began to assemble for the final assault on Schönberg. This would be the regiment's last chance. Out of mortar rounds, low on rifle and machine gun ammo, the 423rd's situation had grown desperate.

Just as the regimental staff was meeting with its battalion commanders, the German LVI Corps launched a massive artillery barrage that swept across the area. The exposed GIs suffered tremendous losses, and one of the battalion commanders died as well.

As the shells continued to fall, a German infantry assault struck the 423rd's rear. The German volksgrenadiers encountered the 590th Field Artillery Battalion, which formed the regiment's rear. The 590th had endured a severe barrage while hunkered down in a small valley. Before they could recover, Germans appeared on the high ground behind them and shot the battalion up with accurate small-arms fire. The 590th had no choice but surrender.

With infantry in their rear and artillery falling in their midst, the men of the 423rd had only one option: drive on for Schönberg. Its battered battalions assaulted forward and ran headlong into heavy resistance. Only two companies managed to reach the outskirts of Schönberg, but they were torn to pieces by German antiaircraft vehicles firing quad 20mm cannons at point-blank range.

By mid-afternoon, it was all over. The regiment's survivors could count only a dozen or fewer bullets left for their rifles. The wounded screamed without succor. No food and little water remained. The regiment surrendered at 4:30 p.m.

Weary soldiers enjoy—as much as possible—a hard-earned cigarette break.

As the 422nd Infantry Regiment tried to break out, the Führer Begleit Brigade rolled into the battle and slammed into the regiment's flank.

The 106th Infantry Division was later rebuilt and sent to the French coast after the Bulge. There, they took the surrender of the German garrison at Saint-Nazaire on April 9, 1945.

The 422nd suffered a similar fate. When it struck out for Schönberg in the morning, its forward elements ran into an ambush along the main road leading from the Losheim Gap to their objective. Laced by accurate machine gun fire, the GIs went to ground. Moments later, the Führer Begleit Brigade and its tanks thundered down the road, heading to Saint-Vith. The panzers cut off part of the regiment. Surrounded and under heavy fire, that portion surrendered first. The rest of the regiment surrendered later that afternoon, though several groups did try to escape and evade and make it back to friendly lines. One group of four hundred managed to avoid the Germans for two days before getting caught and surrendering on the 21st. Altogether, only about 150 men from the 422nd Infantry reached safety.

Between seven and nine thousand American GIs had been lost. It was the worst disaster suffered by the United States Army since the fall of the Philippines. Among those captured by the Germans were future literary great Kurt Vonnegut, whose writing was later deeply influenced by his experience as a prisoner of war. Buffalo Bill's grandson, who was an officer in the 106th Infantry Division, also became a captive of the Third Reich.

The 7th Armored Division rolled into the Saint-Vith area just in time to help blunt the first German drives on the vital crossroad town.

14

INCIDENT AT POTEAU

WHILE THE GIS OF THE 422ND AND 423RD INFANTRY REGIMENTS fought for their lives on the Schnee Eifel, another crisis brewed far to their rear. For the Germans to reach the Meuse River, it was absolutely essential that they take two key road centers in the Ardennes: Saint-Vith and Bastogne. Right behind the Schnee Eifel lay Saint-Vith. With good, paved roads, Saint-Vith offered the Germans relief from their traffic snarls, which by December 17 had approached the levels of Los Angeles at rush hour. Not only would the capture of Saint-Vith give the Germans a springboard from which to assault west, cross the Salm at Vielsalm, then drive to the Meuse; it also gave them access to north-south-running roads that tied into the network already captured in the Losheim Gap.

And on December 17, not much stood between the Germans and this prize besides the headquarters element for the 106th Infantry Division and a few hundred men from the 81st and 168th Engineer Combat Battalions. The 168th set up a defensive line about a mile east of Saint-Vith on a hilly area known as Pruemberg. There, they dug in along the road that led east to Schönberg.

American troops dig in along the edge of a woodline and cover down on a wide, snow-covered field. Veteran U.S. troops learned it was better to emplace along a tree line instead of inside it, as the Germans usually pounded the woods with artillery.

Traffic snarls bedeviled the 18th Volksgrenadier Division all day on the 17th. As they encircled the 422nd and 423rd Infantry Regiments, elements of the division moved west as fast as they could. In their rear, however, chaos reigned. Already, bad roads were churned to swamps of icy mud by heavy vehicles and tanks. There were more units than roads to handle them, and the German military police trying to unsnarl the situation found themselves too few in number and too spread out. The traffic jams simply overwhelmed them. As a result, armor couldn't get to the front lines, and the Germans could not carry out a mad dash to seize Saint-Vith through a coup de main. Units sat and idled away what little fuel their vehicles possessed. Artillery battalions could not join the fray, as they too were stuck in a sea of armored vehicles well behind the lines.

And so, the defenders of Saint-Vith earned a short respite. And the time the Germans gave them proved vital in the end.

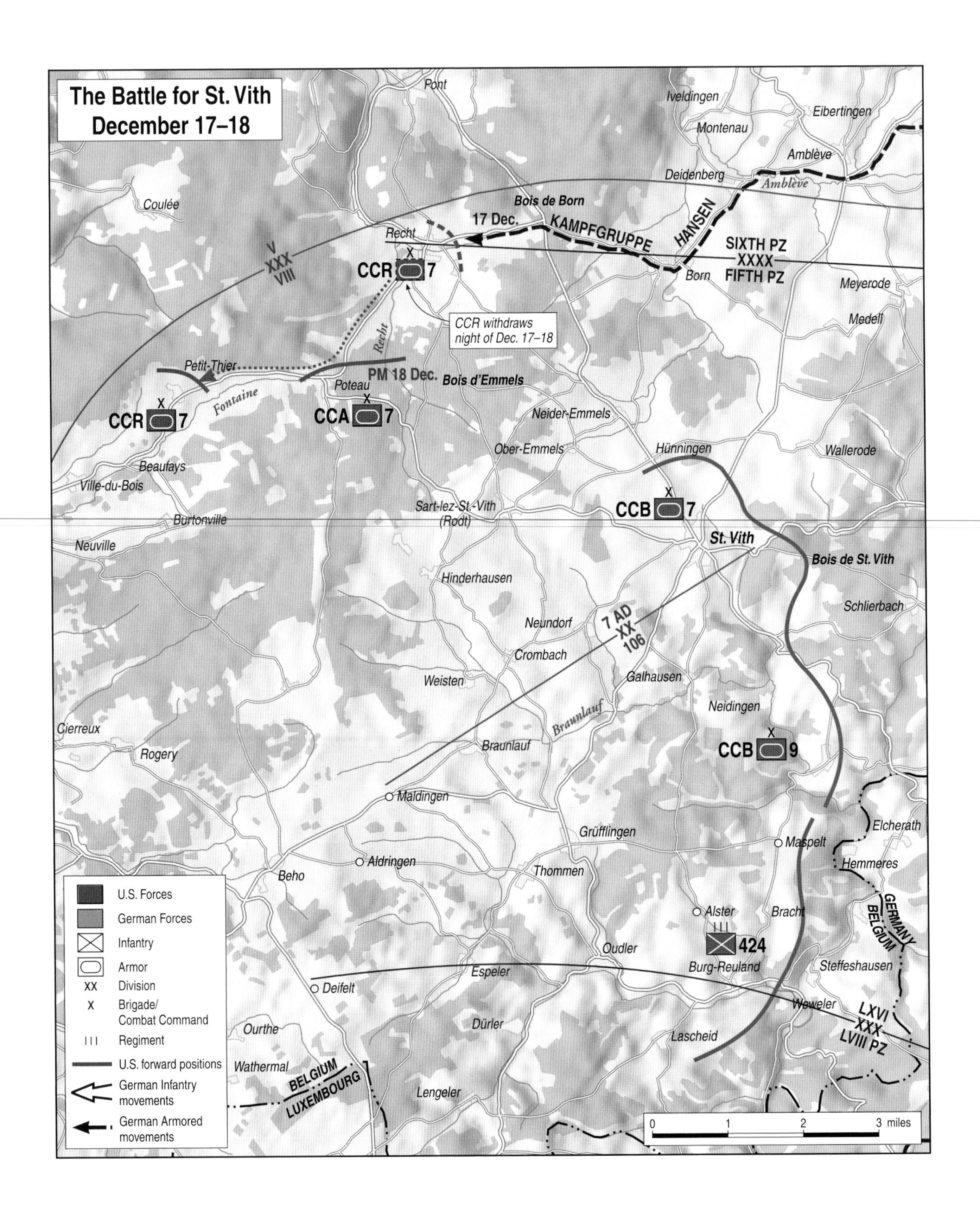
The Battle for St. Vith
December 17–18
U.S. Forces
German Forces
Infantry
Armor
XX Division
X Brigade/
Combat Command
III Regiment
U.S. forward positions
German Infantry movements
German Armored movements
0 1 2 3 miles
CCR 7
CCA 7
CCB 7
CCB 9
424
CCR withdraws night of Dec. 17–18
17 Dec.
PM 18 Dec.
KAMPFGRUPPE HANSEN
SIXTH PZ
XXXX
FIFTH PZ
V
XXX
VIII
7 AD
XX
106
LXVI
XXX
LVIII PZ
BELGIUM
LUXEMBOURG
GERMANY
BELGIUM
Bois de Born
Bois d'Emmels
Bois de St. Vith
St. Vith
Pont
Iveldingen
Eibertingen
Montenau
Amblève
Deidenberg
Coulée
Recht
Born
Meyerode
Medell
Petit-Thier
Poteau
Neider-Emmels
Ober-Emmels
Hünningen
Wallerode
Beaufays
Ville-du-Bois
Burtonville
Neuville
Sart-lez-St.-Vith
(Rodt)
Hinderhausen
Schlierbach
Neundorf
Crombach
Weisten
Galhausen
Neidingen
Cierreux
Rogery
Braunlauf
Maldingen
Grüfflingen
Maspelt
Elcherath
Hemmeres
Aldringen
Beho
Thommen
Alster
Bracht
Oudler
Burg-Reuland
Steffeshausen
Espeler
Deifelt
Weweler
Dürler
Ourthe
Lascheid
Wathermal
Lengeler

Behind the lead elements of the 18th Volksgrenadier Division, massive traffic jams wrought havoc on the German timetable. Units couldn't move forward, artillery couldn't redeploy to support the spearheads, and supplies couldn't get forward through the traffic jams. The situation was so bad that it caused the attack on Saint-Vith to be delayed by several vital days.

A muddy still from a German propaganda film shows the traffic situation east of Saint-Vith. General von Manteuffel and Field Marshal Model were beyond themselves with anger and frustration over the situation.

Lt. Jean Klein and Lt. Claude Jones examine some material pulled from a destroyed German staff car. While rolling for Saint-Vith on December 16, a column of 7th Armored Division artillery and tanks stumbled onto a German convoy. They shot it up and forced the few German survivors to flee. The photo was taken by Corporal Bell from the 167th Signal Company.

Oregonian Cpl. Harold Newhouse and Pennsylvania native Cpl. Ray Ganopsky clean an M2 .50-caliber machine gun atop their camouflaged armored vehicle during a lull in the fighting. The men belonged to the 40th Tank Battalion, attached to Combat Command R, 7th Armored Division.

Men of the 7th Armored Division outside Saint-Vith. Most of the surviving photos (including this one) of that division from the Bulge were taken during the counterattack around Saint-Vith in mid-January. In December, the armored infantry had yet to receive the winter clothing they wear in this photograph.

The track commander of the 7th Armored watches as a Lockheed P-38 Lightning makes a close-air-support run on German targets near Saint-Vith. His M5 Stuart light tank is covered with tree branches to break up its silhouette.

The 7th Armored Division began to reach Saint-Vith on the 17th. Their journey to the center of the fighting in the Ardennes was not an easy one. They encountered traffic jams of their own as fleeing American units and Belgian refugees frequently clogged their line of march. Worse, one of the division's assigned north-south roads went right through a sector taken by Kampfgruppe Peiper. When the 7th Armored Division's operations officer, Col. Church Matthews, tried to run this gauntlet, SS troopers appeared and shot up his Jeep. As he fled, the Germans cut him down, leaving the division without one of its most important officers.

Still, by afternoon, Combat Command R and Combat Command B from the 7th Armored Division reached the Saint-Vith area. Both were sent northwest to stem the German advance around the city. Elements of the 1st SS Panzer Division had pushed along a road through the Losheim Gap and now threatened to cut across Saint-Vith's rear. Elements of both combat commands met the Waffen-SS at a small town called Recht. That evening, Maj. Karl Rettlinger, commander of Kampfgruppe Hansen's jagdpanzer battalion, assaulted into

Recht. Rettlinger, who held the Knight's Cross and had been wounded five times on the Eastern Front, was a tank ace with thirty vehicles to his credit. He and his fellow panzer crews made short work of the less experienced American tankers. In a forty-five-minute fight, they forced Combat Command R and Combat Command B to pull back out of town.

While the 7th Armored Division fought its first pitched battle with the 1st SS Panzer Division, the remains of Colonel Devine's 14th Cavalry Group pulled back to various towns north and northwest of Saint-Vith. All day long, small columns of M8 Greyhounds, Jeeps, and M5 Stuarts darted through, between, around, and in some cases behind the German spearheads. Parts of the 32nd Cavalry Reconnaissance Squadron reached Wallerode, while the squadron's survivors limped into Born, northwest of Saint-Vith.

That night, Colonel Devine, who had moved his headquarters to Poteau, set out to reach Saint-Vith and report personally to General Jones. The situation was so fluid that in the darkness, Devine's small column ran headlong into a German panzer force. He and his men stood no chance, and the panzers made short work of the American cavalry troopers. Only Devine himself and two other officers escaped the ambush. They managed to reach Saint-Vith on foot, where after reporting what happened, General Jones refused to believe that they'd been hit by German armor so far in his rear. He summarily relieved Colonel Devine, who was evacuated from theater through medical channels.

Kampfgruppe Hansen arrives outside of Recht.

A company commander from the 1st SS Panzer Division checks his map at a road junction not far from Malmedy.

At 2:00 a.m. on December 18, Kampfgruppe Hansen, 1st SS Panzer Division, assaulted out of Recht and pushed the 7th Armored back toward Poteau. As the battle unfolded in the darkness, it engulfed elements of the 14th Cavalry Group still in the area. Shortly before dawn, Kampfgruppe Hansen caught a column of jeeps, armored cars, and antitank guns belonging to the 14th Cavalry Group right outside of Poteau. The cavalry troopers stood no chance against the heavily armed panzers they faced, and the Germans demolished the entire column and set its few survivors to flight.

Shortly after sunrise, a German combat cameraman arrived on the scene and photographed the aftermath of this engagement. The 3rd Armored Division later captured this anonymous photographer's film, along with three other rolls shot on the 16th and 17th elsewhere in the Ardennes. These photographs became some of the most iconic images from the Battle of the Bulge, and remain virtually the only ones available to historians that depict the German side of the battle.

continued on page 193

German troops move through the wreckage of the 14th Cavalry Group's column outside Poteau.

A Waffen-SS trooper loots a 14th Cavalry Group M8 armored car caught in the ambush at Poteau.

The remains of the column caught on the road to Poteau.

SS panzer troops enjoy American cigarettes found among the ruins of the 14th Cavalry Group's vehicles.

M8 armored cars stood no chance against SS panzers. The vehicles belonged to the 18th Cavalry Squadron.

A German cameraman films a staged assault by a trio of SS panzer grenadiers alongside the smoking wrecks of the 14th Cavalry Group's column.

A Waffen-SS trooper carries his rifle at his hip and moves past the carnage his unit inflicted on the 14th Cavalry Group column.

A German combat correspondent's camera fell into the hands of the 3rd Armored Division. There were a few unexposed frames left on the last roll, so the Americans snapped some pictures of their M4 Shermans before sending the film up the chain of command.

This page: SS troopers march past abandoned vehicles along the American column.

An M4 camouflaged with branches engages the Germans in a Belgian village. The 7th Armored Division showed up just in time to make a stand outside of Saint-Vith.

continued from page 189

Poteau had to be held at all costs. The main east-west road to Saint-Vith ran from Vielsalm through Poteau. If Kampfgruppe Hansen captured the town, the American main supply route to Saint-Vith would be cut.

Combat Command R dug in its heels. After getting its nose bloodied at Recht, the unit fought with exceptional resolve and slowed Kampfgruppe Hansen's advance long enough for the 7th Armored Division's commander, Brig. Gen. Robert W. Hasbrouck, to send help. Knowing that Saint-Vith's future hung in the balance, Hasbrouck threw all of Combat Command A into the fight. The fresh troops and tanks made the difference, and the 1st SS Panzer Division suffered another setback. Poteau held.

At this key moment, the Germans made another mistake. Kampfgruppe Hansen was ordered back north. Had the Germans reinforced Hansen and made a serious effort for Poteau, they could have taken the town and then advanced west to Vielsalm and its bridges over the Salm. Not only would that have given them the gateway to the Meuse River, it would have trapped the rest of the 106th Infantry Division and the 7th Armored Division in a pocket around Saint-Vith. Instead, Kampfgruppe Hansen ended up getting entangled in the fighting around Stavelot for much of the next few days. Another opportunity slipped away.

A platoon of M10 tank destroyers is seen outside Saint-Vith from a passing U.S. liaison plane.

15

THE LUCKY SEVENTH

WHILE THE BATTLE FOR POTEAU RAGED, the defense of Saint-Vith came together as the 424th Infantry Regiment and elements of the 9th Armored Division took up positions south of the city. The American line now formed a fifteen mile L, with the 424th and 9th Armored on the base, and Combat Command A, 7th Armored Division, at Poteau at its tip. In between were other elements of the "Lucky Seventh" and the engineers dug in at Pruemberg under Lt. Col. Thomas Riggs.

On December 18, one regiment from the 18th Volksgrenadier Division tested the engineers' defenses. The grenadiers attacked without artillery support—their guns were stuck in traffic back around Schönberg—and the engineers drove them off three times. After that, the front directly east of Saint-Vith fell quiet for three critical days.

For Field Marshal Model and General Manteuffel, the holdup outside of Saint-Vith drove them to distraction. Both of them descended on the 18th Volksgrenadier Division's headquarters and demanded that the unit get back into the fight. But words alone would not unsort the traffic jams holding up the advance, which were now made worse as the Sixth Panzer Army drifted into Manteuffel's battle space and clogged up the roads even more with its armored vehicles.

Finally, late on December 20, the 18th Volksgrenadier Division managed to get all three of its regiments back on line. To the southeast, the 62nd Volksgrenadier Division, though badly chewed up, prepared to attack the 424th Infantry Regiment and 9th Armored Division again. To support the infantry units, Manteuffel brought up the Führer Begleit Brigade, whose Tiger Is inspired much dread whenever they appeared. Elements of the II SS Panzer Corps also joined the fight to the north and northwest of Saint-Vith.

The Germans attacked all along the American lines the next morning. To the far south, the 424th Infantry and the 9th Armored fought furiously around Neubrück. The volksgrenadiers attacked in relentless waves, ignoring casualties. Sheer momentum pushed them forward, and

Von Manteuffel (left) and Model (saluting) were both gravely concerned by the delay at Saint-Vith. To get to the Meuse River, the Germans had to take the crossroads town, and as long as it remained in American hands, the traffic situation in the Losheim Gap and the Schnee Eiffel area would remain a major obstacle to pushing the offensive forward.

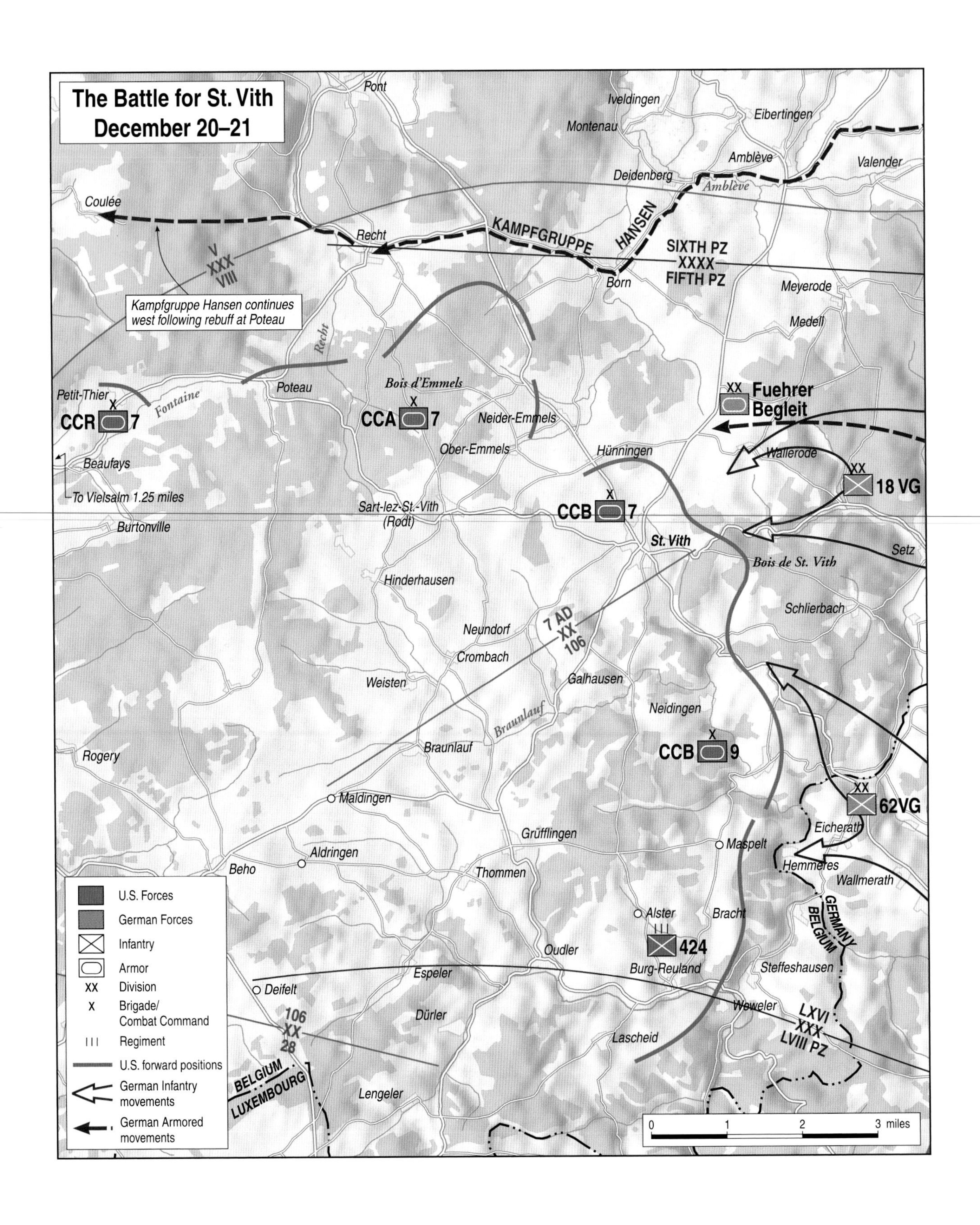
The Battle for St. Vith
December 20–21
Pont
Iveldingen
Montenau
Eibertingen
Amblève
Valender
Deidenberg
Amblève
Coulée
Recht
KAMPFGRUPPE
HANSEN
SIXTH PZ
XXXX
FIFTH PZ
Born
Meyerode
Medell
V
XXX
VIII
Kampfgruppe Hansen continues west following rebuff at Poteau
Recht
Petit-Thier
Fontaine
Poteau
Bois d'Emmels
Fuehrer Begleit
CCR 7
CCA 7
Neider-Emmels
Ober-Emmels
Hünningen
Wallerode
18 VG
Beaufays
To Vielsalm 1.25 miles
Sart-lez-St.-Vith (Rodt)
CCB 7
Burtonville
St. Vith
Bois de St. Vith
Setz
Hinderhausen
Schlierbach
7 AD
XX
106
Neundorf
Crombach
Weisten
Galhausen
Neidingen
Braunlauf
Braunlauf
CCB 9
Rogery
Maldingen
62VG
Eicherath
Grüfflingen
Maspelt
Aldringen
Hemmeres
Beho
Thommen
Wallmerath
Alster
Bracht
GERMANY
BELGIUM
424
Oudler
Burg-Reuland
Steffeshausen
Espeler
Deifelt
Weweler
LXVI
XXX
LVIII PZ
106
XX
28
Dürler
Lascheid
BELGIUM
LUXEMBOURG
Lengeler
U.S. Forces
German Forces
Infantry
Armor
Division
Brigade/ Combat Command
Regiment
U.S. forward positions
German Infantry movements
German Armored movements
0 1 2 3 miles

American troops examine a Tiger I captured in Tunisia at the end of the North African Campaign, one of the first to fall into Allied hands. The Führer Begleit Brigade included a heavy panzer unit composed of these dreaded tanks. For two years, the Allies had faced Tigers in North Africa, Sicily, and Italy. In every instance they were employed, the fear of the Tigers played a significant role in the outcome of the battle.

gradually the 424th gave ground. The 27th Armored Infantry Battalion held off the Germans as long as it could, but its men were overwhelmed later that day. A company of grenadiers broke through the 27th's lines and surged into Neubrück, where they surrounded the battalion command post, which was located in a thick-walled hotel. The 27th's commanding officer, Lt. Col. Fred Cummings, joined his staff at the upstairs windows and blazed away at the Germans dashing around in the streets below. Some twenty grenadiers died as they assaulted the hotel. Finally, the Germans secured a foothold in the basement. The fighting raged in rooms and hallways. Finally, out of ammunition, Cummings and a few survivors surrendered. But one of his officers escaped and managed to find help. He led an armored counterattack that momentarily pushed back into town and liberated the battalion commander and the remains of his staff.

Still, the pressure was too great. The 62nd Volksgrenadier Division drove on for Saint-Vith, the exhausted men of the 424th Infantry and 9th Armored fighting gallantly as they fell back.

Meanwhile, right at the junction of the American L stood a small, scratch force pulled together around the Lucky Seventh's 38th Armored Infantry Battalion. Under command of Lt. Col.

The U.S. Army conducted a series of tests against captured Tigers and Panthers to see which of its antitank weapons would be effective against these German panzers. Part of the test is reproduced here and shows the effectiveness of the British 6 pounder (U.S.-designated 57mm) antitank gun against these two vehicles.

A Tiger destroyed by American P-47s. The Allies discovered that the best way to knock out a Tiger was with a fighter-bomber.

The M1917 Browning medium machine gun ranked as one of the most effective infantry weapons used by the U.S. Army during the war.

An antitank gun crew loads their weapon at Vielsalm, just in case the Germans broke through behind Saint-Vith and tried to cross the Salm River at this location.

William H. G. Fuller, the 38th stiffened a line that included the engineers, part of the 87th Cavalry Reconnaissance Squadron, and a company from the 23rd Armored Infantry. Together, they formed a polyglot blocking position composed of about 1,100 men that stretched from the main road to Schönberg up across a northeast-running road to Roth in the Losheim Gap. It was here that the 18th Volkgrenadier Division's main effort converged on the American lines.

When Fuller arrived, he took over command of all troops in the sector while Lt. Col. Thomas Riggs became his XO. This didn't sit well with Riggs, who had masterfully handled the defense of the Pruemberg line on the 18th. Fuller was an unknown to his engineers. To counter any armored thrusts, Fuller's defense included a platoon of M36 Jackson tank destroyers and a company of M4 Shermans.

At 2:00 p.m., December 21, the Germans unleashed a massive artillery and rocket barrage onto Fuller's battle group. The dug-in defenders weathered the bombardment and then drove off a probing attack from the 295th Volksgrenadier Regiment west of Wallerode. That triggered another round of artillery strikes, which were directed by forward observers with telling accuracy. All day long, shells and rockets pummeled the 38th Armored Infantry Battalion and the engineers. The men could only hunker down in their foxholes while medics braved hurricanes of shrapnel to save wounded GIs.

Near Wallerode, a platoon from the 23rd Armored Infantry Battalion traverses open ground. The cameraman, Technician 5th Class Hugh F. McHugh, was killed only moments after taking this photograph.

The next infantry assault struck the 38th along either side of the Schönberg road sometime after 4:00 p.m. Mounted by the 294th Volksgrenadier Regiment, the initial assault waves poured through a thick, wooded area and surprised a platoon of Shermans. Under intense fire, all but one of the M4 tank commanders died in their turrets. The platoon fell back. The grenadiers charged forward as elements of the 293rd Volksgrenadier Regiment joined the fight.

The Americans stopped the attack cold. Some of the German assault companies got lost in the woods, and the confusion that this caused killed both regiments' momentum. The Germans fell back and called up panzers and assault guns for the next effort.

Meanwhile, another massive artillery barrage pounded the Pruemberg line. Then the 295th Regiment tried again. Its grenadiers charged out of Wallerode and across open ground. There, a platoon of Shermans struck them hard from their right flank while A Company, 38th Armored Infantry Battalion, called in 105mm howitzer fire. The combined shock of tank and artillery shells lacing their ranks broke the 295th, and the regiment reeled backwards to the safety of Wallerode again.

And still, nebelwerfers and heavy artillery pounded the American lines. For hours the shells fell, ripping apart trees, cutting communication lines, and killing the American defenders in their shallow foxholes. By nightfall, the 87th Cavalry Reconnaissance Squadron and the 81st Engineer Combat Battalion had fewer than eighty men left. They sat astride the 294th Volksgrenadiers' main axis of advance, and were sure to get hit again.

7th Armored Division Sherman tanks, loaded with armored infantry, head for the fighting around Saint-Vith.

A patrol from the 7th Armored Division outside of Wallerode.

A German nebelwerfer launcher on a tracked platform. Dubbed "Screaming Meemies" by the GIs, these multiple rocket launchers were deadly effective indirect-fire weapons.

A wrecked Tiger I from the Führer Begleit Brigade, seen in the aftermath of the battle.

An ambulance negotiates through the ruins of Saint-Vith. Colonel Hurley Fuller was evacuated via ambulance from the town after he told General Clarke he couldn't continue in command east of town.

Colonel Fuller had enough. With his line ravaged by steel and high explosive, his men isolated into little knots of stalwart defenders, usually centered around a machine gun or bazooka team, Fuller sought out Lieutenant Colonel Riggs and put him in command of the Pruemberg sector. Fuller, explaining he was going back to Saint-Vith to "seek out alternative positions," drove to Brigadier General Bruce C. Clarke's headquarters and told his superior officer he couldn't handle his responsibilities anymore. Clarke shipped him out that night as a medical casualty.

At their crucial hour, Fuller's men had been abandoned by their leader. Thomas Riggs rose to the challenge. Moving everywhere along the battle-scarred line, he coaxed and encouraged the men as they steeled themselves for another assault.

They didn't have long to wait. Two hours after Fuller decamped, the Germans threw everything they had in one final, furious assault. The last Shermans in the area faced off in the darkness against a platoon of Tiger Is. Flares blinded the American gunners, and the Tigers slaughtered the M4s. Then came the volksgrenadiers, moving swiftly in the darkness. American machine guns chattered. Bazooka teams with raw nerve and courage waited to get flanking shots on Tigers and passing half-tracks. The German grenadiers focused on the American heavy weapons. But every time a bazooka team got wiped out, volunteers risked their lives to retrieve their weapons and train them on succeeding waves of German armor.

The machine gun crews didn't last long. Riggs later estimated that most did not survive more than fifteen minutes before tank and automatic weapons fire wiped them out. Still, there were no shortage of GIs and engineers willing to get those guns back in the fight. They knew their survival depended on these machine guns and their killing power.

On the far right, the 183rd Volksgrenadier Regiment struck the seam between the 7th and 9th Armored Divisions' lines. By 9:30 p.m., the men in the Pruemberg area had been flanked, and now German armor was spilling into Saint-Vith itself.

East of Saint-Vith, the American machine gun crews did not last long. The veteran German infantry made them their highest priority. Lieutenant Colonel Riggs later estimated that few machine gun teams lasted more than fifteen minutes during the battle, but there were always volunteers ready to get the guns back in action.

A Panther takes a direct hit from a bazooka that blew its track off. Usually, the best a bazooka team could hope for was a disabling shot like this one that would immobilize the German panzer.

7th Armored Division M4 Sherman tanks in the snow outside of Saint-Vith.

An American officer inspects the ruins of Saint-Vith in January after the town was recaptured by the 7th Armored Division. All but a handful of buildings had been destroyed, causing intense suffering to the local civilian population.

Still, Riggs and his men held out. Supported by the 814th Tank Battalion's M36 Jacksons, Bravo Company, 23rd Armored Infantry, repulsed every attack for over four hours. Between assault waves, the Germans pounded them with artillery and mortar fire. The men reached the edge of human endurance, but still they fought on.

At 10:00 p.m., the Germans broke through and overran the 38th's battalion command post. Riggs, moving about in the night, evaded the Germans and forty-five minutes later received a radio order telling him to take his command and attack west into Saint-Vith.

A quick meeting with his surviving officers confirmed what he already knew: after all that his men had endured, they were in no shape to attack anything. Knowing they were surrounded now, he ordered his company commanders to save what they could and get out of harm's way. They'd held against dreadful odds for an entire day. Now, they could only hope to survive.

All along the Pruemberg line, pockets of battle-weary Americans slipped off into the night. Riggs tried to lead 150 men around south of Saint-Vith, but with half his men wounded, they made little headway, and the Germans soon captured them. Riggs spent the rest of the war in a POW camp.

Von Manteuffel leading from the front, urging his SS tank crews forward. He was unhappy with the 18th Volksgrenadier Division's rate of advance outside of Saint-Vith, and he stayed at the unit's headquarters to keep the pressure on its commander to get results.

Only twenty-one men of A Company, 23rd Armored Infantry, made it back to American lines. Twenty-three men of A Company, 38th Armored Infantry Battalion, reached safety, led by their commanding officer, Capt. Walter Austrey. Altogether, only 200 of the 1,100 defenders of Pruemberg returned to American lines. Half of those men were wounded or suffering from complete exhaustion and had to be evacuated. The disaster left General Clarke's Combat Command B, 7th Armored, with only a single company of infantry.

It was one of the greatest last stands in American history, yet today Pruemberg has no traction in the American memory. The defenders delayed the capture of Saint-Vith by one vital day. And with the Germans racing against time, it was a delay they could not afford.

Nevertheless, by midnight, the Stars and Stripes no longer flew in Saint-Vith. In the days to follow, the Germans tried to exploit their success, but three things tripped them up. First, Saint-Vith acted like a magnet to shivering German soldiers, eager to find protection from the elements inside the city's remaining buildings. Second, when the 7th Armored Division finally pulled out of Saint-Vith on the night of December 21st, it left behind large amounts of supplies and equipment. The Germans picked up on this, and wholesale looting occupied Manteuffel's spearheads for many hours. Finally, instead of clearing up their traffic problems, the converging units became even more entwined and hopelessly snarled in traffic jams. It would take days to sort this out. In the meantime, the Americans pulled back to Vielsalm and dug in along the Salm River. The chance of exploiting the breakthrough all the way to the Meuse slipped away once again.

The 28th Infantry Division had served in the AEF during World War I. These Pennsylvania National Guardsmen are seen here being inspected by General Pershing in 1918.

16

THE KEYSTONE OF SKYLINE DRIVE

THE GERMANS AND THE PENNSYLVANIA NATIONAL GUARDSMEN of the 28th Infantry Division were well acquainted by December 1944. Dubbed the "Bloody Bucket" Division by the defenders of the Third Reich, the Pennsylvanians had seen action in the Normandy hedgerows around Saint-Lô during the summer of 1944. They'd paraded through Paris and then had driven across France to strike into the Siegfried Line at Binsfeld during the heady days of September. The following month, the Pennsylvanians flung themselves at the German defenses in the Hürtgen Forest, taking savage losses that all but exhausted their veteran riflemen. The division was pulled out of the line, attached to the First Army, and sent south to cover a twenty-five-mile sector of the southern Ardennes.

Deployed along the Our River, the 28th Infantry Division found itself in a heavily wooded and hilly region with few decent roads and way too much territory to defend. Without any other recourse, the Pennsylvanians established platoon and company strong points, usually around a village or town, along the Our River. With many gaps and little reserves, the 28th Division was spread so thin that it could only hope to slow down, not stop, any German assault.

To the division's rear, the only north-south road of any consequence was dubbed Skyline Drive. It served as the main supply line for the division. It was also a key road for the Germans to take if they were to get across the Our River and break out westward.

General Norman Cota, who landed under heavy machine gun fire in the second wave at Omaha Beach, commanded the Keystone Division that December. His leadership on Omaha Beach played a key role in saving the day at Dog White, and during the fighting there on D-Day, he coined the phrase, "Rangers lead the way!" His actions that day earned him a Distinguished Service Cross and, ultimately, a divisional command.

Unbeknownst to the Pennsylvanians along the Our River, Manteuffel's Fifth Panzer Army would make its main effort through their lines on December 16, 1944. Under the 28th

Major General Norman Cota had earned high marks for his performance on Omaha Beach with the 29th "Blue Gray" Division. He subsequently took command of the 28th Infantry Division, and his reputation suffered after the Battle of Hürtgen Forest.

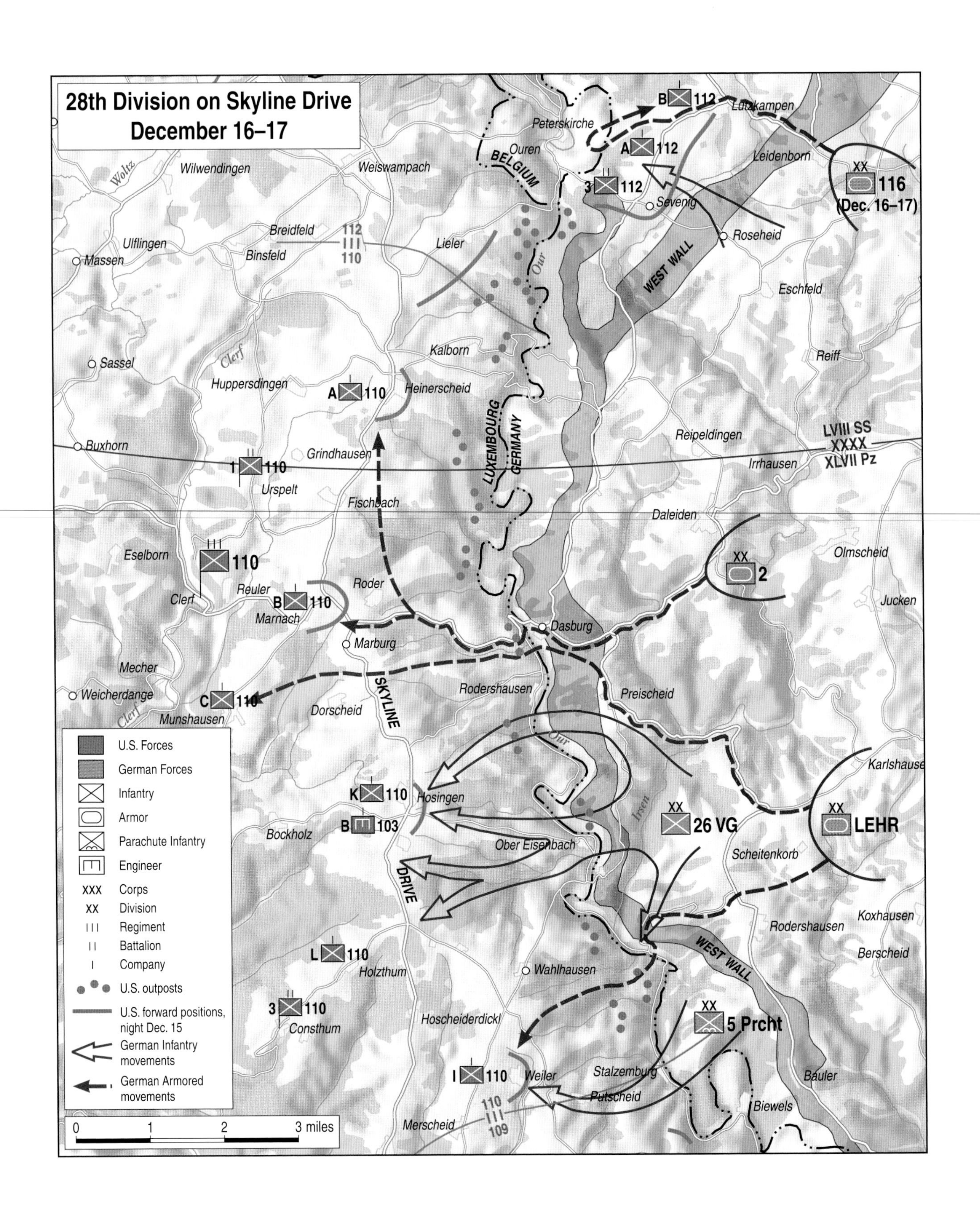
28th Division on Skyline Drive
December 16–17
Peterskirche
B 112
Lutzkampen
A 112
Ouren
BELGIUM
Leidenborn
Wilwendingen
Weiswampach
3 112
Sevenig
116 (Dec. 16–17)
Roseheid
Breidfeld
112
110
Ulflingen
Binsfeld
Lieler
Massen
WEST WALL
Our
Eschfeld
Kalborn
Reiff
Sassel
Clerf
Huppersdingen
A 110
Heinerscheid
LUXEMBOURG
GERMANY
Reipeldingen
LVIII SS
XXXX
XLVII Pz
Buxhorn
Grindhausen
1 110
Irrhausen
Urspelt
Fischbach
Daleiden
Olmscheid
Eselborn
110
2
Reuler
Roder
Jucken
Clerf
B 110
Marnach
Dasburg
Marburg
Mecher
Weicherdange
C 110
SKYLINE
Rodershausen
Preischeid
Munshausen
Dorscheid
Karlshause
K 110
Hosingen
B 103
26 VG
LEHR
Bockholz
Irsen
Ober Eisenbach
Scheitenkorb
DRIVE
Rodershausen
Koxhausen
L 110
Holzthum
Berscheid
Wahlhausen
3 110
Consthum
Hoscheiderdickt
5 Prcht
I 110
Weiler
Stalzemburg
Putscheid
Bauler
Biewels
Merscheid
109
U.S. Forces
German Forces
Infantry
Armor
Parachute Infantry
Engineer
XXX Corps
XX Division
III Regiment
II Battalion
I Company
U.S. outposts
U.S. forward positions, night Dec. 15
German Infantry movements
German Armored movements
0
1
2
3 miles

In December 1944 the 28th Infantry Division had been strung along the southern sector of the Ardennes in a series of company- and platoon-level outposts designed to defend the Our River and Skyline Drive. It was a quiet, heavily wooded sector with few roads. Prior to its deployment to the Ardennes, the 28th had seen intense close-quarters combat in the Hürtgen Forest, where it had taken devastating losses. It had been moved to Skyline Drive to rest and absorb replacements.

Division's nose, the Germans concentrated the entire XLVII Panzer Corps on its front. To the north, elements of the LVIII Panzer Corps faced off against one of Cota's infantry regiments. And to the south, part of the Seventh Army, including the 5th Fallschirmjäger Division and the 352nd Volksgrenadier Division would hit the Keystone Division's right flank.

Altogether, Norman Cota's command faced the 2nd Panzer Division; Panzer Lehr Division; the 15th, 26th, 352nd, and 560th Volksgrenadier Divisions; and various corps and army assets, including an engineer battalion, a flak battalion, and a battalion each of Jagdpanzers and Sturmgeschützes. All these units had one key objective: cross the Our River, push west, and get to Bastogne as soon as possible. Bastogne, like Saint-Vith, was the hub of all the decent roads in this sector of the Ardennes. Without Bastogne in German hands, the panzers had no chance to reach the Meuse.

Never had an American infantry division faced such overwhelming power. And on December 16, the Germans attacked through the fog and caught the Pennyslvanians completely by surprise.

On the far left of the 28th Division's line, the 112th Infantry Regiment reacted with exceptional vigor as the first German assault waves crossed their front. The 116th Panzer Division sent out two shock companies of grenadiers with orders to infiltrate around the regiment's strong points and unhinge Cota's northern flank. Things did not go well for the Germans in these two units. One company was virtually wiped out in a crossfire as they moved across a dangerously

A Sturmgeschütz III failed to make it across the Our River.

Two captured German soldiers assist a wounded American back to an aid station. The 112th Infantry Regiment chopped up the first German attack waves, capturing almost an entire company of panzergrenadiers from the 116th Panzer Division.

An American GI guards a couple of infiltrators. Infiltration tactics worked well in the Losheim Gap and elsewhere around the Schnee Eiffel. They failed completely during the first day on the 112th Infantry Regiment's front.

The M18 Hellcat combined the decent hitting power of the 76mm cannon (an adaptation of the British 17 pounder) and remarkable speed. With the pedal to the metal, the M18 could reach an incredible fifty-five miles per hour.

exposed stretch of terrain. Another got behind the 112th Infantry and closed to within a few hundred yards of the regimental command post before it was stopped cold. A local American counterattack captured virtually the entire company.

For the first two days of the offensive, the 112th's companies faced off against battalions of assaulting Germans, supported by panzers and flame-throwing armored vehicles. The regiment refused to give ground, forcing the 116th Panzer to deploy a company of Panthers to try to crack open the line. The Panthers rolled forward and shot up machine gun nests with their 75mm cannons. The Americans countered that move by sending forward a platoon of speedy M18 Hellcats, whose 76mm gun and extraordinary maneuverability led to the destruction of four Panthers. All but one of the M18s succumbed to German fire.

Later that day, as the Germans pressed their attack and began to seep around the company strong points, gun crews from the 229th Field Artillery Battalion found themselves in point-blank duels with panzers and supporting infantry. The gunners bore-sighted their 105s and blasted the German tanks into burning wreckage. At the same time, using M16 antiaircraft half-tracks to tear apart the dismounted panzer grenadiers with their quad .50-caliber machine guns, the Americans drove the attackers off.

Just before dark on December 17, General Cota ordered the 112th Infantry to pull back across the Our River. At this point, the company strong points had become rocks in a river of German armor and infantry. Pulling out meant moving through a fluid situation with the enemy all around them. Amazingly, most of the 112th got across the Our in good shape. That night, the 1st Battalion, 112th, actually used a bridge already in German hands. The battalion commander formed up his men, placed a German-speaking officer at the head of the column, and audaciously marched right across. As they moved among the panzer grenadiers guarding the bridge, the American officer called out random orders in German to complete the ruse.

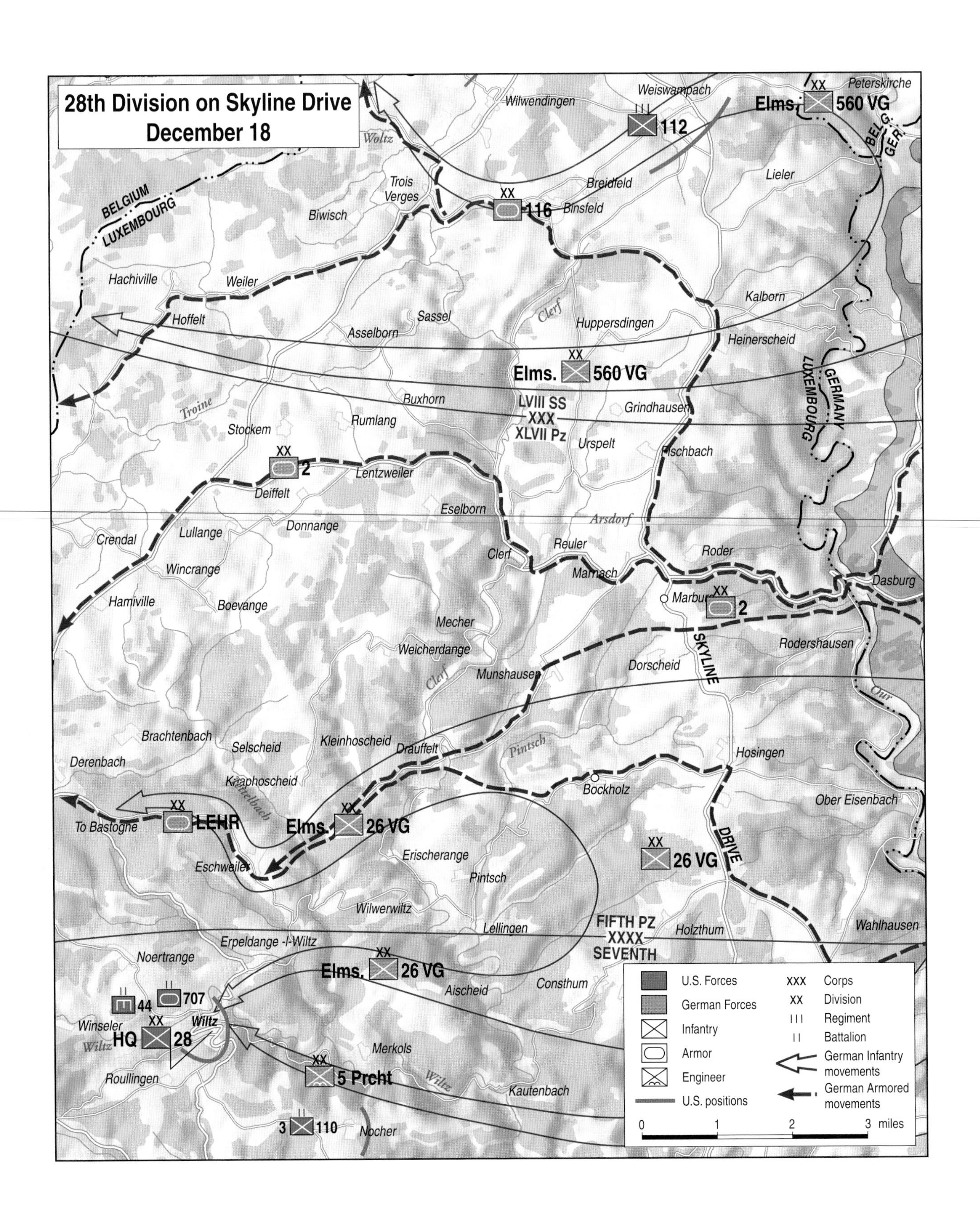
28th Division on Skyline Drive
December 18
BELGIUM
LUXEMBOURG
GERMANY
LUXEMBOURG
BELG.
GER.
Elms. 560 VG
112
116
Elms. 560 VG
LVIII SS
XXX
XLVII Pz
2
2
LEHR
Elms. 26 VG
26 VG
FIFTH PZ
XXXX
SEVENTH
Elms. 26 VG
44
707
HQ 28
5 Prcht
3 110
SKYLINE
DRIVE
To Bastogne
Wilwendingen
Weiswampach
Peterskirche
Trois Verges
Biwisch
Breidfeld
Binsfeld
Lieler
Hachiville
Weiler
Hoffelt
Sassel
Asselborn
Huppersdingen
Kalborn
Heinerscheid
Buxhorn
Rumlang
Stockem
Grindhausen
Urspelt
Lentzweiler
Deiffelt
Eselborn
Crendal
Lullange
Donnange
Clerf
Reuler
Marnach
Roder
Dasburg
Wincrange
Hamiville
Boevange
Mecher
Weicherdange
Munshausen
Dorscheid
Rodershausen
Brachtenbach
Selscheid
Kleinhoscheid
Drauffelt
Derenbach
Hosingen
Bockholz
Ober Eisenbach
Eschweiler
Erischerange
Pintsch
Wilwerwiltz
Lellingen
Holzthum
Wahlhausen
Noertrange
Erpeldange -l-Wiltz
Consthum
Aischeid
Winseler
Wiltz
Merkols
Roullingen
Kautenbach
Nocher
Woltz
Troine
Arsdorf
Pintsch
Our
U.S. Forces
German Forces
Infantry
Armor
Engineer
U.S. positions
XXX Corps
XX Division
III Regiment
II Battalion
German Infantry movements
German Armored movements
0 1 2 3 miles

By dawn on December 18, most of the 112th had reassembled at Weiswampach. There the Pennsylvanians stayed throughout the day, but the men watched in dismay as long lines of German armor passed by their right flank at Trois Vierges. Ultimately, the regiment fell back again, but while doing so was ordered by General Cota back to Weiswampach. The regimental commander decided Cota had lost touch with the situation, so he drove to the 106th Infantry Division's headquarters and put his regiment at General Jones' disposal. Jones, already down two regiments thanks to the fighting in the Schnee Eifel, was overjoyed to receive a surprise infusion of an intact regimental combat team.

At the same time, the 109th Infantry Regiment served as Cota's far right flank. It was hit by elements of the Fifth Panzer Army and the Seventh Army. Forced back from the Our, the 109th lost contact with Cota's center—the 110th Infantry—and soon lost all communication with 28th Divisional Headquarters. The regiment withdrew and joined the Third Army's 4th Infantry Division to the south.

It was that middle regiment that the hammer blow fell upon during those first chaotic days of the Battle of the Bulge. The 110th Infantry Regiment, commanded by Col. Hurley Fuller, covered the only paved road to Bastogne from the Our River.

As the German offensive began, General Cota recognized the significance of the 110th Infantry Regiment's position. He also knew his center had to hold. He called Hurley Fuller and told him, "No one comes back." Fuller acknowledged. Cota pressed him again to make sure he understood. Fuller replied, "No one comes back, sir."

Very few men did. But with their blood, they saved Bastogne.

The dreaded "Meatchopper," an M16 antiaircraft half track with quad .50-caliber machine guns, could unleash simply staggering carnage on infantry in the open with its four heavy weapons. The .50-calibers would literally tear men apart.

The U.S. Army had nothing that could stand toe-to-toe with a Panther. Instead, the American tank crews had to rely on stealth, speed, and surprise to close with and destroy the better armored German panzer. A good fight was one in which the tank losses were even.

Private First Class Floyd Duncan, a rifleman with the 110th Infantry Regiment, stands guard from his shallow foxhole shortly before the German offensive began.

A GI climbs aboard a demolished German armored vehicle just outside of Hosingen. The town, held by a battalion minus from the 110th Infantry Regiment, lay in the path of much of Manteuffel's Fifth Panzer Army. For two days, the Americans held out against furious attacks by panzers and infantry. Finally, on the morning of December 18, the GIs inside Hosingen fired their last rounds of ammunition and were forced to surrender. Their last stand helped block the way to Bastogne, giving the 101st Airborne and 10th Armored Divisions the time needed to beat the Germans to that strategically vital city.

17

WHEN THE ODDS WERE FIFTEEN TO ONE

★ ★ ★ ★ ★

THIRTY-ONE THOUSAND GERMAN SOLDIERS AND PANZER CREWS slammed into the two thousand men under Colonel Fuller's command on December 16. His companies were spread all along a north-south line in mini-fortresses in key villages and intersections. Fuller's command post was located in the vital town of Clerf, which lay in a bend of the Clerf River. There, the paved road the Germans needed so much ran west across the river and on to Bastogne. Take Clerf, and Cota's center would be compromised. The entire division's position along Skyline Drive would be rendered untenable.

Clerf had always been in Manteuffel's sights. He assigned it top priority and told the XLVII Panzer Corps to take it by the end of the first day of the offensive. As a result, the 110th faced both the veteran 2nd Panzer Division—regarded by the Americans as the best Wehrmacht armored formation—and the well-blooded 26th Volksgrenadier Division, which had seen extensive combat on the Eastern Front.

The Germans hit the 110th with engineers and infantry on December 16. Getting panzers across the Our River became a serious issue that day. Only the bridges at Dasburg and Gemund could support their weight, so the initial fighting on Skyline Drive centered on infantry-versus-infantry battles for the 110th Regiment's strongholds at Hosingen, Munshausen, and other little towns.

Hosingen proved to be a vital position. Skyline Drive ran right through it, and just to the south was a secondary road that ran west toward Bastogne from Gemund. For the

The Browning M1919 light machine gun provided the rifle companies with an extremely useful support weapon. Weighing thirty-one pounds, it had a 1,500-yard effective range and a six hundred-rounds-per-minute rate of fire.

Germans, taking Hosingen was the only way to exploit their bridgehead at Gemund and get the panzers rolling for their main objective.

The town was held by a combined force of two companies of infantry and a handful of engineers. All through the 16th, they beat off attack after attack by two regiments of volksgrenadiers. Frustrated, the Germans brought up self-propelled guns and flamethrowers and through brute firepower managed to grab a toehold in the southern part of town. The Americans refused to surrender. Instead, the GIs fought street to street and room to room, despite a dwindling ammunition supply. On the night of the December 17, a small force of Sherman tanks managed to fight its way into town and join up with its embattled defenders. And while the arrival of armor gave the GIs a boost, the tanks didn't bring any rifle ammunition with them. Through the night, the fighting raged until by morning, the surviving American troops were down to three magazines of rifle ammunition apiece. By 10:00 a.m. on December 18, even that was gone. Without any means to fight on, the Americans surrendered.

The Pennsylvanians defending Munshausen, a town west of Hosingen, fought a similar pitched urban battle. As the Germans from the 2nd Panzer and the 26th Volksgrenadier

The shattered remains of a Hetzer jagdpanzer lie in the mud just outside of Hosingen. Two companies of infantry, a handful of engineers, and a few Sherman tanks withstood overwhelming odds at Hosingen and took a heavy toll on the Germans trying to force their way through the town to open up Skyline Drive.

U.S. artillery played a vital role in small-unit actions on the 28th Infantry Division's front, allowing isolated pockets of American defenders to hold off vastly superior forces—for awhile at least.

Divisions closed around their village, the men barricaded the streets with overturned trucks. They fought against overwhelming odds for two days and then attempted to break out and get across the Clerf River. Only a handful survived.

As these strong points fought on with increasing desperation, the main battle took shape around Marnach and Clerf itself. Here, Colonel Fuller gathered as many men as he could and made his last stand.

On the 16th, the 2nd Panzer Division made a concerted drive to take Clerf. The Americans at Marnach barred the way. Cota fed Fuller what reinforcements he could, which included some Shermans from the 9th Armored Division's Combat Command R. These particular tankers had never seen combat before, and as they counterattacked around Marnach, they were hit hard by antitank guns and panzerfausts. The few surviving Sherman crews pulled out and disappeared. That afternoon, Cota dispatched one company of the 707th Tank Battalion to buttress Fuller's center. These Shermans rolled into a hornet's nest of panzer grenadiers and German armor, and their counterattack bogged down almost immediately. Later, he released his reserve battalion, which was from the 110th, back to Fuller. The 28th Division now had only one company of light tanks in reserve.

The next morning, Fuller ordered his 2nd Battalion to counterattack down the road from Clerf to Marnach. But the effort was like throwing pebbles into a tornado. Supported by the last of the division's reserve, a company of M5 Stuart light tanks from the 707th Tank Battalion, the Pennsylvanians ran straight into a wall of firepower. Sturmgeschützes and Panthers, supported by infantry armed with panzerschreks and panzerfausts, lit up Fuller's counterattack and demolished the M5 company. Within hours the counterattack had been crushed by the sheer weight of the German forces around Marnach.

A German soldier with a panzerfaust at the ready. The Shermans sent to reinforce Colonel Fuller's command around Clerf came from an inexperienced company of the 9th Armored Division and drove headlong into a strong force of German infantry, well equipped with panzerfausts and panzerschrecks. A close-range tank-infantry duel erupted, and the green American tank crews took heavy losses.

Employing field-expedient camouflage. American gunners have tried to conceal their tank destroyer with bed sheets pulled from the local houses.

By 9:30 a.m., the 2nd Panzer's spearhead of twelve Panzer IVs and thirty half-tracks full of grenadiers was rolling out of Marnach for Clerf. A platoon of Shermans barred the way, and a furious, small-scale tank battle ensued. The M4 crews managed to knock out four of the Panzers, but lost three of their own tracks in return. However, one of the German tanks had been destroyed on a narrow stretch of winding road, barring the way into Clerf for the other panzers in the column. The spearhead had to find another way into town until the burning tank could be pushed out of the way. That bought Colonel Fuller and his men a little bit of time.

Meanwhile, in other outposts along Skyline Drive, desperate mini-Alamos took place. The 3rd Battalion, 110th Infantry Regiment, absorbed numerous attacks from the 26th Volksgrenadiers on December 17. The remnants of the battalion made a last stand at Consthum, south of Clerf. There, elements of the 26th Volksgrenadier Division, supported by sturmgeschützes, shattered the battalion and put its survivors to flight. Only two hundred men made it out.

As darkness fell, the Germans found their way across the Clerf River bridge and began to approach Colonel Fuller's command post. Located in a stoutly constructed hotel, Fuller's men hunkered down and obeyed General Cota's "No one comes back" order.

By 6:30 p.m., the Germans surrounded Fuller's command post. The regimental phone operator grimly announced to divisional headquarters that "This switchboard is closed." While the GIs and Fuller kept the German infantry at bay, they had no antitank defenses. Soon, some of the 2nd Panzer Division's Panzer IVs pressed so close to the hotel that their 75mm barrels actually pressed through windows before they opened fire.

The hotel began to collapse around Fuller and his headquarters staff. Fuller ran to his room, where he found it full of GIs seeking cover from the tank fire. Just then, an explosion rocked the room and wounded several of the men. It was time to get out. Colonel Fuller, leading a blinded GI by the hand, got his small band of survivors through a window and across a ladder laid out as a walkway to a nearby cliff. Shortly after scaling the cliff, though, they encountered a German patrol in the darkness. Fuller and his men ended up as prisoners of war.

The 110th Infantry ceased to exist as an integrated fighting force, though pockets of determined Pennsylvanians held out through the next day. One group took refuge in a castle near the Clerf River bridge. From there, they sniped at passing German infantry until the 2nd

Some of the quartermaster personnel assigned to the 28th Infantry Division managed to get their hands on a shipment of snowshoes. These were employed on special resupply missions later in the battle.

The 707th Tank Battalion's M5 Stuart light tanks were the last reserves General Cota had under his command. He sent them to reinforce Colonel Fuller so that Clerf could be held. The M5s sped into the fight, only to encounter Sturmgeschütz IIIs and Panthers. The M5s didn't stand a chance.

A knocked-out Panzer IV sits in the snow. During the Bulge, the 2nd Panzer Division still relied heavily on this older, though less logistically demanding, medium tank. One Panzer IV from the division was knocked out on a narrow stretch of road just outside Clerf. It blocked the main road into town, and while it burned the Germans couldn't move it. Instead, they were forced to find an alternate way into the town, further delaying the drive to get to Bastogne.

Exhausted survivors from the 28th Infantry Division pull back through Bastogne. The men who saved Bastogne, the valiant defenders of Skyline Drive, never have received the credit they deserved for helping blunt the German offensive to the Meuse. Their stand along the Our River totally upset the Fifth Panzer Army's schedule and set the stage for the mammoth battle for Bastogne.

Panzer Division grew weary of such treatment and drove a tank through the castle gates. Some eighty defenders staggered out of the castle and into captivity.

Altogether, the 110th and its reinforcing units lost 2,700 men defending Clerf and the strongpoints around Skyline Drive. General Cota was now a commander without a command. The 112th Infantry Regiment was up north fighting with the 106th Infantry Division around Saint-Vith, and the 109th Infantry Regiment had joined up with the 4th Infantry Division. Cota, with just a scratch force of stragglers and headquarters troops, could no longer bar the way to Bastogne. Manteuffel's panzers and volksgrenadiers had torn a fifteen-mile hole in the First Army's lines.

But it had come at a steep price in blood and time. The 110th's last stand at Clerf and Hosingen had delayed the drive on Bastogne by forty-eight critical hours. And by a razor's edge, those forty-eight hours proved to be decisive. The Americans would win the race to Bastogne thanks to the dogged last stand of the Keystone Division.

Bastogne served as a hub for the Ardennes road and rail network. Capturing it would be essential if the Germans were to actually stand a chance of getting across the Meuse River.

18

OLD CROCK AND FRITZ

AS THE PENNSYLVANIANS HELD OUT IN LITTLE POCKETS all around Skyline Drive, the XLVII Panzer Corps pushed hard to get untangled from these fragmented firefights and race to Bastogne. As parts of the Panzer Lehr and 2nd Panzer Divisions rolled across the Clerf, American units were racing for Bastogne as well. By early afternoon, December 18, thousands of men and vehicles were converging from all compass points on the plum prize of the Ardennes. He who controlled Bastogne controlled the road network south of Saint-Vith.

Both General Omar Bradley and General Middleton, commander of VIII Corps in whose sector Bastogne lay, recognized the strategic significance of the Belgian city. On the afternoon of the 16th, Bradley committed the 101st Airborne Division (Screaming Eagles) to Bastogne. He also took Combat Command B, 10th Armored Division, away from Patton's Third Army and sent it north to support the paratroopers.

These two units needed time to get to Bastogne. The 28th Infantry Division had bought the Americans two days. Now, with the 2nd Panzer Division's spearheads driving hard for the city, Middleton needed to pull a rabbit out of his hat and scrape together something to slow the Germans down.

He didn't have much on hand, just Combat Command R, 9th Armored, three battalions of engineers, and a few battalions of artillery. Middleton deployed the engineers around Bastogne proper. They drew M1s and machine guns, went out east of town, and dug in. In the meantime, Combat Command R sped east to buy Bastogne some time.

Divided into two forces, Task Force Harper and Task Force Rose, Combat Command R received orders from Middleton to block the road at Lullange and Allerborn. Neither position could support the other, but at least they had a battalion of M7 Priest self-propelled 105mm guns they could count on to give them artillery support.

continued on page 227

Major Gen. Maxwell Taylor (left) shakes hands with Gen. Anthony McAuliffe, his divisional artillery chief. Taylor happened to be stateside in Washington, D.C., when the German offensive began, so McAuliffe took the 101st Airborne into Bastogne.

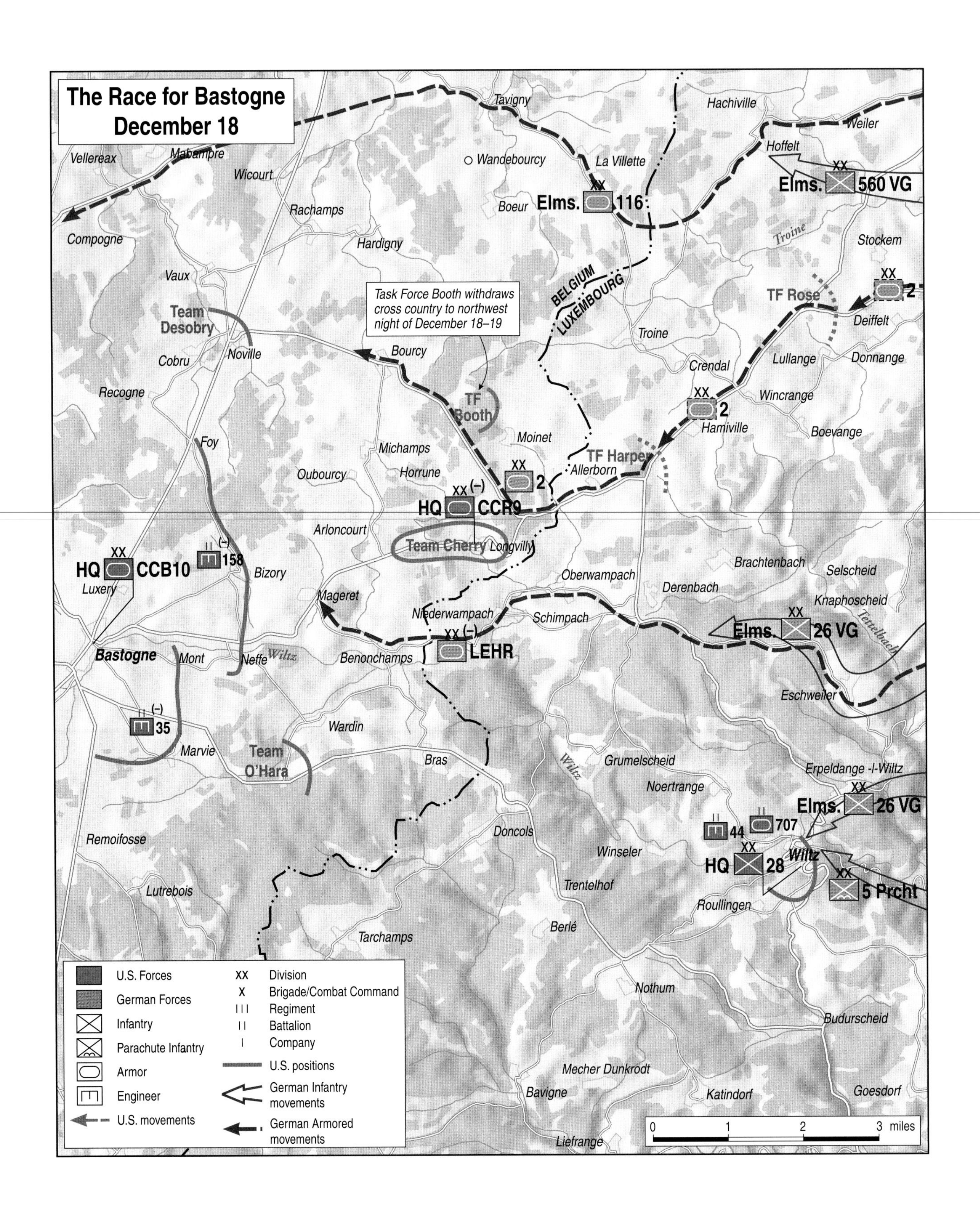
The Race for Bastogne
December 18
Task Force Booth withdraws cross country to northwest night of December 18–19
Vellereax
Mabampre
Wicourt
Tavigny
Hachiville
Weiler
Hoffelt
Wandebourcy
La Villette
Elms. 560 VG
Rachamps
Boeur
Elms. 116
Compogne
Hardigny
Troine
Stockem
Vaux
BELGIUM
LUXEMBOURG
TF Rose
2
Deiffelt
Team Desobry
Noville
Cobru
Bourcy
Troine
Crendal
Lullange
Donnange
Recogne
TF Booth
2
Hamiville
Wincrange
Boevange
Foy
Moinet
Michamps
TF Harper
Allerborn
Oubourcy
Horrune
2
HQ CCR9
Arloncourt
Team Cherry
Longvilly
HQ CCB10
158
Luxery
Bizory
Brachtenbach
Selscheid
Oberwampach
Derenbach
Knaphoscheid
Mageret
Niederwampach
Schimpach
Tettelbach
Elms. 26 VG
Bastogne
Mont
Neffe
Wiltz
Benonchamps
LEHR
Eschweiler
35
Wardin
Marvie
Team O'Hara
Bras
Wiltz
Grumelscheid
Erpeldange -l-Wiltz
Noertrange
Elms. 26 VG
44
707
Remoifosse
Doncols
Winseler
HQ 28
Wiltz
5 Prcht
Lutrebois
Trentelhof
Roullingen
Berlé
Tarchamps
U.S. Forces
German Forces
Infantry
Parachute Infantry
Armor
Engineer
U.S. movements
XX Division
X Brigade/Combat Command
III Regiment
II Battalion
I Company
U.S. positions
German Infantry movements
German Armored movements
Nothum
Budurscheid
Mecher Dunkrodt
Bavigne
Katindorf
Goesdorf
Liefrange
0 1 2 3 miles

General Middleton in the field with the commander of one of his infantry divisions.

An M20 scout car from the 10th Armored Division. The 10th served with the Third Army, and at first Patton was loath to give this veteran unit up to his neighbors to the north.

Though M4 Shermans were unable to stand with the Panthers and Tigers, the M4 was a multi-role platform whose versatility made the tank enormously useful. With its 75mm gun, it could function in an antitank role and infantry-support role. Some M4s, like the ones seen here, came equipped with 105mm howitzers and could provide indirect-fire missions for frontline units.

A unit pulling out of Bastogne passes one heading into the battle. Behind the defenses coalescing around Bastogne's outskirts to the north, east, and south, panicked stragglers and rear-echelon support units bugged out. To some in the 101st Airborne, it seemed disgraceful.

The aftermath of a tank battle.

The twisted remains of one of the M7 Priests that had been supporting Task Force Rose and Task Force Harper.

continued from page 223

At 8:30 a.m., December 18, the 2nd Panzer Division's reconnaissance battalion blundered into Task Force Rose's roadblock. With much of the division still hung up around Skyline Drive and inside Clerf, the recon element couldn't count on much help. They backed off and waited for help. Later that morning, a few tanks shook loose from the Pennsylvanians and rumbled up to Lullange. Under a smoke screen, they charged the roadblock with the recon battalion's lighter armored vehicles. A confused tank skirmish erupted, but Task Force Rose managed to hold on.

All afternoon, the Americans at the roadblock traded shots with the 2nd Panzer Division. The 116th Panzer Division made things more complicated when its panzers overran the 73rd Field Artillery Battalion's positions and the M7 Priests supporting Task Force Rose had to fall back. Without the 105s to help hold off the 2nd Panzer Division's spearheads, the Americans faced getting overrun. Middleton ordered them to hold fast, and both Rose and Harper did so. As the day wore on, the 2nd Panzer Division, as well as part of Fritz Bayerlein's Panzer

continued on page 230

A field of Panthers knocked out by U.S. antitank weapons. The German spearheads took heavy losses driving on Bastogne, even after they burst through the 28th Infantry Division's defenses on Skyline Drive.

The streets of Bastogne during the battle.

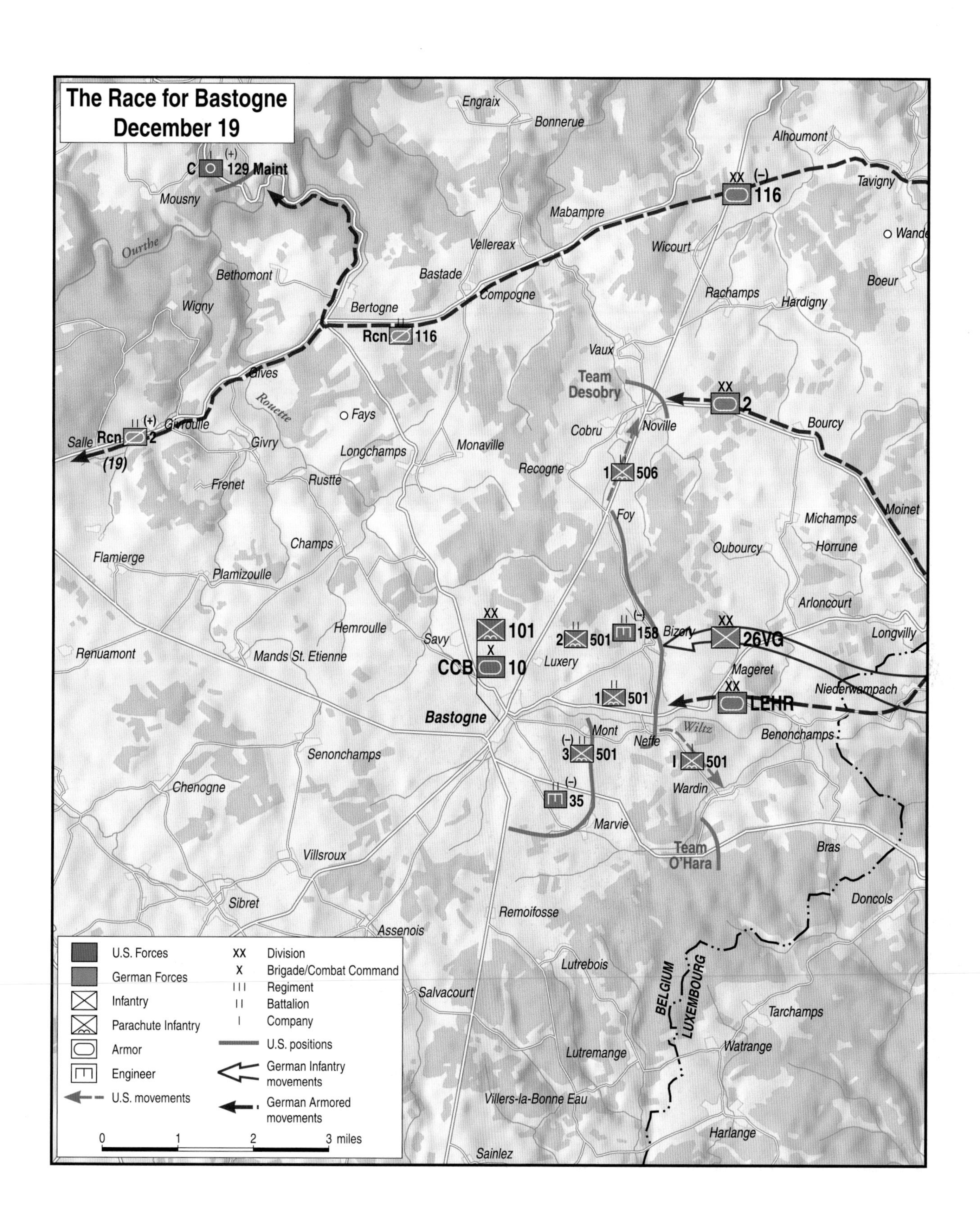
The Race for Bastogne
December 19
C 129 Maint
Mousny
Ourthe
Bethomont
Wigny
Gives
Rouette
Fays
Giviroulle
Salle
Rcn 2
(19)
Givry
Frenet
Rustte
Longchamps
Monaville
Champs
Flamierge
Plamizoulle
Hemroulle
Renuamont
Mands St. Etienne
Savy
Engraix
Bonnerue
Mabampre
Vellereax
Bastade
Compogne
Bertogne
Rcn 116
116
Alhoumont
Tavigny
Wicourt
Wande
Boeur
Rachamps
Hardigny
Vaux
Team Desobry
Noville
Cobru
2
Bourcy
Recogne
1 506
Foy
Michamps
Moinet
Horrune
Oubourcy
Arloncourt
101
CCB 10
2 501
158
Bizory
26VG
Longvilly
Luxery
Mageret
Niederwampach
1 501
LEHR
Bastogne
Mont
Neffe
Wiltz
Benonchamps
3 501
I 501
Wardin
Senonchamps
Chenogne
35
Marvie
Team O'Hara
Bras
Villsroux
Sibret
Assenois
Remoifosse
Doncols
Lutrebois
BELGIUM
LUXEMBOURG
Salvacourt
Tarchamps
Watrange
Lutremange
Villers-la-Bonne Eau
Harlange
Sainlez
U.S. Forces
German Forces
Infantry
Parachute Infantry
Armor
Engineer
U.S. movements
XX Division
X Brigade/Combat Command
III Regiment
II Battalion
I Company
U.S. positions
German Infantry movements
German Armored movements
0 1 2 3 miles

Elements of the 101st Airborne Division march into Bastogne on December 18. The Americans won the race into the town.

continued from page 227

Lehr Division, flowed around both American blocking positions. As dusk settled over the icy Belgian countryside, Combat Command R, 9th Armored Division, found itself surrounded.

That evening, Middleton gave Task Force Rose permission to withdraw. But escape now was problematical. At 8:00 p.m., the Germans pounded Task Force Harper with artillery and then unleashed a blistering attack spearheaded by Panthers. The Americans hung on until midnight, but by the early hours of December 19, TF Harper had been shattered. The 9th Armored Division would no longer pose an obstacle to the Germans.

Yet, while Combat Command R's brave men stood and died, Combat Command B, 10th Armored Division, rolled into Bastogne after dark. Its tanks and armored infantry were desperately needed. Problem was, there were so many approaches to Bastogne that Middleton had to divide the combat command into three battalion-sized elements. Each one would have to hold a key village outside of the city, buying more time so the 101st Airborne's crack paratroopers could get into Bastogne and dig in.

The 10th Armored Division split into three teams: Cherry, Desobry, and O'Hara. Team Cherry sped east to backstop Combat Command R, 9th Armored Division, while O'Hara deployed around Wardin to the southeast and Desobry dug in at Noville to the north. The Americans won the race to Bastogne, but only by the narrowest of margins.

As Combat Command B, 10th Armored, fanned out and prepared to take on three panzer divisions, the 101st Airborne reached Bastogne in soft-skinned trucks. Pulled out of reserve billets in France, the division hadn't had time to draw its full ration of ammunition and cold weather gear. In the darkness, as American stragglers streamed past them, the plucky paratroopers stripped the fleeing GIs of their rifle and machine gun ammo, grenades, and anything else that could be of use in the coming fight.

As the 101st entered town, many of its Belgian residents packed up what little they could and limped west to avoid the fighting. With little food and clothing, they suffered tremendous privation that winter.

An aerial view of Bastogne shows the spider web of roads that converged on the city.

A paratrooper from the 101st Airborne squats in his frozen foxhole at a checkpoint on the edge of Bastogne. Curious Belgian civilians look on.

The 101st Airborne solidified its status as one of the legendary units of World War II with its resolute defense of Bastogne. Yet, it had not seen as much combat as the 82nd Airborne had. Its first taste of battle came during the D-Day drop and the fighting in Normandy. Later, it saw its second major operation in Holland during Operation Market-Garden. The Ardennes and Bastogne was the division's third campaign.

A lull in the action gives soldiers time to dig in.

A wrecked Sherman is salvaged near Bastogne. This one was clearly engaging German antitank forces at its two o'clock position when two direct hits on the right-hand star knocked it out. Sherman crews learned that their biggest danger came from a penetration hit that detonated their ready ammunition supply. Veteran crews learned they usually had a few seconds before the ammo started to cook off, so they made it standard practice to bail out immediately after taking a hit that penetrated their armor.

With the arrival of the Screaming Eagles, General Middleton initially did not designate an overall commander for the Bastogne forces. The 101st's commander, Maj. Gen. Maxwell Taylor, was actually in the States at the time, so Brig. Gen. Anthony McAuliffe, the 101st Airborne's artillery commander, took the outfit into Belgium. His presence made the 10th Armored's leader, Col. William Roberts, leery of coming under command of a foot-slogging paratrooper instead of another armor officer. Tankers always dreaded coming under command of infantry officers, as they inherently felt they would be misused on the battlefield.

Roberts, who had first seen combat at Château-Thierry during the summer of 1918, was leather hard, a warrior to the core. So was McAuliffe, who had gone through jump school in his forties to be able to serve with the 101st. Leaping out of airplanes, he explained to a friend, was pretty rough for an "old crock like me." The line spread through the ranks of the Screaming Eagles, and McAuliffe earned "Old Crock" as his nickname ever after.

At first, both officers would report to Middleton and just cooperate with each other. That didn't last long, though, and Middleton realized he needed to unify the command structure at Bastogne. Ultimately, he put McAuliffe in charge. The arrangement ended up working out just fine.

As McAuliffe and Roberts got acquainted, the first regiment of the 101st to enter Bastogne, Col. Julian Ewell's 501st Parachute Infantry Regiment, beat feet for Mageret, just east of Bastogne. The 3rd Battalion, 501st, dug in deep, overwatching the main road through town. The 506th headed north of town. By midnight, the American defenses at Bastonge

American vehicles clutter the streets of Bastogne.

On the narrow Belgian roads available in the Ardennes, an armored division would be spread out for miles. When passing units intermingled with it, huge traffic snarls ensued.

consisted of a layer of blocking positions established by the 10th Armored Division, with the 101st digging in furiously behind them in a horseshoe-shaped line around the city.

Out east of Bastogne, Team Cherry deployed near Longvilly. As the men established fields of fire and started to dig in, dazed survivors from the 28th Infantry Division and the 9th Armored Division's road blocks staggered into their lines. Stray vehicles sought refuge behind them as well. Soon, Team Cherry's rear was jammed with trucks, half-tracks, and jeeps from various shattered units. Some of the men hefted their M1s and joined Team Cherry. Others just wanted to get out of harm's way.

To the south, Fritz Bayerlein's Panzer Lehr spearheads reached the outskirts of Mageret at 9:00 p.m., December 18. The Germans were now only a few miles from downtown Bastogne. Riding in the lead panzer, Bayerlein brought his track to a stop, bailed out of it, and sought out a Belgian civilian. He asked the man if he'd seen any Americans in the area. The Belgian, no friend of the Nazis, lied to the general's face and told him he'd seen almost a hundred armored vehicles drive through town earlier in the day.

Bayerlein, now convinced he had a full American armored division in his sector, ordered his panzers to pause and set up defensive positions. While they did, Colonel Ewell's paras reached the area and dug in furiously. Had Bayerlein pushed on, he might have been able to get all the way into Bastogne. Instead, he sat in the snow and awaited a counterattack that never came.

Demolished American vehicles lie abandoned in the snow after Team Cherry was wiped out by German jagdpanzers from Fritz Bayerlein's division.

The next morning, disaster struck Team Cherry. Longvilly was several miles from the main American line of resistance taking shape east of Bastogne. The tankers found themselves surrounded by elements of the 2nd Panzer Division and Panzer Lehr. The 2nd Panzer struck them from the east, and a battle raged all morning long. It became all too clear that Team Cherry faced just too much firepower to hold for long. Just before noon, the order to retire to Bastogne went out. Team Cherry assembled behind a rear guard that soon absorbed another armored attack. While they fought furiously, the rest of the force stacked up on a road that ran west out of town.

The column ran straight into dozens of straggling American vehicles. Strung out along the country lane, Team Cherry's tanks, armored cars and half-tracks made little progress west.

Enter Panzer Lehr. After Bayerlein had spent the night outside Mageret with his spearhead kampfgruppe, his lead elements were joined by the division's other two battle groups. One, Kampfgruppe Fallois, reached Neffe, just east of Bastogne, at 8:00 a.m. on December 19. Again, Bayerlein feared a counterattack and became ultra-cautious. Instead of pushing into the city, he sent his jagdpanzer battalion north, where it crested a hill and came across the target of all targets: Team Cherry's massive traffic jam.

The Jagdpanzers unleashed a firestorm of armor-piercing (AP) shells on the trapped Americans. Frantic M4 crews tried to get off the road and deploy, but they simply didn't have the chance. Sherman after Sherman exploded in flames. Half-tracks blew apart as AP shells tore through their gas tanks. The stricken GIs aboard the vehicles bailed out and scattered under a hail of machine gun fire.

When the massacre ended, Panzer Lehr's tank hunters had destroyed or captured over a hundred vehicles, including twenty-three Shermans, fifteen M7 Priests, and fourteen armored cars. Team Cherry ceased to exist.

The 2nd Panzer Division ran into Team Desobry at Noville. Thinking they faced light resistance in this town on the northern edge of Bastogne, the XLVII Panzer Corps commander ordered the 2nd Panzer to launch a frontal assault and clear the way to Meuse. Instead of light opposition, the 2nd Panzer ran into a firestorm and suffered irreplaceable losses.

GIs on the move outside of Bastogne.

Meanwhile, even as the slaughter west of Longvilly continued, most of the 2nd Panzer Division swung north and tried to push on to the west. Earlier that morning, reconnaissance discovered Team Desobry ensconced in Noville. The 2nd Panzer Division's commanding officer, Meinrad von Lauchert, tried to bypass the American-held town. His forward elements crept along a ridge just outside of Noville, concealed by ground fog. Suddenly, the fog lifted, and both sides discovered they were only a few hundred yards from each other. A furious, close-range tank battle erupted that sent the 2nd Panzer's spearhead reeling backwards.

Later that morning, General Heinrich von Lüttwitz, commander of the XLVII Panzer Corps, arrived on the scene and conferred with Lauchert. Lüttwitz grew convinced that Noville was thinly held. Instead of bypassing it, he ordered Lauchert to take it. Problem was, most of the 2nd Panzer was strung out on muddy back-country roads from Noville back behind Longvilly. It would take time to assemble the forces needed to take the town.

That afternoon, the 2nd Panzer Division struck Team Desobry once again. The Panzers and their supporting grenadiers swarmed all over the hard-pressed American force. But to the south, the 1st Battalion, 506th PIR, heard the fighting. Lieutenant Col. James LaPrade ordered his men forward, and the paratroopers sprinted to the sound of the gunfire. The sudden arrival of the paratroopers threw the 2nd Panzer off its game. A brutal armor-infantry battle raged all afternoon and into the evening. Between panzer attacks, the Germans pummeled Noville with deadly accurate artillery barrages. One shell hit the 1st Battalion, 506th's command post, killing Lieutenant Colonel LaPrade and wounding Colonel Desobry in the head. His

When the fight at Noville broke out, the 1st Battalion, 506th PIR, was just to the south. Its commander ordered the battalion forward, and the paratroops rushed to the sounds of gunfire. Before the Germans finally drove them out of Noville, the battalion suffered two hundred casualties. But they had helped thrash the 2nd Panzer Division.

The great strength of the M18 Hellcat was its size, agility, and speed. If used to maximum effect, it could be a very difficult opponent for a Panther or Tiger crew.

The 2nd Panzer Division lost thirty-five of its tanks taking Noville. This Panzer IV was opened like a tin can by an American antitank weapon.

Dead German panzergrenadiers littered the open fields after the battle for Noville. Some five hundred were killed or wounded in the pitched fighting for the town.

As the fighting raged outside the city limits, the din of battle convinced many of the remaining Belgian families to abandon their homes and get out of Bastogne.

men loaded Desobry into an ambulance, which sped off for Bastogne, but ran into Germans south of Noville, who captured the colonel and the vehicle's other occupants. The fighting continued through the night. But the Americans held.

The next morning, the Germans tried again. At 5:30 a.m., Lauchert launched the bulk of his division at Team Desobry and the 506th PIR. The battle grew desperate. Communication with Bastogne became problematical. Team Desobry's surviving eight Shermans ran low on AP ammunition, and one panzer charge was only repelled with the help of twelve M18 Hellcats and their 76mm cannon.

As the defenders of Noville clung to their positions, the 2nd Panzer Division outflanked them and drove the 3rd Battalion, 506th PIR, out of Foy. This cut Noville off from the rest of the Bastogne garrison, a situation that demanded an immediate response. McAuliffe ordered Foy retaken, and in the afternoon he told Team Desobry and the 1st Battalion, 506th, to get out of Noville. The counterattack at Foy succeeded in temporarily recapturing the town. Meanwhile, Team Desobry and the paratroopers fought their way south. By the time the battle ended late that afternoon, the 1st Battalion, 506th, had lost over two hundred men killed, wounded, and missing. Team Desobry also lost about two hundred men, along with five Shermans, twelve half-tracks, and a platoon of Hellcats.

As grim as these casualties were, Lauchert's 2nd Panzer Division suffered even worse. Beneath thirty-five funeral pyres burned some of the best tanks in the division. Scattered around their ruined hulks lay the corpses of over five hundred panzer grenadiers. The fighting at Noville cost the 2nd Panzer two days and almost half its armor and a battalion of infantry.

Private William J. Ottersbach, a Kentucky native, cleans his rifle during a lull in the fighting around Bastogne. Ottersbach belonged to the 3rd Battalion, 327th Glider Infantry Regiment. The photo was taken by Pfc. E. J. Martin from the 162nd Signal Company.

Men of the 10th Armored Division stand guard over some German prisoners taken at Mageret.

Searching for survivors buried in the ruins of a building that collapsed during a German bombardment of Bastogne.

The ruins of Bastogne.

Lauchert wanted to pursue the retreating Americans. He saw a chance to strike at Bastogne from the north and take it with a swift coup de main while its defenders were still disorganized in this sector. Lüttwitz refused to allow it. He ordered Lauchert to take his division west to continue the race to the Meuse.

By now, the 2nd Panzer Division was low on fuel. Throwing together what units he could, Lauchert followed orders and drove west. His lead units crossed the Ourthe River and then ran out of gas.

Without capturing Bastogne, getting fuel to the panzer spearheads would be an agonizingly slow process. The back-country roads around the city were muddy swamps that bogged down the soft-skinned vehicles trailing behind the fighting elements.

As the 2nd Panzer Division struggled north of Bastogne, Panzer Lehr swung around to the south and tried to penetrate the American defenses there. On the afternoon of December 19, Kampfgruppe Fallois drove headlong into Team O'Hara dug in at Wardin. The Germans managed to push the 10th Armored Division element out of the town, but O'Hara's men rallied at Marvie and drove off further attacks.

That night, Fritz Bayerlein ordered Kampfgruppe Poschinger to attack from the east into Bastogne. By now, part of the 26th Volksgrenadier Division had arrived on the scene. Its men assaulted the American lines at Bizory.

The twin attacks failed. The 101st held firm. As a result, Lüttwitz gave Bayerlein permission to bypass Bastogne to the south. Leaving behind Kampfgruppe Hauser to support the 26th Volksgrenadier Division, the rest of Panzer Lehr drove around Bastogne and rolled west through the snow and mud. On the 21st, Bayerlein's tanks reached the Ourthe River, and here his lead units ran out of gas. The race to the Meuse would have to wait until the Germans took Bastogne.

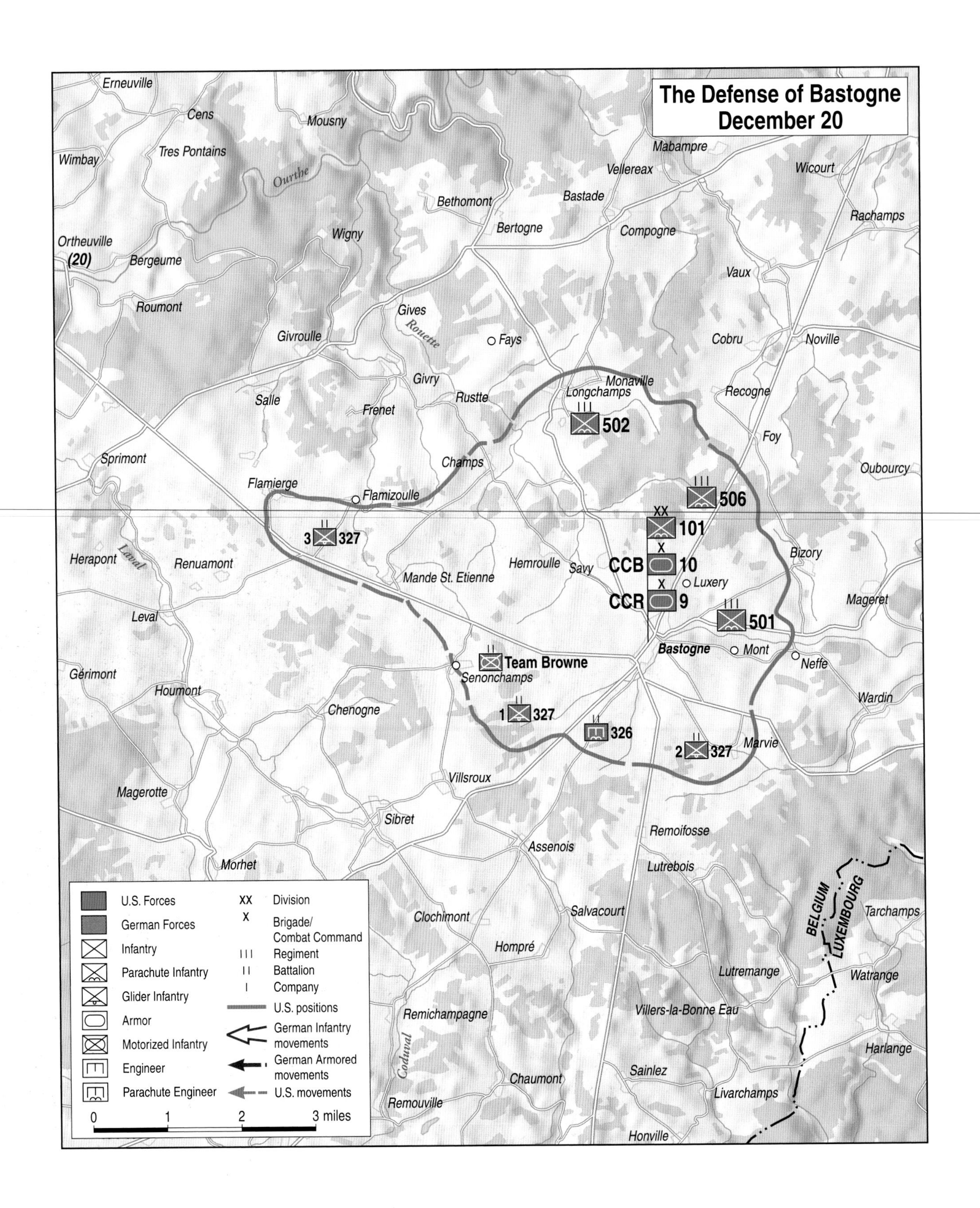
The Defense of Bastogne
December 20
Erneuville
Cens
Mousny
Wimbay
Tres Pontains
Ourthe
Mabampre
Vellereax
Wicourt
Bethomont
Bastade
Rachamps
Bertogne
Compogne
Ortheuville
(20)
Bergeume
Wigny
Vaux
Roumont
Gives
Rouette
Fays
Givroulle
Cobru
Noville
Givry
Monaville
Longchamps
Recogne
Salle
Frenet
Rustte
502
Foy
Sprimont
Champs
Oubourcy
Flamierge
Flamizoulle
506
101
3
327
Herapont
Laval
Renuamont
Hemroulle
Savy
CCB
10
Bizory
Mande St. Etienne
Luxery
CCR
9
Mageret
501
Leval
Bastogne
Mont
Neffe
Team Browne
Gérimont
Senonchamps
Houmont
Wardin
Chenogne
1
327
326
2
327
Marvie
Villsroux
Magerotte
Sibret
Remoifosse
Assenois
Morhet
Lutrebois
BELGIUM
LUXEMBOURG
Tarchamps
Clochimont
Salvacourt
Hompré
Lutremange
Watrange
Villers-la-Bonne Eau
Remichampagne
Harlange
Coduval
Sainlez
Chaumont
Livarchamps
Remouville
Honville
U.S. Forces
German Forces
Infantry
Parachute Infantry
Glider Infantry
Armor
Motorized Infantry
Engineer
Parachute Engineer
XX Division
X Brigade/ Combat Command
III Regiment
II Battalion
I Company
U.S. positions
German Infantry movements
German Armored movements
U.S. movements
0 1 2 3 miles

Now surrounded by two panzer divisions plus the 26th Volksgrenadier Division, McAuliffe's men faced a critical lack of key supplies. First, the fighting over the past few days drained Bastogne's ammunition stocks. Draconian rationing of the remaining supply took place, and each gun was allowed to fire only ten rounds a day. Worse, hundreds of wounded GIs lay in aid stations around the city, but most of the 10th Armored Division's medical personnel and supplies had been captured by Panzer Lehr when it hooked around Bastogne on its way to the Meuse. The wounded suffered without adequate treatment for days, and the aid stations became grimly overcrowded as the fighting continued.

The paratroopers holding the perimeter also faced critical shortages of mortar and machine gun ammunition. The 10th Armored Division gave McAuliffe's men what it could, but the ammo situation remained critical. Another few days, and the airborne troops would be forced to throw rocks to stave off the Germans.

On Christmas Day in Bastogne, men of the 101st walk past dead paratroopers who were killed the night before.

While McAuliffe's command included ample artillery, Bastogne soon ran critically short of ammunition for the guns. McAuliffe was forced to ration the dwindling stock on hand, and at its worst, the guns were limited to fewer than ten shells per day.

Taking care of the wounded inside Bastogne became extraordinarily difficult after the Germans surrounded the town and overran the 10th Armored Division's medical personnel. Supplies ran low, and there was a shortage of surgeons, doctors, and nurses.

Cold and dirty, but resolute, men of the 101st pick up rations and supplies inside Bastogne, then head back to the frontline foxholes to share their finds with their buddies.

A glider has just brought in a load of ammo for the Bastogne's Long Toms. Once the weather cleared on the 23rd, the artillery ammunition situation improved a little bit. The 101st brought in glider-loads full of 105mm and 155mm shells for the big guns.

Yet, on the other side of the lines, the Germans faced their own issues. Many of the panzers around the city were immobilized with empty fuel tanks. The supply convoys carrying gas to them crawled along narrow lanes and could not adequately support the divisions in the area. Ammunition and food grew scarce as well.

On December 22, Bayerlein decided to try to take Bastogne through a ruse. He drafted a letter to McAuliffe. In it, he stressed that the Americans in the city were now surrounded and faced annihilation from an entire corps of artillery. He gave McAuliffe two hours to surrender; otherwise Bayerlein threatened to unleash his artillery and demolish Bastogne through sheer weight of firepower.

Bayerlein gave the letter to a pair of staff officers, who approached the American lines at 11:30 a.m. under a flag of truce. When they delivered the letter to McAuliffe, the pugnacious general simply replied, "Nuts!" The response puzzled the pair of German officers, who were led back to the front lines by Col. Joseph W. Harper, the commander of the 327th Glider Infantry Regiment. As they departed, one of the Germans asked what McAuliffe's reply meant. Harper answered, "It's the same as 'Go to hell!'"

He paused for a moment as the Germans digested this, then added, "And I'll tell you something else: If you continue your attack, we'll kill every goddamned German who tries to break into this city."

The German saluted, said that many Americans would die in the fighting to come. Unfazed, Colonel Harper replied, "On your way, Bud. And good luck to you." He later wished he'd never said that last line.

Old Crock had called Fritz's bluff.

Exhausted German prisoners are marched through Bastogne.

The American generals who ran the campaign in Western Europe. Front row (left to right): George S. Patton, Omar Bradley, Dwight D. Eisenhower, and Courtney Hodges. Second row: Keen, Charles H. Corlett, J. Lawton Collins, Leonard Gerow, and Elwood "Pete" Quesada. Third row: Allen, Hart, and Tjoraon.

19

ROOSEVELT'S HIGHEST-PAID BUTCHERS

WHILE THE FIGHTING TOOK SHAPE AROUND BASTOGNE, the senior American leadership in theater gathered at Verdun to discuss the brewing crisis. During the meeting, Eisenhower asked General Patton how long it would take for him to strike north from France and relieve Bastogne.

Patton replied that he could have three divisions attacking north in forty-eight hours. The other generals around the table guffawed. Eisenhower blurted, "Don't be fatuous, George!"

The truth was, George Patton recognized an opportunity the moment the Germans crashed into the Ardennes. His Third Army sat on the southern side of the Bulge, and the farther west the Germans went, the deeper they stuck their head in a noose, as far as Patton was concerned. Before the Verdun conference, he had his staff begin to make plans to turn III Corps north with the intent of counterattacking into the Bulge's exposed southern underbelly. If the First Army could do the same thing, the two forces could meet in the middle and cut off the Sixth and Fifth Panzer Armies. The German forces on the western front would be decimated.

For now, though, Bastogne needed to be relieved. Getting to McAuliffe would be the immediate objective.

Over the next two days, the III Corps disengaged from the front in Eastern France, crossed behind several other Third Army divisions, and took up assault positions south of Bastogne. They accomplished all of this in a heavy snow storm. And true to his word, Patton was ready to counterattack by December 21.

To lead the attack, Patton selected his pet division. The 4th Armored had come into France via Utah Beach. It saw heavy combat in the Normandy bocage and later took part in the race across France. The men of the 4th soon earned a stellar reputation for professionalism, deadliness, and speed. In fact, the German propaganda machine took a special dislike to the 4th. In radio broadcasts, the Nazis called the division "Roosevelt's highest-paid butchers."

continued on page 253

Ike and Patton had a prickly relationship, but they needed each other. At the Verdun conference, Patton shocked Ike by promising to launch a three-division counterattack against the southern flank of the German penetration within two days.

Verdun was the fortress city that in 1916 became the site of one history's bloodiest battles. During the first days of the Bulge, Eisenhower sat down with his senior leaders to work out the American reaction to Hitler's desperate gambit.

Private Ken Boyer of Rome, New York, served as a gunner with Patton's most favored unit, the 4th Armored Division. Boyer belonged to the 37th Tank Battalion.

Captain J. F. Brady, another New Yorker from Long Island, led Company R, 35th Tank Battalion, across France during the fall of 1944. The 4th Armored saw considerable combat before the Bulge, gaining Patton's trust with its speed and fierce spirit. Brady had earned two Purple Hearts and a Silver Star by early October alone.

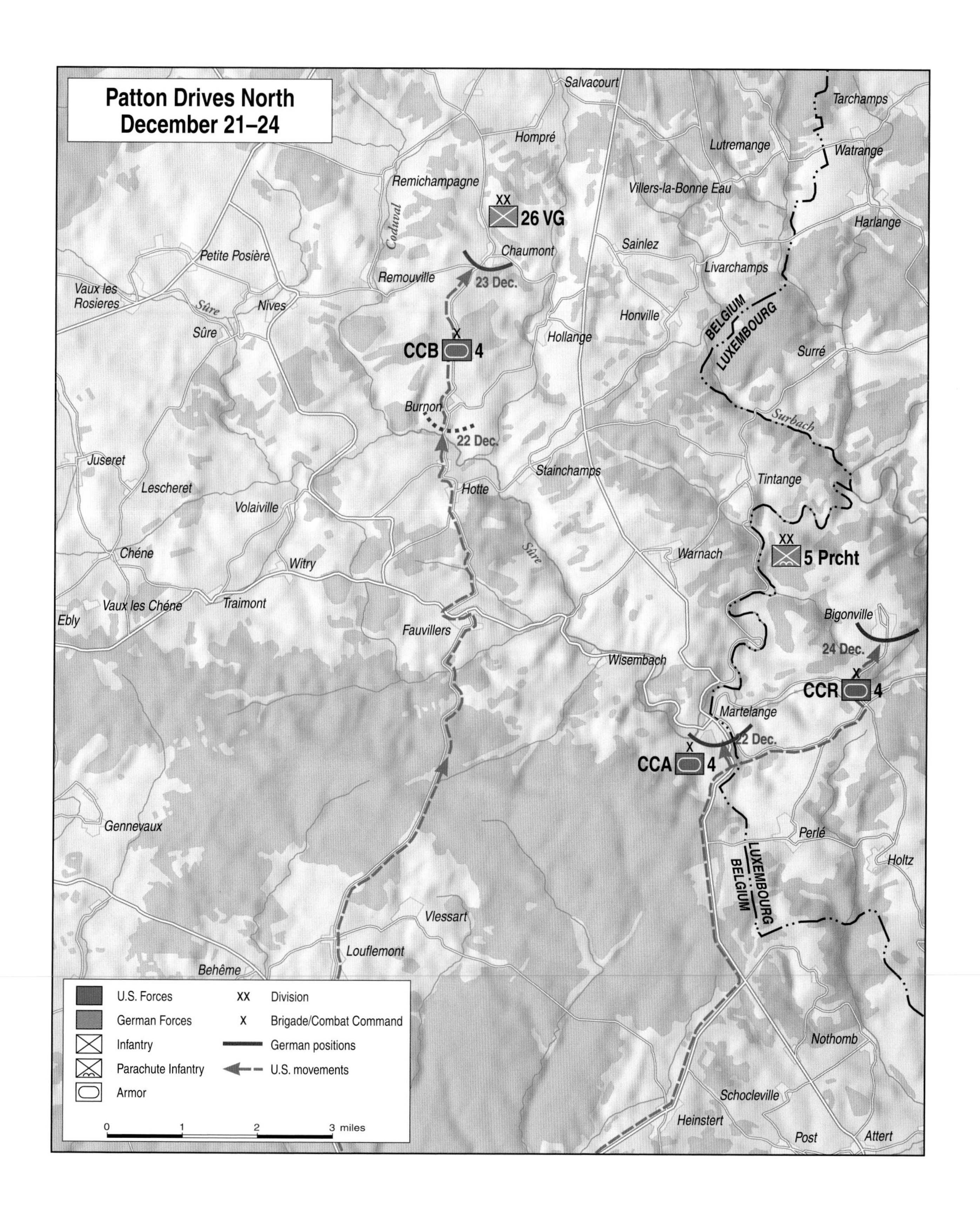
Patton Drives North
December 21–24
Salvacourt
Tarchamps
Hompré
Lutremange
Watrange
Remichampagne
Villers-la-Bonne Eau
XX
26 VG
Harlange
Coduval
Sainlez
Chaumont
Petite Posière
Livarchamps
Remouville
23 Dec.
Vaux les Rosieres
Sûre
Nives
Honville
BELGIUM
LUXEMBOURG
Sûre
CCB
4
Hollange
Surré
Burnon
Surbach
22 Dec.
Juseret
Stainchamps
Tintange
Lescheret
Hotte
Volaivile
XX
5 Prcht
Warnach
Chéne
Sûre
Witry
Bigonville
Vaux les Chéne
Traimont
Ebly
Fauvillers
24 Dec.
Wisembach
CCR
4
Martelange
22 Dec.
CCA
4
Perlé
Gennevaux
LUXEMBOURG
BELGIUM
Holtz
Vlessart
Louflemont
Behême
U.S. Forces
German Forces
Infantry
Parachute Infantry
Armor
XX Division
X Brigade/Combat Command
German positions
U.S. movements
Nothomb
Schocleville
Heinstert
Post
Attert
0
1
2
3 miles

An M4 Sherman of the 8th Tank Battalion, 4th Armored Division, crosses a canal during the drive across France. The 4th Armored Division moved fast and hit hard.

Creighton Abrams (right) stands next to the tank he drove into Bastogne. Abrams commanded the 37th Tank Battalion, 4th Armored Division. It was his unit that ultimately reached Bastogne first during Patton's counteroffensive against the south side of the Bulge.

continued from page 249

Another time, the Germans derisively labeled Creighton Abrams, commander of the 4th Armored Division's 37th Tank Battalion, a Jew. Abrams wasn't a Jew, but he asked American reporters not to let the Germans know about that.

When Patton called on the 4th Armored that December, the division didn't let him down. In nineteen hours, the 4th covered 150 miles through snow flurries to get into position to lead the attack to Bastogne. That in itself was a logistical masterpiece, one of the greatest of the war in Europe.

Joining the 4th Armored were two veteran units, the 80th and the 26th Infantry Divisions. The 26th had a long history of killing Germans—it spent 210 days in combat during World War I and took part in both the Saint-Mihiel and Meuse-Argonne Offensives. Two decades later, the sons of the Great War vets of the Yankee Division landed in France once again. Entering combat in October, the 26th proved to be a tough, effective unit. It also happened to be a federalized National Guard unit, composed of men from Maine, Rhode Island, Vermont, New Hampshire, Massachusetts, and Connecticut.

The 80th was a draftee division, largely made up of men from West Virginia, Pennsylvania, Maryland, and Virginia. The "Blue Ridgers" had joined the fight in France during the final stages of the Normandy breakout in August. During the fierce fighting in Eastern France in the fall of 1944, the 80th proved to be one of the best infantry outfits in the entire Third Army.

Side by side, the three divisions launched Patton's counterattack on December 21 along a thirty-mile front. Facing them were elements of the German Seventh Army, tasked with moving west and covering Manteuffel's southern flank, just in case the Third Army did try to

A member of the 26th Infantry Division, another National Guard unit, rushes for cover during the bloody battle for Aachen. The Yankee Division saw extensive combat prior to Patton's counteroffensive to relieve Bastogne.

A Browning M1919 light machine gun team in action during the Battle of Aachen. The 26th Infantry Division saw every type of close-quarters fighting during this battle, and by the time it joined Patton's counteroffensive against von Manteuffel's Fifth Army, its men were seasoned urban warriors.

A patrol from the 26th Infantry division is taken under fire. After the Bulge, the 26th took part in the drive into Germany and helped secure the Fulda Gap, which for future generations of American soldiers would become a key piece of European real estate.

GIs from the 317th Infantry Regiment, 80th Infantry Division, greet a young French girl during the drive to the German frontier in late August 1944. Another of Patton's blooded veterans, the men of the 80th Infantry Division, a draftee division, were selected by the general to spearhead the drive to Bastogne, along with the 26th ID and 4th Armored.A

intervene in the Ardennes. Colonel Ludwig Heilmann's 5th Fallschirmjäger Division would be III Corps' main adversary in the days to come. Arrogant, stubborn, and full of fight, Heilmann was an old-school paratrooper with extensive combat experience. He'd been cut off in Sicily and fought his way across fifteen miles of British-held territory to get back to German lines. Later, in Italy, Heilmann commanded the regiment of paratroopers who held the Abbey at Monte Cassino. He understood how the U.S. Army fought, and he knew how to fight a defensive battle.

South of Bastogne, Heilmann created a series of strong points along Patton's line of march. Fortifying small villages and road choke points, the fallschirmjägers dug in deep and waited for the American assault Heilmann knew would surely come soon. His job was to slow Patton down long enough so that the Fifth Panzer Army units besieging Bastogne could finally capture the city.

A new race took form between the 4th Armored Division's ability to forge a corridor to Bastogne before McAuliffe could be overrun. The race began on December 21. At first, III Corps made excellent progress. By noon the following day, the 4th Armored had covered half the distance to Bastogne. Twelve miles separated Patton's corps and McAuliffe's beleaguered defenders. But those dozen miles became a deadly gauntlet for the American tankers and armored infantrymen.

At a small town called Martelange, a die-hard company of fallschirmjägers blew up a vital bridge over the Sure River, then held out until 3:00 a.m., December 23, before being driven off. It took Combat Command A, 4th Armored, all day on the 23rd to get across the Sure River.

Men of the 26th Infantry Division prepare to assault north into von Manteuffel's left flank.

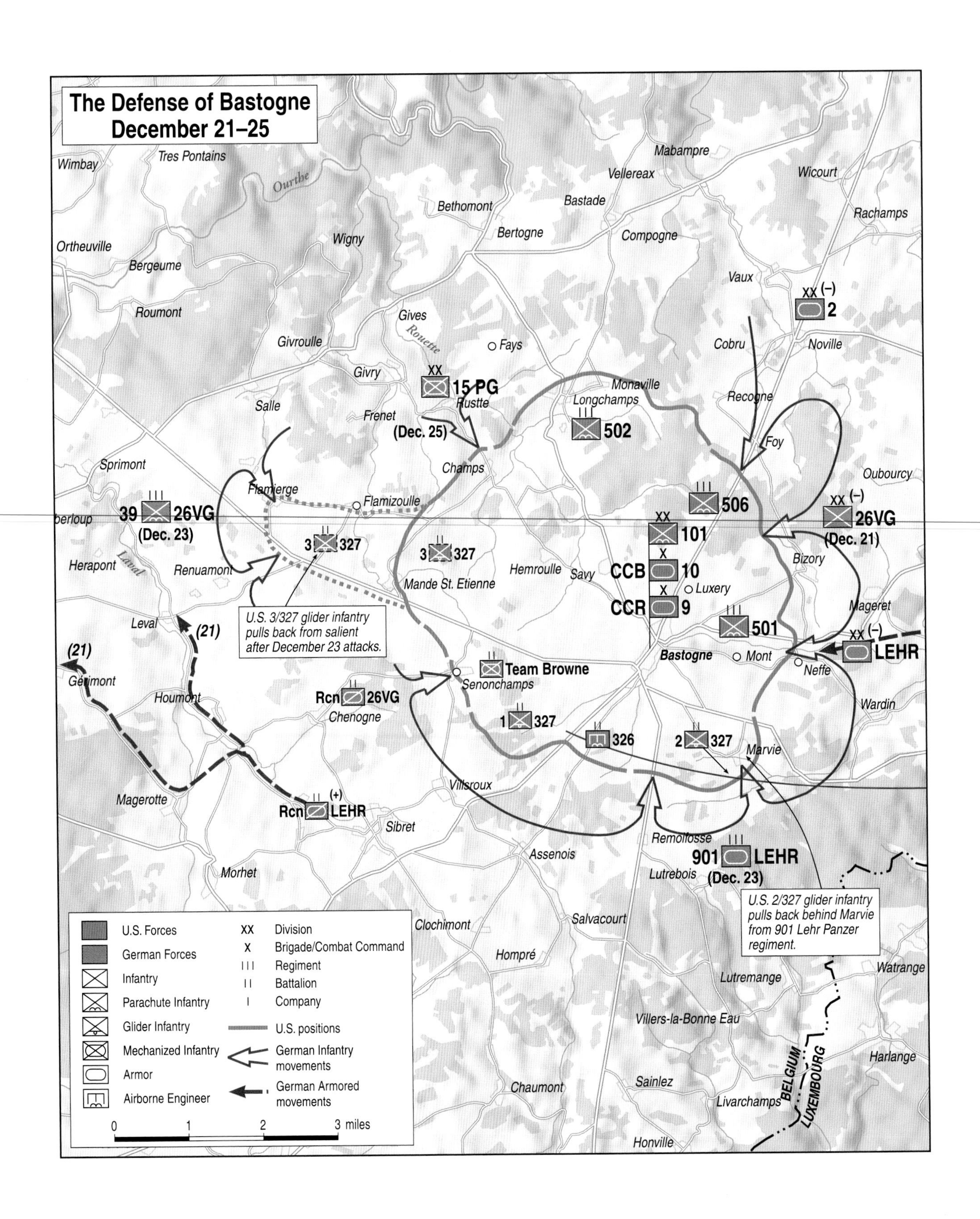

The Defense of Bastogne
December 21–25
Wimbay
Tres Pontains
Ourthe
Bethomont
Bastade
Mabampre
Vellereax
Wicourt
Rachamps
Ortheuville
Bergeume
Wigny
Bertogne
Compogne
Vaux
Roumont
Gives
Rouette
Fays
Givroulle
Cobru
Noville
XX (–) 2
Givry
XX 15 PG
Rustte
(Dec. 25)
Salle
Frenet
Monaville
Longchamps
502
Recogne
Foy
Champs
Sprimont
Flamierge
Flamizoulle
Oubourcy
39 26VG
(Dec. 23)
erloup
506
XX 101
XX (–) 26VG
(Dec. 21)
3 327
3 327
Herapont
Laval
Renuamont
Mande St. Etienne
Hemroulle
Savy
X CCB 10
X CCR 9
Luxery
Bizory
Leval
(21)
(21)
U.S. 3/327 glider infantry pulls back from salient after December 23 attacks.
501
Mageret
XX (–) LEHR
Bastogne
Mont
Neffe
Gérimont
Team Browne
Senonchamps
Houmont
Rcn 26VG
Chenogne
Wardin
1 327
326
2 327
Marvie
Villsroux
Magerotte
Rcn LEHR (+)
Sibret
Remoifosse
901 LEHR
(Dec. 23)
Assenois
Lutrebois
Morhet
U.S. 2/327 glider infantry pulls back behind Marvie from 901 Lehr Panzer regiment.
Clochimont
Salvacourt
Hompré
Watrange
Lutremange
Villers-la-Bonne Eau
Harlange
Chaumont
Sainlez
Livarchamps
BELGIUM
LUXEMBOURG
Honville
U.S. Forces
German Forces
Infantry
Parachute Infantry
Glider Infantry
Mechanized Infantry
Armor
Airborne Engineer
XX Division
X Brigade/Combat Command
III Regiment
II Battalion
I Company
U.S. positions
German Infantry movements
German Armored movements
0 1 2 3 miles

The 4th Armored Division heads north to relieve Bastogne.

The 35th Tank Battalion drives north. The 4th Armored ran into stiff resistance from German fallschirmjägers attached to the Seventh Army. The Seventh's job was to cover Manteuffel's southern flank as his units raced for the Meuse.

Nearby, Combat Command B ran into similar problems at Bondorf, where another bridge was blown. The German paratroops held the village all day on the 22nd and fought on even after Combat Command B surrounded them. Finally, out of ammunition, the fallschirmjägers surrendered. Combat Command B took four hundred prisoners.

Pressing on, Combat Command B captured Burnon on the morning of the 23rd. Chaumont, the next village en route to Bastogne, turned out to be heavily defended by elements of the 14th Fallschirmjäger Regiment, reinforced by a number of 88mm flak guns. The 4th

At Chaumont, Combat Command B, 4th Armored Division, ran into heavy resistance from the 14th Fallschirmjäger Regiment, which was supported by 88mm flak guns that played havoc on attacking American tanks.

The 4th Armored at Chaumont. A dead American lies in the foreground as the advance continues.

At Warnach, German paratroopers caught elements of Combat Command A's armored infantrymen in soft-skinned trucks like this one. Packed into the back of these vulnerable rigs, the infantrymen suffered dreadfully.

Armored called in fighter bombers, who savaged Chaumont with bombs and .50-caliber machine gun fire. Even so, it took until the afternoon for Combat Command B to clear the town and continue the advance north.

Before the Americans got far, Heilmann counterattacked with almost thirty Sturmgeschütz III assault guns. Strongly supported by fallschirmjägers, the armored onslaught threw Combat Command B back in disarray. Chaumont was lost to Heilmann's Luftwaffe troops, and the 4th Armored Division left eleven Shermans burning around the village by nightfall.

The next day, Combat Command B tried to retake Chaumont. The fighting lasted all day, and still the Germans clung to the village as the sun set.

Nearby, Combat Command A ran into even worse trouble. After taking Martelange, its tanks and armored infantry rolled into Warnach. At first, it appeared the village was deserted, and the lead Shermans passed through it without interference. Moments later, the command's infantry motored into town aboard unarmored trucks. Suddenly, fallschirmjägers appeared in windows and doorways to lace their vehicles and shoot up the men as they bailed out of their rigs.

The close-quarters street fight grew chaotic and exceptionally violent. The Shermans retuned to town and blasted away at the German paratroops from point-blank range. Room to room, house to house, the Americans fought their skilled and deadly foe. The Germans, by now experts at urban warfare, kept infiltrated behind the Americans. A few snipers or a machine gun team would get into a house that Combat Command A had already cleared. Lying low, the Germans would wait until an opportune moment to open fire and surprise the Americans with small-arms fire from their supposedly safe rear area. It wasn't until lunchtime on Christmas Eve that Warnach finally fell into American hands for good.

continued on page 263

Stiff resistance from the fallschirmjägers stalled the 4th Armored Division's advance. To get the offensive going again, something creative needed to be done.

101st Airborne troops attend a Christmas service in Bastogne. As the 4th Armored Division struggled to reach Bastogne, the city's defenders spent Christmas Day beating back another major German attack and then tried to celebrate as best they could.

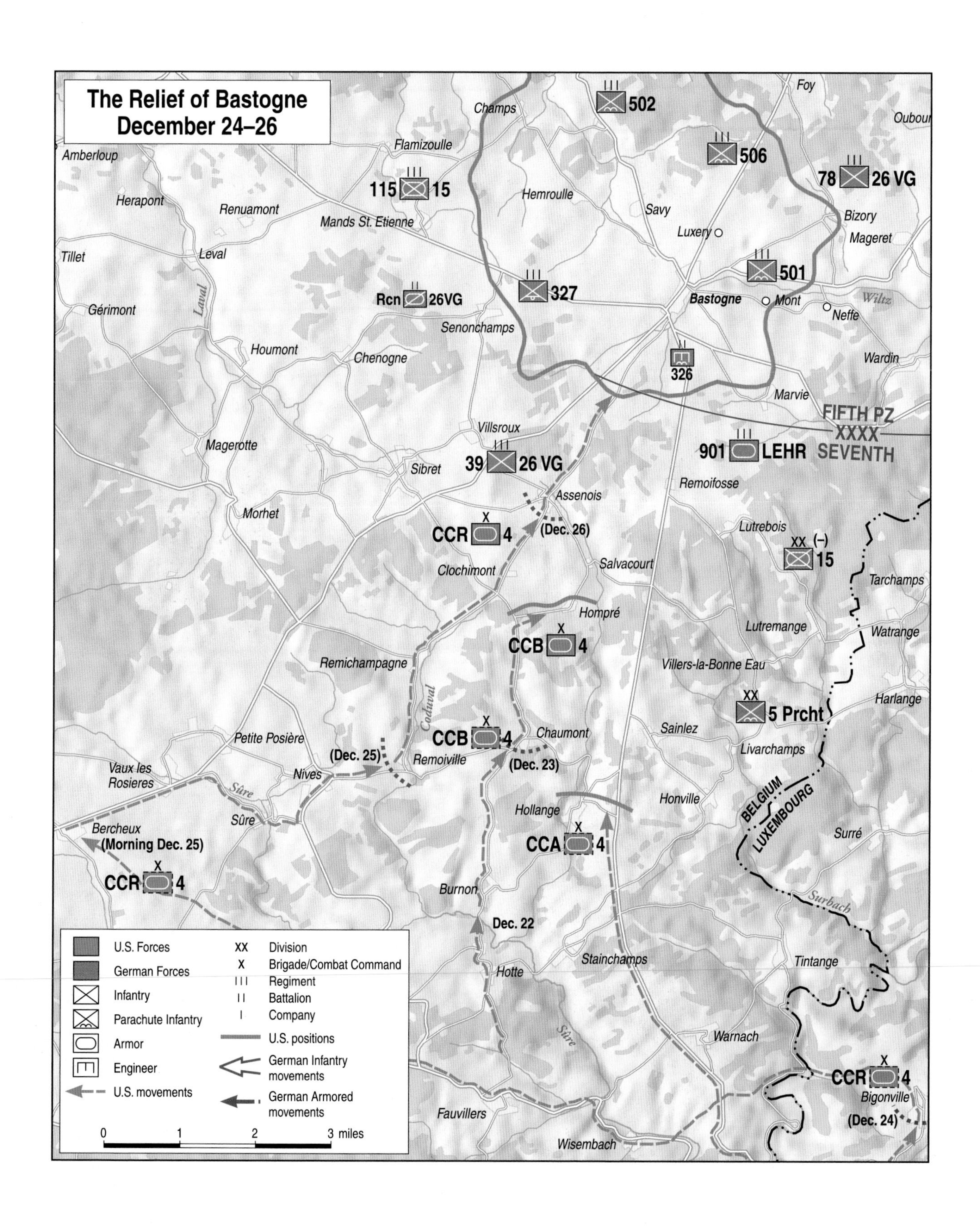
The Relief of Bastogne
December 24–26
Champs
502
Foy
Oubour
Flamizoulle
506
78
26 VG
Amberloup
115
15
Hemroulle
Herapont
Renuamont
Savy
Bizory
Mands St. Etienne
Luxery
Mageret
Tillet
Leval
501
Rcn
26VG
327
Bastogne
Mont
Neffe
Wiltz
Gérimont
Laval
Senonchamps
Houmont
Chenogne
326
Wardin
Marvie
FIFTH PZ
XXXX
SEVENTH
Villsroux
Magerotte
901
LEHR
39
26 VG
Sibret
Remoifosse
Assenois
Morhet
CCR
4
(Dec. 26)
Lutrebois
15
Clochimont
Salvacourt
Tarchamps
Hompré
CCB
4
Lutremange
Watrange
Remichampagne
Villers-la-Bonne Eau
Harlange
Coduval
5 Prcht
Petite Posière
CCB
4
Chaumont
Sainlez
(Dec. 25)
Remoiville
(Dec. 23)
Livarchamps
Vaux les Rosieres
Nives
Sûre
Honville
BELGIUM
LUXEMBOURG
Sûre
Hollange
Bercheux
(Morning Dec. 25)
CCA
4
Surré
CCR
4
Burnon
Surbach
Dec. 22
Stainchamps
Tintange
Hotte
Sûre
Warnach
CCR
4
Bigonville
(Dec. 24)
Fauvillers
Wisembach
U.S. Forces
German Forces
Infantry
Parachute Infantry
Armor
Engineer
U.S. movements
XX Division
X Brigade/Combat Command
III Regiment
II Battalion
I Company
U.S. positions
German Infantry movements
German Armored movements
0
1
2
3 miles

Resupplying Bastogne became much easier after the weather broke on December 23. For days, the C-47s of the Ninth Air Force delivered hundreds of tons of ammunition, medical supplies, and rations.

continued from page 259

Patton's counteroffensive had bogged down. Bastogne hung in the balance. It looked like the Germans might win this fight after all.

At 3:30 a.m., the Germans launched another bid for Bastogne. Heilmann's masterful defense had given Manteuffel time to bring up the fresh 15th Panzergrenadier Division, whose men were well-blooded veterans of the Italian campaign.

The division struck Bastogne from the northwest, hitting a seam between the 501st Parachute Infantry Regiment and the 327th Glider Infantry Regiment. The division's panzers rolled right over a company of glider infantry and fanned out behind the American frontlines, searching for targets of opportunity. Moments later, assault waves of panzer grenadiers closed with the glider men and ran smack into a wall of firepower. As dawn broke over the frozen landscape, both sides refused to give up. The 327th took severe losses, but the panzer grenadiers did not shatter the regiment. Nearby, the 501st gave ground, but it didn't crack either.

Meanwhile, teams of fast-moving M18 Hellcats sought out the Panzers roaming in the 101st Airborne's rear. Sharp tank battles erupted in the woods behind Rolle as panzer after panzer was brought to bay. Some ran afoul of prowling Hellcats. Others stumbled across 105mm howitzers, dug in to support the paratroopers. The gun crews fired over open sights and took out several German tanks. Lacking infantry support, the panzers also fell prey to bazooka-armed Screaming Eagles. By the time the assault ended, the 15th Panzergrenadier Division had lost hundreds of grenadiers and all eighteen of the panzers that had broken through the lines. McAuliffe's men had held once again.

By Christmas afternoon, things were looking up for Bastogne's defenders. The Germans had launched two attacks in the past two days. On the 23rd, Kampfgruppe Hauser overran a company from the 327th Glider Infantry and captured Hill 500 near Marvie on the south side of the perimeter. But the Germans couldn't exploit that success, and the attack failed. The Christmas morning assault turned into a fiasco.

Besides weathering these attacks, the garrison benefitted from a sudden weather change. On the night of the December 22–23 the temperature dropped precipitously and the skies cleared up. The ground around Bastogne froze, allowing armored units to move across country at last. More importantly, clear skies enabled air support. All day long, hundreds of C-47 transports delivered 441 tons of supplies. Gliders crash-landed inside the perimeter to bring much needed artillery ammunition to the howitzer crews. And behind the lines, Ninth Air Force fighter-bombers ranged out in search of German supply convoys. Over the next few days, they did so much damage that one German officer said at night the burning vehicles knocked out by the Thunderbolt squadrons stretched like a torchlight procession from Bastogne back to the Siegfried Line.

Hitler now became obsessed with Bastogne. Losing all perspective, he ordered the city taken at all costs. To make it happen, he sent word to Sepp Dietrich to redeploy the II SS Panzer Corps against Bastogne's northern flank. The Waffen-SS units began a long, perilous journey from the north side of the Bulge to the south, racing with Patton to get to Bastogne first.

The resupply effort delivered 441 tons of supplies on December 23 alone. The sight of American aircraft overhead once again energized the defenders and urged on Patton's divisions.

Men of the 4th Armored push on across open, rolling terrain during the final stages of the drive to Bastogne. With the ground frozen, the division's Shermans and other tracked vehicles could move cross-country. This helped restore mobility to the battlefield and played a major role in cracking the German defenses south of the city.

To get III Corps moving again, Gen. John Millikin swung the 4th Armored Division's Combat Command R behind the rest of the division, moving it from the right flank to the far left. It was a masterful stroke, and when CCR crushed the German defense at Remonville, the way to Bastogne had almost been opened.

III Corps had no time for recovering wrecked vehicles. Instead, they were simply pushed aside so the offensive could continue. Recovering could wait for later.

By Christmas Eve, III Corps's advance north had all but stalled. To get it moving again, the corps commander, Gen. John Millikin, decided to try a daring left hook against the far side of the 5th Fallschirmjäger Division's defensive line. For the past few days, Combat Command R, 4th Armored Division, had been engaged on Combat Command A's right flank at a town called Bigonville. Here, Combat Command R fought a pitched battle with dug-in Germans who only surrendered when they finally ran out of ammunition around lunchtime on Christmas Eve.

After Bigonville was cleared, Millikin ordered Combat Command R to swing west behind the rest of the 4th Armored Division and then pull up on the left flank of Combat Command B and strike north again. Colonel Wendell Blanchard, Combat Command R's commander, relished the opportunity. He led his command to the left with great vigor. He also had learned a lesson from Bigonville: the German fallschirmjägers were going to defend every town and hamlet between his men and Bastogne. He took that lesson to heart.

On Christmas Day, Blanchard's men attacked. The first obstacle they came to was Remonville. Unsure if there were any German paratroopers in it, but not wanting to take any chances, Blanchard called down the wrath of God upon the small village. Four full battalions

GIs from the 4th and 10th Armored Divisions link up outside of Bastogne. By the morning of the 26th, the relief of the city was imminent. German resistance began to collapse, and the 4th Armored Division was able to break through at last.

of artillery blasted the place to smoldering rubble. When Combat Command R assaulted into town, they found a battalion of dazed fallschirmjägers who were unable to offer much resistance. Almost 330 of them surrendered by nightfall. Blanchard had pierced Heilmann's main line of resistance. Bastogne lay only four miles away.

The next day, the frozen ground allowed Combat Command R's Shermans to maneuver cross-country, a tactical advantage that played no small role in the successes of the day. In quick succession, Blanchard's men stormed Remichampagne and Clochimont. With P-47s swarming overhead, the 4th Armored Division rolled on for Assenois, the last obstacle between Combat Command R and Bastogne.

Here, a desperate and bloody fight developed. The town was held by elements of the 5th Fallschirmjäger Division as well as some volksgrenadiers. They made Combat Command R earn every house and building. Through the afternoon, the battle waxed and waned through the town. Both sides closed to grenade range, and in some cases the fighting devolved into room-to-room mini-engagements.

A 4th Armored Division 76mm-equipped Sherman is inspected by men of the 354th Fighter Group. These pilots had been providing close air support for III Corps once the weather had cleared.

More Germans are rounded up under the watchful eyes of an M4 crew.

Signs of a broken army.

With the armored infantry occupied, Blanchard tried to push his armor through town. Five Shermans and a half-track made a dash through the firefight. As they rolled north of the village, daring German soldiers dashed out into the road and threw Teller mines under the column. One exploded and destroyed the half-track, which caused the two trailing Shermans to lose contact with the lead three. The three in the van kept going, and they reached Bastogne at 4:50 p.m. on December 26. As they got into the city, McAuliffe was there to greet them. "Gee, I'm mighty glad to see you," he quipped.

Not long afterward, the Germans gave up at Assenois. Blanchard's men took another four hundred prisoners and then opened up the road to Bastogne so the first relief and supply columns could get into the city.

The siege of Bastogne had been lifted. And while there remained much fighting ahead, the arrival of the 4th Armored Division demolished the last hopes the Germans had of getting across the Meuse River.

Despondent German POWs march past an M2 half-track rolling forward to continue the counteroffensive.

Ike put Monty in charge of the Bulge's north shoulder, a move that provoked bitter reaction from Bradley. The decision made good military sense, since Bradley's communication lines with the northern units in the First Army had been overrun by the German advance. Nevertheless, Monty caused considerable friction, and his over-cautious nature did not sit well with the American offensive spirit once the shoulder had been stabilized.

20

THE PRICE OF OVER-CAUTION

IN THE DAYS THAT FOLLOWED THE RELIEF OF BASTOGNE, the Germans continued to fling their dwindling resources at Patton's Third Army and VIII Corps. By this time, the SS units as well as Manteuffel's panzer divisions were running out of able bodies and running tanks. Exhaustion and a chronic shortage of supplies and gas plagued the German spearheads as the Ninth Air Force immolated their logistical support units every time the weather cleared.

The day after the Verdun conference, Eisenhower took a drastic step and handed command of the First and Ninth Armies over to Field Marshal Bernard Law Montgomery, the controversial British hero of El Alamein and Normandy. Montgomery made some very wise tactical decisions in the days that followed, which helped strengthen the defense of the Bulge's northern shoulder. But when it came to offensive operations, Montgomery was born cautious. He also didn't understand how vastly superior American logistics were to what he was used to in the British Army. As a result, Eisenhower pushed for days for Monty to launch a counteroffensive while the Germans were fixated on Bastogne. When he finally did begin the offensive of January 3, 1945, Ike reportedly exclaimed, "Praise God from whom all blessings flow!"

A 26th Infantry Division GI smiles despite the freezing weather.

The problem was the offensive began too far to the west. The Americans had a golden opportunity to hit the Germans at both shoulders and pinch the Bulge off at its base. This would have bagged part of the Seventh Army along with the Fifth and Sixth Panzer Armies. Field Marshal Walter Model feared this was coming, as did Hitler. But Monty's cautious ways caused this opportunity to slip away.

In the weeks that followed, the Third Army and the First Army flattened out the Bulge and pushed the Germans east. The Lucky Seventh returned to Saint-Vith and recaptured the city on January 17. The Germans resisted fiercely, contesting every crossroads and every hard-won village. Nevertheless, even Hitler admitted defeat by the end of the first week of

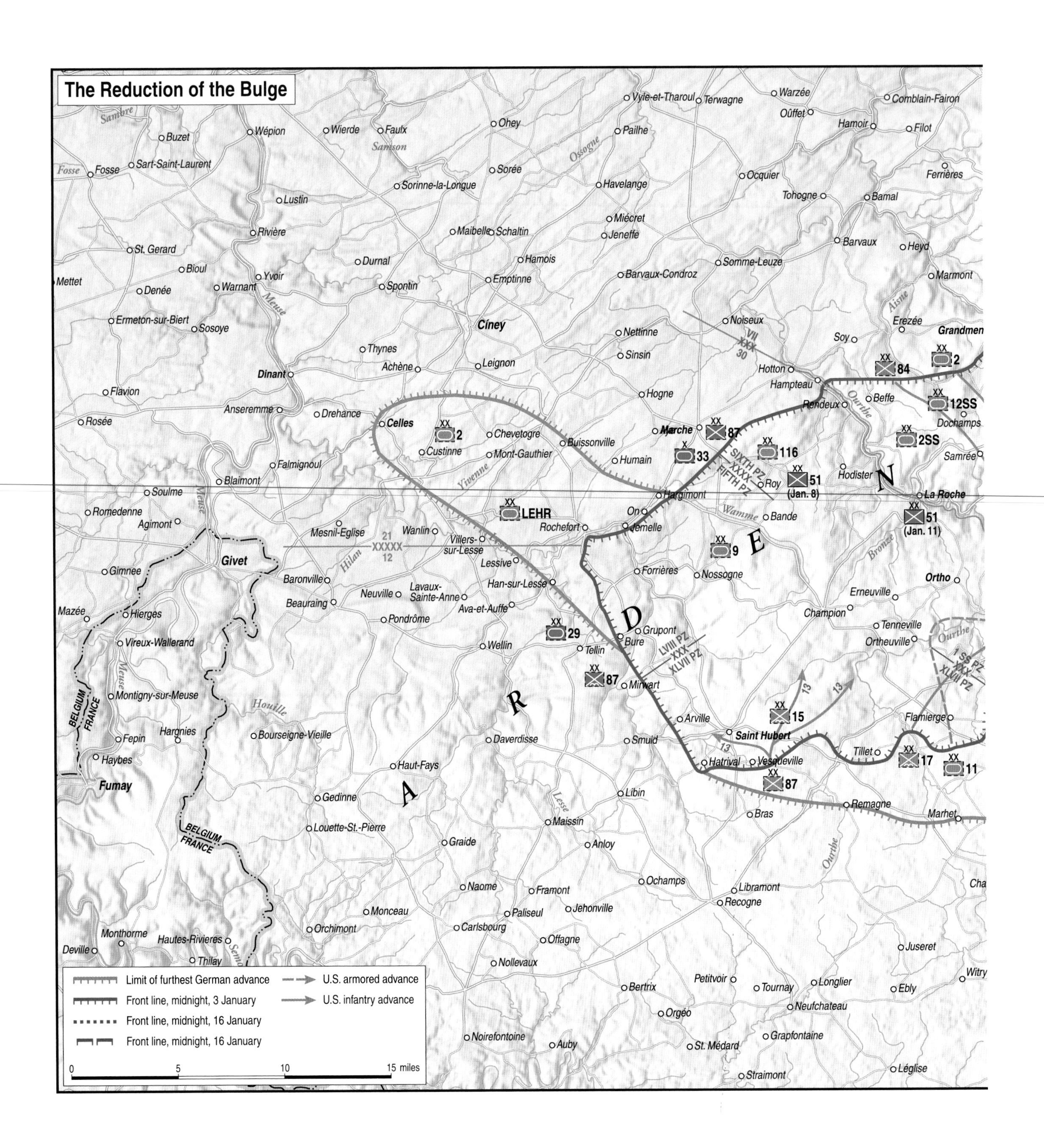
The Reduction of the Bulge
Limit of furthest German advance
Front line, midnight, 3 January
Front line, midnight, 16 January
Front line, midnight, 16 January
U.S. armored advance
U.S. infantry advance
0
5
10
15 miles
Dinant
Ciney
Marche
Celles
Rochefort
Givet
Fumay
Saint Hubert
La Roche
Hotton
Ortho
LEHR
(Jan. 8)
(Jan. 11)
SIXTH PZ
FIFTH PZ
BELGIUM
FRANCE
A
R
D
E
N

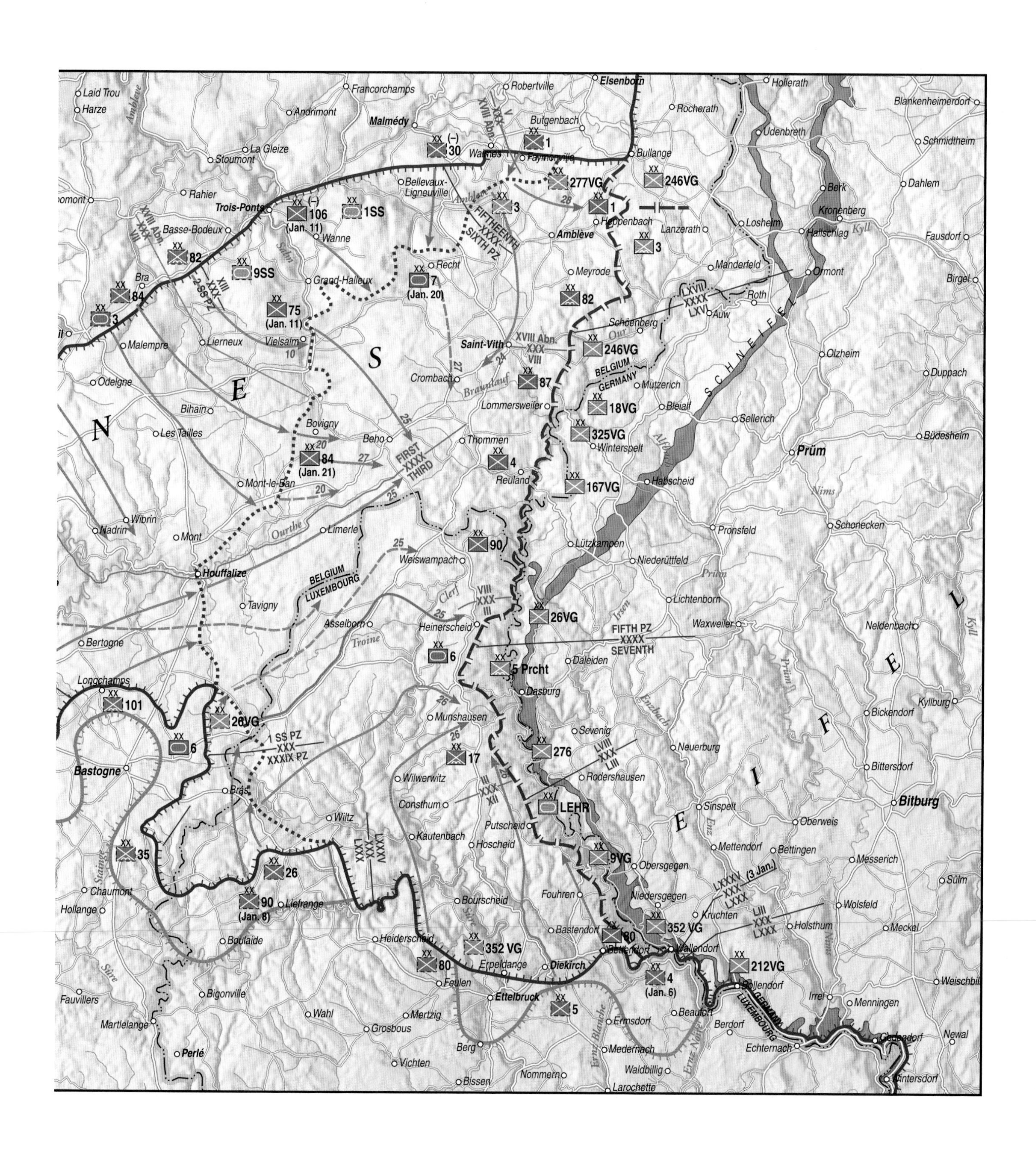
Laid Trou
Harze
Amblève
Andrimont
Francorchamps
Robertville
Elsenborn
Hollerath
Rocherath
Blankenheimerdorf
Malmédy
Butgenbach
Udenbreth
Schmidtheim
30
1
La Gleize
Stoumont
Waimes
Faymonville
Bullange
246VG
277VG
Bellevaux-Ligneuville
Dahlem
Rahier
Berk
Trois-Ponts
106
(Jan. 11)
1SS
3
1
Heppenbach
Losheim
Kronenberg
Hallschlag
Kyll
Fausdorf
Basse-Bodeux
Wanne
Amblève
Lanzerath
3
82
9SS
Recht
7
(Jan. 20)
Grand-Halleux
Meyrode
Manderfeld
Ormont
Birgel
Bra
84
3
75
(Jan. 11)
82
Roth
Auw
Schoenberg
Our
Vielsalm
Lierneux
Malempre
Saint-Vith
246VG
Olzheim
S
Crombach
Braunlauf
87
Duppach
Odeigne
E
Mutzerich
18VG
Bleialf
Lommersweiler
Bihain
N
Les Tailles
Bovigny
325VG
Winterspelt
Sellerich
Beho
Thommen
Büdesheim
84
(Jan. 21)
4
Reuland
Prüm
Mont-le-Ban
167VG
Habscheid
Nims
Wibrin
Nadrin
Mont
Ourthe
Limerle
90
Lützkampen
Pronsfeld
Schonecken
Weiswampach
Niederüttfeld
Houffalize
Prüm
Clerf
Lichtenborn
Tavigny
26VG
Irsen
Asselborn
Heinerscheid
Waxweiler
Neldenbach
Bertogne
Troine
6
Daleiden
5 Prcht
Dasburg
Longchamps
101
26VG
Munshausen
Sevenig
Kyllburg
Bickendorf
6
17
276
Neuerburg
Bastogne
Bras
Wilwerwitz
Rodershausen
Bittersdorf
Consthum
LEHR
Sinspelt
Bitburg
Wiltz
Putscheid
Oberweis
35
Kautenbach
Hoscheid
Mettendorf
Bettingen
26
9VG
Obersgegen
Messerich
Chaumont
90
(Jan. 8)
Liefrange
Bourscheid
Fouhren
Niedersgegen
Sülm
Hollange
Kruchten
Wolsfeld
Boulaide
Heiderscheid
352 VG
Bastendorf
80
352 VG
Holsthum
Meckel
80
Erpeldange
Diekirch
Bettendorf
Wallendorf
212VG
Sûre
Feulen
4
(Jan. 6)
Bollendorf
Weischbil
Bigonville
Ettelbruck
5
Irrel
Menningen
Fauvillers
Wahl
Mertzig
Ermsdorf
Beaufort
Berdorf
Martlelange
Grosbous
Berg
Medernach
Echternach
Newal
Perlé
Vichten
Waldbillig
Bissen
Nommern
Larochette
BELGIUM
GERMANY
BELGIUM
LUXEMBOURG
GERMANY
LUXEMBOURG
SCHNEIFEL
EIFEL
FIRST
XXXX
THIRD
FIFTHEENTH
XXXX
SIXTH PZ
FIFTH PZ
XXXX
SEVENTH
1 SS PZ
XXX
XXXIX PZ
LVIII
XXX
LIII
III
XXX
XII
VIII
XXX
III
XVIII Abn.
XXX
VIII
LXVII
XXXX
LXVI
LXXXV
XXX
LXXX
LIII
XXX
LXXX
(3 Jan.)

Members of the Waffen-SS fall into American hands. The failure of Hitler's last-gasp offensive devastated German morale on the Western Front.

January. He ordered Dietrich's Sixth Panzer Army out of the Bulge. It would be hastily refitted and sent back into battle a few weeks later in Hungary, where the Russians would ultimately destroy it.

By January 28, 1945, the Americans had returned to the December 15 starting lines. The Bulge had been erased. Neither side had scored a strategic victory, though both had opportunities to do so. In the end, the failure of the Ardennes offensive crushed Germany's last slender reed of hope that it could avoid invasion and end the war on its terms.

The cost of this last hope was brutally high. The Third Reich squandered almost twenty percent of its remaining tanks. The U.S. Army destroyed or captured half of the armored vehicles employed in the Ardennes Offensive. Somewhere between seventy thousand and one hundred thousand German soldiers and Waffen-SS troopers died, suffered wounds, and fell into American hands during the month of fighting in the Bulge.

The 82nd Airborne Division's artillery joined the barrage that started the general American counteroffensive in early January. Instead of pinching the Bulge off at its base—and bagging most of the Fifth and Sixth Panzer Armies in the process, Montgomery elected a more conservative approach and sought to flatten out the Bulge, driving west to east. It was another frustrating lost opportunity, part of the price of coalition warfare.

As the Germans were thrown back, P-47s and B-26 Marauders ranged behind the lines and savaged vehicle convoys, railheads, and road junctions.

A kiss on New Year's Day. A 3rd Infantry Division patrol liberating Havelange, Belgium, runs into a friendly local.

Revenge of the Lucky Seventh. Men of the 7th Armored Division pause in the snow outside Saint-Vith, whose defense claimed so many of their brothers the month before. In mid-January, the division recaptured the city in a bold offensive stroke.

With the Allies ascendant on the Western Front, the Third Reich stood no chance. The Russians were coming with a juggernaut of fire and steel, and they would show Germany no mercy. The Sixth SS Panzer Army was hastily refitted after the Bulge and sent east to try to stem the Soviet tide in Hungary. Instead, Dietrich's men faced annihilation.

A Panther lies on its back, demolished by American air power in the Bulge. The Germans lost half of their remaining panzers on the Western Front in a month of fighting in the Ardennes.

Such losses, combined with the desperate state of the Third Reich, devastated the Wehrmacht's morale on the Western Front. The average soldier understood that defeat was inevitable. Germany would soon be under foreign occupation.

The Americans suffered ghastly losses as well. The Ardennes cost America the lives of 10,276 of its sons. Another 47,493 returned home with Purple Hearts. Another 23,218 went missing or spent the war in Nazi POW camps.

By the fall of 1944, the U.S. Army was already struggling with an extreme shortage of trained riflemen. The Bulge turned the shortage into a crisis that ultimately had an unintended consequence. Desperate to fill the ranks, SHAEF reached into the logistics system and sought

Buddies from the 317th Infantry Regiment share a smoke at last. Staff Sgt. Abraham Aranoff and Pvt. Henry Beyer remained in the Bulge fighting with their regiment for twenty-seven straight days. Filthy and exhausted, they enjoyed a well deserved break. The photographer was M. H. Miller with the 167th Signal Company.

More wrecked and irreplaceable German armor lies in the mud of the Ardennes in the wake of the battle.

volunteers for frontline duty from the ranks of the segregated African-American transport units. Stalwart patriots stepped forward, believing they were finally going to get to break Army's color line once and for all. It didn't work out that way. Instead of integrating these black volunteers into white infantry companies, as was the original plan, provisional units were formed with black enlisted men and NCOs. A few African-American officers joined the ranks, but for the most part these provisional units were led by white officers. They were attached to infantry regiments and sent forward in time to fight their way across Germany in the spring of 1945.

The Battle of the Bulge will hopefully remain the largest battle ever fought by the United States Army. During the six weeks the battle lasted, the army endured an epic crisis, faced tremendous odds in local situations, and showed the world that the American fighting soldier

A GI helps a Sherman negotiate a narrow Belgian road. The poor condition of the roads in the Ardennes significantly affected the German offensive from the outset. Traffic jams delayed the advance, alternate routes frequently had to be found as vehicles bogged down in muddy lanes, and as the traffic stacked up, the panzers idled away their precious fuel supply.

The Battle of the Bulge exhausted the U.S. Army's ready supply of infantry replacements. A crisis developed that was never fully solved, and even as the American army drove into Germany, most of its frontline rifle companies remained perpetually under strength.

In response to the manpower crisis, African-American volunteers were allowed to join frontline infantry and armored divisions. Culled from the ranks of the logistical echelons, these men often took reductions in rank and pay to be able to join the fight.

Despite the deaths and wounding of their closest friends, the physical hardships, the omnipresent fear, and inadequate supplies, the American soldier prevailed, as always, with resolute spirit and irreverent humor.

could stand and take the worst punishment Hitler's elite formations could deal out. The story of the Bulge is the story of a crisis and how an Army and its character weathered that storm. Units broke. Others surrendered. There were cowards and shirkers, to be sure. But all along the line that winter, courage was not a rare commodity. Men like Col. Hurley Fuller, Lt. Col. Fred Cummings, and Pfc. Richard Cowan set the example with their spirit and resolve. In doing so, the defenders of the Ardennes established and reinforced a tradition of dogged self-sacrifice and valor. Such a hard-earned tradition has an immeasurable effect on any organization, and for the U.S. Army it serves today as part of the cornerstone of its sense of professionalism and dedication. Today, whenever American soldiers roll into battle, the ghosts of the Keystone Division, the Lucky Seventh, and the Blue Spaders ride with them. Their fighting spirit will always ensure that the heart of the United States Army beats strong and proud.

The Bulge remains the largest battle ever fought by the United States Army. The level of human misery experienced by the men in the frontlines has rarely been eclipsed. Between the weather and the German Army, surviving the Bulge tested every GI to his maximum psychological and physical endurance.

ACKNOWLEDGMENTS

THIS BOOK WAS ORIGINALLY SUPPOSED to be authored by Dana Lombardy and Eric Hammel. Through a variety of circumstances, the project fell to me to complete. There is no way I could have accomplished that without Dana's work at the National Archives and the photographs he acquired there. Eric Hammel's constant support and guidance aided the process tremendously. Eric, you are a close friend, and I especially appreciate everything you've done for me.

Richard Kane, who has been my editor or been involved in four of my fourteen books, is always long on patience and understanding. Richard, it is always an honor to be working with you, and over these years you've become a valued friend. I'm very glad we finally managed to have that cup of coffee. To Scott and everyone else at MBI who have made this book what it is, I know this project has been one that has probably caused hair loss, lack of sleep, and way more stress than was warranted. I want you all to know how much I appreciate your effort and your dedication to seeing the project to its completion. Whatever success it has will be your success.

It took enormous support from many individuals to conduct the research required for this book. Foremost, I'd like to thank my wife, Jennifer, and my children, Ed and Renee, for their patience while I spent many nights away from home working on this manuscript. To my folks, John and Judy Bruning, I thank you for opening your home to me while I was on the road so that I could continue writing.

Mark Flowers, my friend and colleague, offered plenty of input and suggestions on the manuscript. It has been a great pleasure working with you, Mark, in all our endeavors together. Mark is a veteran of the Gulf War and a superb historian of the German Army and the USMC as well.

To the entire 973rd COB cadre—Mark, Jones, Ox, KK, Kyle, Joey, Ben, Spencer, Taylor, Andrew, Joe, Aaron, Shaun, Travis, Tim, Bob, Brad, and everyone else—you guys are a constant inspiration to me. Your help and encouragement through this difficult project was especially valued. To see these tremendous Americans and the contribution they have made to preparing our soldiers for combat in the Middle East, please check out the organization's website at: http://973cob.org.

Shawna Akin and Eric Vinyard made sure my workspace was organized and clean. This is no small task when my office is frequently piled with all sorts of random stuff related to the 973rd's operations! Wading through a mix of training aids, stacks of paperwork, piles and piles of notes, books, printouts, and photographs is not for the organizationally impaired. Eric and Shawna, you make it look easy. Thank you both for everything you do for me.

Andy and Denice Scott, Brenda, and Kayla kept me going during long days. At night, Alex's crew around the corner from my office made sure I was fed. Kali, Amanda, John, Jessica, Jake, Jesse, Alex, Kiki, Samantha, y'all made sure I was well taken care of on those nights I lingered late after closing, writing on my laptop in the corner. Your kindness has always been appreciated. Thank you.

Lastly, I'd like to thank two more individuals for their faithful moral support. Donna Henderson and Julie Coching, I count you both among my most loyal and trusted friends. Thank you for all that you have done for me these many years.

BIBLIOGRAPHICAL NOTES

This book sits atop a vast historiography of the Ardennes Offensive that stretches back sixty-plus years. There have been hundreds, if not thousands, of books on the subject, many by truly great historians and writers. I've listed here some of the most outstanding or notable works.

The starting point for anyone interested in the Bulge has to be the Green Books. This is the U.S. Army's massive series on its operations in World War II. It is by far the best official history to emerge from any branch of service that saw action during the conflict. *The Ardennes: The Battle of the Bulge* by Hugh Cole is the volume that covers the last German offensive in the West. It is indispensable for researchers, historians, and interested readers alike.

Charles McDonald, who was not only a veteran of the battle (see his peerless memoir, *Company Commander,* for details) but also one of the great writers and historians to devote himself to the Bulge. His work *A Time for Trumpets* needs to be on every World War II enthusiast's shelf. Trevor Dupuy's *Hitler's Last Gamble* is another superb general history of the Bulge. Steve Zaloga, another outstanding historian, has written a two-volume overview of the Bulge for Osprey that is fact-packed as well as a quick and lively read: *Battle of the Bulge 1944 (1): St. Vith and the Northern Shoulder* and *Battle of the Bulge 1944 (2): Bastogne.* For a good general survey of the German side of the Bulge, Samuel Mitcham's book *Panzers in Winter* is a very useful work. For fascinating anecdotes, William Cavanagh's *A Tour of the Bulge Battlefield* cannot be beat. It is a fun and informative read with lots of local lore interwoven into a description of a driving tour of the battlefield.

Gerald Astor's book *A Blood-Dimmed Tide* is an enduring classic that provides many firsthand accounts of key moments in the Bulge. Astor's book gets into the nuts and bolts of what life was like for the soldiers in the snow like few books do. This one is also a must-have.

Though I disagree with much of what Russell Weigley concluded about the U.S. Army in Western Europe, his work *Eisenhower's Lieutenants* remains in a class of its own.

To understand the German side of the battle, there are ample works available. Charles Messenger's *Sepp Dietrich: Hitler's Gladiator* is an excellent study of the 6th SS Panzer Army commander. *Kampfgruppe Peiper at the Battle of the Bulge* by David Cooke and Wayne Evans chronicles the nefarious SS leader during the offensive. Charles Whiting's biography *Jochen Peiper* also is a useful reference.

There are two outstanding sources that detail the 82nd Airborne's operations in the Bulge. General James Gavin's *On to Berlin* is a truly engaging read. *All the Way to Berlin,* the memoir of James Megellas, is another must-have for anyone with an interest in the 82nd Airborne.

The 101st at Bastogne is well covered in Stephen Ambrose's famous work, *Band of Brothers.* For the story of the 28th Infantry Division on Skyline Drive, John McManus's book *Alamo in the Ardennes* is in a class of its own. Stanley Weintraub's *11 Days in December* is also a fine account of the climactic days at Bastogne.

For details on the defense of the Twin Villages, William Cavanagh's classic *The Battle East of Elsenborn* provides a depth of detail that is simply amazing. The German side of this action can be found in Hubert Meyer's *The 12th SS: The History of the Hitler Youth Panzer Division, Volume Two.*

Two fascinating books related to the 99th Infantry Division's experiences in the Bulge are George W. Neill's *Infantry Soldier* and Alex Kershaw's *The Longest Winter.*

For details on the saga of the 106th Infantry Division, see Trever Dupuy's *St. Vith: Lion In the Way.* Though dated, it is the standard work on the subject. A more recent look at the 106th is *St. Vith: U.S. 106th Infantry Division* by Michael Tolhurst.

An excellent look at the American leaders who managed the battle is Harold Winton's book *Corps Commanders of the Bulge: Six American Generals and Victory in the Ardennes.*

Nuts! The Battle of the Bulge by Donald Goldstein, Katherine Dillon, and J. Michael Wenger is an engaging photographic overview of the battle.

For details on the USAAF's role in the battle, see Volume III of *The Army Air Forces in World War II,* edited by W. F. Craven and J. L. Crate. Robert Dorr and Thomas Jones' recent work, *Hell Hawks!,* details one 9th Air Force fighter-bomber unit during the campaign in Western Europe and includes a section on the Bulge.

INDEX

British Units

French Units

German Units

GENERAL INDEX